Writings on Cities

'To our mothers, Rachel Kofman and Fernande Lemouton.'

Writings on Cities

HENRI LEFEBVRE

Selected, translated and introduced by

Eleonore Kofman and Elizabeth Lebas

Blackwell
Publishing

BLACKWELL PUBLISHING

350 Main Street, Malden, MA 02148-5020, USA
9600 Garsington Road, Oxford OX4 2DQ, UK
550 Swanston Street, Carlton, Victoria 3053, Australia

English translation first published 1996

9   2006

Library of Congress Cataloging-in-Publication Data

Lefebvre, Henri, 1905–
    Writings on cities/Henri Lefebvre; selected, translated, and introduced by Eleonore Kofman and Elizabeth Lebas.
        p.   cm.
    Translated from the French.
    Includes bibliographical references and index.
    ISBN 0-631-19187-9 — ISBN 0-631-19188-7 (pbk)
    1. Cities and towns. I. Kofman, Eleonore. II. Lebas, Elizabeth. III. Title.
HT153.L345   1996
307.70 — dc20   95–12470
                                                            CIP

ISBN-13: 978-0-631-19187-2 — ISBN-13: 978-0-631-19188-9 (pbk)

A catalogue record for this title is available from the British Library.

The publisher's policy is to use permanent paper from mills that operate a sustainable forestry policy, and which has been manufactured from pulp processed using acid-free and elementary chlorine-free practices. Furthermore, the publisher ensures that the text paper and cover board used have met acceptable environmental accreditation standards.

For further information on
Blackwell Publishing, visit our website:
www.blackwellpublishing.com

Contents

CONTENTS

Acknowledgements

We would like to thank all those who gave us their time and hospitality, which enabled us to deepen our understanding of Lefebvre's ideas, his relationships with architects, urbanists and intellectuals, his influence in France, and not least, the imprint of his personality on his thinking. Thanks also to those with whom we discussed general issues raised in the Introduction.

In particular we would like to mention Roland Castro, Katherine Coit, Jean-Pierre Garnier, Antoine Haumont, Remi Hess, Armelle Lefebvre, Jean-Pierre Lefebvre, Catherine Lefebvre- Régulier, Jean de Matelaere, Makan Rafadtjou, Henri Raymond, Serge Renaudie, Christian Schmid. The bookshelves of Pascal Buléon and Patrice Cotensin suggested some much appreciated, and not obvious, reading.

Special thanks to Finn Barnow for reading the Introduction and Louise Coté-Read for her invaluable corrections of all translations.

We would also like to thank Middlesex University and Nottingham Trent University for financial help and sabbaticals, and the Centre de Recherche sur l'Habitat, Nanterre, where Eleonore Kofman spent part of her sabbatical.

We would like to thank the following copyright holders for permission to translate and reproduce material, as follows: Anthropos for permission to translate *Le Droit à la Ville*. Catherine Lefebvre-Régulier for permission to translate 'Essai de rythmanalyse des villes méditerranéennes'; *Espaces Temps* 33, 1980, pp. 17–19 for permission to translate Lefebvre's article 'Hors du centre, point de salut?'; Éditions Syllepse for permission to translate 'Vue de la fenêtre', chapter 3 from Henri Lefebvre's *Éléments de Rythmanalyse. Introduction à la connaissance des rythmes*. Société Française for 'L'Urbain en question' 33, 1989, pp 44–7.

PART I

Introduction

1

Lost in Transposition – Time, Space and the City

Choice of Works

The title for the introduction reflects an important aspect of our selection and translation of writings on the city by Henri Lefebvre, French Marxist philosopher and sociologist, whose life spanned the century and whose major publications begin in the 1930s and end with his death in 1991. We have modified the title of our introduction from a book called *Lost in Translation* (1989), by Eva Hoffman who recounts, as someone who migrated from Poland to Canada at the age of thirteen years, the acquisition of a language and new forms of social relations. Although our own histories are slightly less linguistically traumatic, we too have been immigrants and operated in another language, sometimes simultaneously. So our choice of 'transposition' stemmed from the fact that we wanted to give a stronger sense of changing places and contexts than might be conveyed by the term translation. And as editors as well as translators, the choice of texts introduces a strong element of filtering and mediation. Elizabeth Lebas (1983), one of the translators of Castells in the 1970s, pointed out that English academics were ignoring other French Marxist urban sociologists; they were attempting to transfer concepts that had evolved in a French context, and which were not necessarily applicable elsewhere. So, whilst translation opens up new worlds, it also closes off those left outside this mediation. Given the list of influential French thinkers, starting from A for Althusser, B for Barthes, Baudrillard, Bourdieu, C for Cixous . . . that have been transposed, the question of mediation is significant.

Yet decontextualization produces other effects than that of taking a work out of the economic, social and intellectual environment in which it is produced. There is what could be called the concertina effect such that the temporal sequence and spacing of the works may be lost, and in this way decontextualized. It can operate both in terms of a temporal delay in translation or in the quick succession of works that reach us, but which were actually produced at longer intervals and in a different order. In the process of reordering, recontextualization takes place. Not only does such recontextualization often lose the conditions in which a work was produced and its relationship with other intellectual currents of this period (Eribon, 1994), it is often transformed into the intellectual concerns and language, including the intellectual conflicts, of the new place and period. Such a process has probably been most clearly in evidence in the United States arising out of an 'uncontrolled international intellectual exportation' (Wacquant, 1993, 254–5) of French philosophy and social theory. Whilst it is obviously not desirable to close off new contextualizations and interpretations, it is also necessary to understand the conditions of production in order to appreciation more fully a work.

David Macey (1993) in his review of three books on Foucault and Lacan commented that we have a perennial problem with what to do with masters, dead or alive. He goes on to make the distinction between introduction, appropriation and reading in the form and intent of mediation. Introduction may involve an initial acquaintance with an author's work or it may consist of ushering in a previously untranslated body of writing. Appropriation consists of trying to fit or reconstruct a work into an existing corpus which may have previously been in opposition or excluded, for example, Foucault and feminism[1] (Braidotti, 1994) or attempts to reconstruct a writer as a postmodernist. A new reading may arise from a repositioning against an early interpretation or from the introduction of new works of an author which widen the available body of texts. Whilst we can heuristically separate the different processes, they are in reality often intermingled, as we shall see in the case of Lefebvre.

Another persona in this act of mediation is the interviewer. In Lefebvre's case there have been numerous short (1986c; 1987; 1989) and book-length (Latour and Combes, 1991) interviews: in addition, self-reflections on his own intellectual trajectory (Lefebvre, 1959; 1975b), as well as a biography (Hess, 1988). All of these capture the

---

[1] Lefebvre also frequently referred to sexuality and gender both in relation to the crisis of the 20th century and the role of psychoanalysis and Freudianism. He had read a number of the feminist classics, such as Kate Millett and Germaine Greer, and discussed the potential of contemporary feminism (1980b, 156–77).

reasons for his interest in time, space, the city and everyday life. In this they compare starkly with Foucault, whose inclusion of spatial metaphors and strategies has also generated interest among an Anglo-Saxon public (Smith, 1993b). We are much more at the mercy of his interviewers (Foucault, 1984; 1986). Despite the spatial nature of his concepts and his interest in the use of space in society (Foucault, 1986), there seems to be a struggle going on to extract his ideas on space and architecture, the latter being seen primarily as an element ensuring a certain allocation of people in space and a canalization of their circulation.

Until recently little of Lefebvre has been translated into English, unlike the situation in other languages such as Spanish, German, Swedish or Japanese. In the 1960s he was the second most translated intellectual, especially in terms of number of languages. His increasing recognition in Anglo-American cultural studies has tended to focus on the production of space, and to a lesser extent urbanism (Harvey, 1973; Soja, 1985; 1989a, b). The recent translation of *Production of Space*, the last and his major work on space, and originally published in French in 1974, has made the richness of his thinking more readily available to readers, who no longer have to depend on partial résumés. Possibly the most striking and neglected aspect to be commented upon in this translation is the debt to Nietzsche, whom Lefebvre sought to conjoin with Marx. The emphasis on the body, sexuality, violence and the tragic, and the production of differential space and plural times, have direct resonances in Nietzschean thought. One of the questions that we could play with is what would have been the impact of *Production of Space* on our understanding of space and society had it been translated soon after its French publication, as occurred in Italy, Spain and Germany. It is hard of course to give an answer to this question, since it may well be that Lefebvre's approach chimes in with current concerns, including the North American attempt to interpret him as a precursor of postmodernism (Dear, 1994; Hamel and Poitras, 1994; Soja, 1989b). Another major translation in progress is that of *Critique of Everyday Life*, the first volume published in 1947, the second volume in 1962 and the third in 1981. The first two are now available in English (1991) with an introduction by Michael Trebitsch. Its significance in French philosophical and social thinking (Huisman, 1993) has been recognized and can now be appreciated by English readers. The everyday was a concept which Lefebvre considered to be his major contribution to Marxism (1988, 78); it can be seen as a level between the individual and history and continues to have much potential for an understanding of the transformation of the world we live in. Yet it would be a pity to limit his important work largely to translations of these few books.

Over a span of sixty years Lefebvre wrote about a wide range of themes, from literature, language, history, philosophy, Marxism, to rural and urban sociology, space, time, the everyday and the modern world. It was his involvement in urban theory and practice which immediately preceded his extended analysis of space and society and which has had a much wider audience in France than the purely spatial. The Anglo-American readership has tended to view his other writing through the prism of the spatial. However, the urban question was not only more influential in the 1960s and early 1970s in France, but has also figured prominently on social and political agendas in the 1980s and 1990s, leading in 1988 to the creation of a Ministère de la Ville (Ministry for the City) (Body-Gendrot, 1993; Kofman, 1993). Though distanced from the greater optimism and possibilities of the 1960s, Lefebvre nevertheless continued to reflect on daily life and the right to the city in a world in which many illusions had been shattered (1989; 1991a).

Our selection was guided by a number of considerations. The intention was firstly, to redress a balance in the translation of his writing and in particular the urban which has been subordinated to the spatial. His urban vision remains relevant for the developed world despite all the transformations in urban life and structures. And secondly, through this urban writing to raise questions about the conceptualization of the city, the rights of its citizens and articulation of time, space and the everyday. Hence the choice of his first major, and highly polemical book on the city Le droit à la ville, completed in 1967 to commemorate the centenary of the publication of Marx's Capital, and which came out before the events of 1968. Its title has become a slogan, as have a number of his aphorisms, and has passed into general usage. We have also translated an introduction from Espace et politique (1973a), which develops at greater length the role of architecture. Some of it has already been translated (Antipode, 1976) and much of it announces the subsequent and more elaborate Production of Space. Next we have included two short interviews published in Espaces Temps in 1986 and La Société Française in 1989. In the first, he was asked specifically to address the issue of centrality, a major theme in his urban writing, and where he also discusses what he likes and dislikes in cities. The second raises questions about the future of the city. Lastly, we move to two pieces written towards the end of his life and published in *Éléments de rythmanalyse. Introduction à la connaissance des rythmes*. These two essays reveal the return in the 1980s to interests that go back to his inter-war years in the interweaving and structuring of temporalities in everyday life, especially the theory of moments. As he himself stated, 'the standing of time as it relates to space is problematic and has yet to be defined clearly' (1974, 408). We have selected, in keeping with the theme of the book, the essay written with Catherine Régulier on Mediterranean cities[2] and a very personal essay 'Seen from the Window', in which starting from his position as subject and his body, he reaches out to the bustling world outside him and links the two. It is worth noting that he considered *Éléments de rythmanalyse* as the fourth volume of critique of everyday life (Ajzenberg, 1994).

In the following section, we outline the evolution of his writing on space, time, the everyday and the city. In doing this we move synchronically and diachronically, an absolute necessity if one is to understand the different sources of inspiration in his work and the continual dialogue within it, which is as he saw his work. Sometimes the reader is directed to the work in question, as when Lefebvre stresses the analogous relations between the territorial, the urbanistic and the architectural (1974, 1986, viii) which can only be understood in terms of relations of logic-dialectic, structure and conjuncture, and which he elsewhere elucidated in *Logique formelle, logique dialectique*, first published in 1947. Yet in *Right to the City*, he also outlines a theory of forms, without the reader being directed to the core concept of formal logic. And similarly other key themes are elaborated elsewhere, such as *habiter*, and its Heideggerian connotations, for which one would have to turn to his preface to the study on the *pavillonaire* (individual house) (1966b) and the slightly mocking description of Heidegger's cult of the artisanal, touchingly sentimental, patriarchal and Germanic dwelling (1965b, 135). For Lefebvre, it was not the home, but the city, which expressed and symbolized a person's

---

[2] This essay originally appeared in *Peuples Méditerranéens*, 37, 1986 and resulted from an invitation from the architect Paul Chemetov to participate in a group Ville et Citoyens to counteract what Chemetov saw as a tendency of architects to justify anything with the threesome of 'animation, communication, space' (Chemetov, 1991).

being and consciousness. Heidegger was the twentieth-century philosopher with whom Lefebvre most engaged, sharing a number of preoccupations concerning existence and the world, but not coming to the
same conclusion. As a philosopher, he says, Heidegger was capable of
the worst and the best, of the archaic and the visionary (1965b,
133–49). And, of course, there is the figure of Nietzsche, who opens
Right to the City, and is present in so many of his themes and writings.
These are just a few of the examples we would give to support a wider
reading of Lefebvre and which we shall seek in the following sections
to interweave in the transposition of his work.

It is also worth pointing out that re-editions of his books often
contain interesting prefaces and act as a sort of autocritique. So for
example in the third edition of *Production of Space* he mentions
several absences – *banlieues*, ghettos, false ensembles, architecture as
usage of space and the role of the military. He attributes these and
other absences to the fact that it was written in a direct, incisive
manner like a pamphlet. If this was meant seriously, then *Right to the
City* would be a tract! What he may well have also meant by this
comment is a comparison with Marx who was accused of only being
an unoriginal pamphleteer, because as Lefebvre notes, he used existing
concepts and reassembled them; the originality lay in submitting them
to a negative and radical critique (1970a, 175–7). So, what may seem
as detours in our account of Lefebvre's urban trajectory, actually lead
us to his central concepts and the writers who have inspired him.

In the last sections we examine the present standing of Lefebvre and
his potential contributions to a number of significant issues. Being
Lefebvrian, it has been said, is more a sensibility, rather than a closed
system; and indeed, many have found his theoretical insights difficult
to apply due to the fluidity, dynamic and openness of his thought. It is
probably encapsulated to perfection by one of his most common
responses, 'yes and no'. Some of his most impressive abilities, apart
from the polymath qualities, were the capacity to elucidate ideas in
advance, whilst holding onto what he was currently discussing; and
secondly to be able to explain highly complex ideas, often using
concrete and personal examples, such as the renovation of Les Halles
in central Paris about which he felt deeply and emotionally.[3]

---

[3] This section has been written on the basis of discussions with people who worked
with Lefebvre, such as Katherine Coit, whose thesis on political activities of local

Crucially it is his ability to move from the abstract to the concrete, from theory to reality, which he performs with the dialectical agility characteristic of his work. This he does through several interlocking methodological steps. The most significant for his writing on the city and the urban are regression–progression, dialectical movement and the theory of forms (see 1980a for a concise exposition). It was in an article on perspectives in rural sociology (1970b) that Lefebvre first elaborated the method of regression–progression, initially outlined in 1953, and adopted and modified by Sartre in his *Critique de la raison dialectique* (Hess, 1988, 182–7). It consists of three procedures (1970b, 73–4):

1 *Description* – observation informed by experience and a general theory.
2 Analytico-regressive – analysis of the reality as described with an effort made to compare and not fall into vague statements.
3 Historico-genetic – the study of modifications of the above structures through their evolution and their subordination to more general structures. Classification of formation and structures in relation to general processes and attempt through explanation and elucidation to return to the present.

He used share cropping as an example but the method of regression–progression was subsequently most fully developed in the *Production of Space*. In it he combines genealogical (returning to the emergence of a concept and exploring its concrete affiliations, detours and associations) and historico-genetic procedures (abstract and total, linked to the general history of society and philosophy). Progression refers to the opposite move, that of beginning with the present and evaluating what is possible and impossible in the future. He always emphasized this was a method taken directly from Marx, reading Marx as the thinker of the possible, and not a realist (1980a). Tendencies and virtualities are always plural and what is impossible today may become possible in the future and vice versa.

The second element is dialectical materialism. Lefebvre's dialectic is not that of Hegel, thesis–antithesis–synthesis, nor one of affirmation–

associational groups he supervised and who was a member of the Groupe de Navarrenx, and Serge Renaudie, an architect who accompanied him to California in 1983–4 as an assistant.

negation–negation found in Marx, but a much more open, ended movement, bringing together the conflictual and contradictory, and linking theory and practice. Examples would be homogeneous and fragmented, ephemeral and durable. The intention is not to deny one or other term nor to transcend them (*dépasser*), but to reveal the continual movement between them. It has to be subversive and negative. At the same time he criticized static binary modes, and tended to suggest series of triads, for example, in music, melody, harmony and rhythm, in nature, energy, space and time, or the true, the beautiful and the good. Each term can be analysed either individually, in a conflictual relation to each other or to another term altogether (1986a, 42). These triads are not intrinsically dialectical, rather dialectical thinking can be brought to bear upon them. The dialectical, he comments, is frequently occluded by metaphors which we use to express the relationship between difference and totality and the negative and positive (1980a, 208). The dialectical is not chaotic, rather it highlights the relationship between form and contents and dissolves stable morphologies to such an extent that stability becomes a problem (206).

Thirdly, the theory of forms is developed in *Logique formelle, logique dialectique* 1968 and was applied to the notion of urban (1965a; ch. 12). Forms are derived from differences of content and in turn codify the practices with which a particular content operates. Their emptiness gives them a great versatility and capacity for renewal and combination. Thus the forms of the Greek *polis* and Roman *urbs* come together in the medieval city. Another example is that of the contractual form covering sexual relations between couples and social relations between employer and worker. The most abstract form of modernity is informatics, which has developed in and out of processes of globalization led by multinational firms and which has dislocated nations, States and markets and extracted resources from all areas of the planet including the depths of the earth, the sea and the sky.

Urbanism and the City

Initial encounters: projects and utopias

Lefebvre's interest in space and play originated in his childhood and his awareness of the changing location of production. He was strongly influenced by surrealism, noted for its fleeting encounters in the city in which the explorer sets out without knowing what lies in store. Lefebvre cites in particular Louis Aragon's *Les paysans de Paris*, whose mythologies for modern times could be constructed from threatened arcades (Passage de l'Opéra) and public pleasure grounds, such as Buttes Chaumont (Melly and Woods, 1991). This is not about aimless wandering in the city but a detailed exhumation of the arcade and its occupants. The arcade is the place of encounter, of gatherings and of *jouissance*, and Lefebvre comments that the contrast between the pleasures and desires of the arcade and the functional and divided spaces in the streets must have inspired the surrealists (1973c, 191). Later, Walter Benjamin[4] dissected the arcades of the past century and the possibility of recapturing them through fleeting and dialectical images.

The other group that shared his fascination and critique of the colonization and fragmentation of everyday life was the Situationist International formed in 1958 largely in reponse to what it considered to be the complacency and complicity of the orthodox Left and pre-war surrealism (for an analysis see Plant, 1990 and 1992; Wollen, 1990). Guy Debord, the main theoretician, had been a pupil of Lefebvre in the 1950s and Lefebvre introduced Raoul Vaneigem, another situationist theoretician, to him.

The Cobra group (the acronym being derived from a combination of artists in Copenhagen, Brussels and Amsterdam) too came into the Situationist International. As a group of artists critical of Western rationalism and interested in non-Western art and irrational forms, they came together in November 1948 and survived until 1951 (Stokvis, 1987). They rejected however the surrealist emphasis on individual consciousness and replaced it with the more Jungian focus on collective archetypes. The leaders, Dotremont, a Belgian poet and calligrapher, Asger Jorn (1914–73), a Danish artist-philosopher and Constant Niewenhuys (born in 1920), a Dutch painter, were particularly influenced by Marxism. In their future society, art would not be elitist but would be for everybody and made by anybody. Constant saw his own life as exemplifying a series of dialectical alternations.

---

[4] Benjamin wrote in Paris in 1939 a major treatise on the arcades that was not published until 1982 in Frankfurt and 1993 in Paris. Benjamin had read Lefebvre (Anderson, 1976, 37).

Jorn's dislike of functionalism in architecture led him to organize the *Mouvement international pour un Bauhaus Imaginiste* in 1953. This merged with the Lettrist International in 1957 and later with the Situationist International in 1958. In 1960 Jorn and Constant left the SI which they found too polarized politically under Debord's leadership. Cobra members helped to develop a number of urban and environmental themes such as *urbanisme unitaire* (unitary urbanism), psychogeography, *dérive* (drift) and *détournement*. Constant, whose writing *Pour une architecture de situation* (1953) influenced Lefebvre (1986a, 13) and inspired his ideas of experimental utopias, worked with the Dutch architect Aldo van Eyck to create a New Babylon project, for which he constructed a series of models from 1956 to 1969. This city of the future would materialize when technology had taken over many laborious functions, enabling people to evolve into homo ludens (Stokvis, 1987, 23). The nomadic inhabitants of this experimental utopian city with changing zones for free play could chose their own sensory environment, organization of space and so on.

On the other hand, the notion of situations, central to the SI's strategies of engagement, were constructed encounters and creatively lived moments in existing urban settings that could produce modes for the transformation of the city. Psychogeography[5] could reveal the sudden changes of ambience in the environment. The Situationists also adapted the dadaist and surrealist practice of the *dérive* which represented a model for human relationships. It was however more a means of displacement and dislocation in an existing setting than an aimless wandering (Plant, 1992, 59–60).

Lefebvre however found these strategies interesting but partial, too individualistic and theatrical. The situation, a concept derived from existentialism, and also present in surrealism (Latour and Combes, 1991) was for him unsituated (1970a, 169). His use of the term was more general and broader. It could be applied to individuals and groups or to the world as it affected all peoples. So for example, modernity is a situation and not an essence (1966a, 328–31). Meanings stem and feed into situations.

---

[5] Debord (1994) produced a psychogeography of Paris entitled *A Discourse on the Passions of Love.*

For Lefebvre, it was, as he wrote later, a sort of unfinished love affair with the situationists (1975b, 110). Even in the early days it was a relationship of critical friendship. Though they were influenced by his idea of revolutionary romanticism (1971), which referred to the discord arising from the contradiction of the progressive individual in the modern world, they criticized him for failing to go beyond the present order. His theory of moments, which combined the absolute and consciousness of its passing, was deemed too abstract (see Hess, 1988, ch. 18). By the early 1960s relations were strained and the break came over several pages written by the Situationists on the Commune (1965a) for Lefebvre and which he did not acknowledge.[6]

Different types of spaces figured as poles of Lefebvre's existence. He regularly returned to the very traditional and barely changing home of his roots, and lived there for two years before his death. Thus what the French call *la France profonde* obviated the need to travel to the Third World. At the other extreme, bustling Paris attracted him despite its intellectual elitism and intrigues. Florence was for pleasure and Los Angeles for fascination (1986c). These two sides represented his *côté charnel* and *côté valeur d'usage* (carnal and use value sides). The rural pole was of course the stable dwelling at the heart of Heidegger's thought, of which Lefebvre was critical because of its bearing on Heidegger's trivialization of everyday life and mistrust of the city, its encounters and chatter. Heidegger's images are derived from the rural world of meditation and solitude, especially forests and mountains (Ansay and Schoonbrodt, 1989, 466). For Lefebvre this was only one element of his dialectical existence, but it certainly left its mark in his glorification of the peasant community in his early work on everyday life (1958). It was in fact through rural sociology that Lefebvre had entered the CNRS in 1948 and submitted his thesis on the Vallée de Campan.[7]

---

[6] Hess (1988, 228) concludes that although all the major Situationist ideas could be found in Lefebvre, they radicalized him and that, in turn, the international aspect of their activities stimulated his thinking on the emergence of the global (*mondial*). The relationship between Lefebvrian and Situationist concepts awaits a serious study.

[7] Lefebvre studied land rents in particular and it is interesting to note that in his last interview he comments that land rents have reappeared in the city whilst the countryside and agriculture have come to the fore. The rural world is again a site of invention, and not just of traditions (Latour and Combes, 1991, 87). Hess (1988, 175–6) notes the relevance of all the work Lefebvre did on land rents and revenue to the question of oil.

Lefebvre's shift into the study of the urban and the city resulted from a disenchantment with the possibilities open to him in rural sociology. He was unable to express what he wanted due to the intellectual climate of the 1950s in the Communist Party and was never invited to work on these themes in socialist countries. His exclusion from the Communist Party (1957) liberated his thought, as he describes in his autobiography *La somme et le reste*. He could continue to combine the spontaneous romantic and the lucid thinker (Blanchot, 1971, 98). The move into the urban permitted him once again to partake of more general intellectual discussions; he felt very isolated in undertaking rural research. The adventure of the century was for him the continual reworking of his earlier ideas in conjunction with new currents of the period, for he had an acute sense of emerging intellectual trends (conversation with Armelle Lefebvre and Jean de Matelaere).

His realization of the urban as a moment had occurred earlier when he visited New York before the Second World War and then Bologna in 1950 (1980b, 234). He became increasingly aware that the urban revealed the contradictions of society, acutely demonstrated by the sudden invasion of a new town Mourenx,[8] in south-western France, not far from his birthplace of Navarrenx, which with its existing ramparts presents quite a different aspect (1962, 7th prelude). Here, as in the Tuscan countryside, he understood not only the dramatic transformation of the raw materials of first into second nature but also the crisis of the city and the extension of the urban in which town and country had little distinctive meaning, unlike the older and increasingly disintegrated historic cores. The urban constituted this new form of sociability where town and country had been abolished. As from the early 1960s, the French State, increasingly freed from its heavy investment in colonialism, turned wholeheartedly to the reconstruction of French space and reorganizing capitalism (1987). He states too that it was during this period that it came to be understood explicitly and implicitly that the object of science was space rather than time. But it was the confused and paradoxical notions of space that troubled him, a response to the attempt by technicians to remodel France and insert it into an emerging European and global space

[8] Mourenx, built between 1957 and 1960 to house workers from the Lacq gas fields, rises starkly in a profoundly rural landscape. The town is relatively compact because it largely comprises blocks of flats, some of which are 12 storey high.

(1974/1986, preface), and it was this which led him to focus on the production of space in the early 1970s. His objective was to show that space was political, and that it had been remodelled by technocratic rationality rather than primarily to mount a critique of the nineteenth-century prioritization of time. He devoted attention in the 1950s and 1960s to the waning star of history (1971; 1970c), the nature of historicity (1965a,b) and the expulsion of history by structuralism and technocratic rationality (1965b, 185–7).

At the beginning of the 1960s, influenced by the Situationists, he still believed in the possibility of a new urbanism and wrote about experimental utopias ('Utopie expérimentale: pour un nouvel urbanisme', in 1970b). An experimental utopia is the exploration of what is humanly possible based upon the image and the imaginary (*imaginaire*), constantly subjected to critique and referring to a problematic derived from the real, that is a feedback mechanism. He envisaged a ludic city, such that work would be organized around residence, and in which everyday life would be transformed, and people would be in charge of their lives. The worst utopias are those which do not call themselves as such but which, in the name of positivism, impose the harshest constraints (1970b, 155).

During this period he was involved in conducting market research, in which many left-wing people were employed. Indeed one of the part-time researchers later to be a famous writer, Georges Perec, was sent to undertake fieldwork.[9] Observation and curiosity of the world in which we live is the basis of intuition, questioning, critique and

---

[9] Perec knew Lefebvre well, for he frequented the New Left of which Lefebvre was one of the older members, and whom Perec called a sad clown. Lefebvre employed Perec to be part of a team undertaking the study of the everyday life of a mining community in Caen (Normandy) in 1960 that was likely to be closed, and in 1961 in a rich farming community in the Oise at a time when the Common Agricultural Policy had just been set up. David Bellos notes that *Critique de la vie quotidienne* treated philosophically the same social themes that Perec would later write about (1994, 212). He comments that Perec picked up from his fieldwork experiences the idea that life can be apprehended from the objects that people desire and acquire, that their daily routine does not take away the significance of these objects nor their ability to feel passionately about them. Perec's novel *Les choses* (1965) describes the everyday life of a young middle-class couple and their idea of happiness, which remains inaccessible to them because of their subjugation to things. For Perec as well, the detailed recovery of everyday life is a means of retrieving and preserving memory against change, as for example through his study of the occupants of a building (1978) or a series of places (1974).

transformation. Becoming a real sociologist begins with observation, however banal or trivial, as he advised his students at Nanterre to do in their journey from Saint Lazare station (Hess, 1988, 232). The findings of market research were relevant to Marxists interested in the consequences of lives increasingly oriented around consumption and the acquisition of objects. Lefebvre coined the term *société bureau-cratique de consommation dirigée* (bureaucratic society of organized consumption) which was taken up and shortened by students at Nanterre to consumer society.

As Professor Henri Lefebvre, director of the Institut de Sociologie Urbaine at Nanterre from 1965, he was concerned about changing the teaching of urbanism so as to make it interdisciplinary. Yet at the end of the 1980s he commented on the continuing neglect of urban questions in university teaching (see the second interview in this book). He also took part in debates and conferences in his capacity as a sociologist. In one of the debates organized by the Centre d'Études Socialistes, he was attacked by Jean Balladur, one of the two architect-urbanists on the panel, as an abstract sociologist for his analytical conception of urbanism (1967c). This refers to all organization of space that juxtaposes constitutive elements of people's living environ-ment into an architecture and urbanism of zoning. It excludes archi-tecture, starting as it does with land as property and produces a surface urbanism based on juxtaposition of functions. In contrast organic urbanism is three dimensional, integrating urban functions with and through architecture. Although there was some misunder-standing arising from Lefebvre's comment about the separation of architecture and urbanism in terms of levels, Balladur's talk revealed the insights of a practising architect-urbanist. Lefebvre had primarily spoken of the myth of technocracy which hid behind a language of techniques to mask the lack of will to invest and criticized all the left-wing parties for failing to pay attention to urban questions during an electoral period (the 1967 legislative elections). He then made some concluding remarks about reconstructing the city, which it is worth quoting in full:

> Space is nothing but the inscription of time in the world, spaces are the realizations, inscriptions in the simultaneity of the external world of a series of times, the rhythms of the city, the rhythms of the urban population, and in my opinion, as a sociologist, I suggest to you the idea that the city will only be rethought and reconstructed on its current

ruins when we have properly understood that the city is the deployment
of time, and that it is this time, . . . of those who are its inhabitants, it
is for them that we have to finally organize in a human manner. (1967c,
10)

The Institut de Sociologie Urbaine was one of the two major urban
institutes in France in the 1960s and undertook many studies under
contract, for example for the Ministère de l'Équipement.[10] In a study
of the *quartier* (neighbourhood) he attacked its ideological use and the
tendency to move from description to normative positions. The significance of his short introduction on a study of four *quartiers* (1967b)
was acknowledged by subsequent research on everyday life (Giard and
Mayol, 1994). In another research report, on the attitudes of urban
dwellers to the *habitat pavillonaire* (detached housing), Lefebvre
wrote a substantial preface, in which he combined what had been
previously separate, that is linguistic (semantic and semiological)[11] and
Marxist analyses (critique of alienation, ideologies and everyday life)
(1966b; 1970b).

Lefebvre refers to Bachelard (1957) and the disappearance of the
house of yore which served as a means of integrating thought, memory
and dreams. Heidegger too warns against construction solely in economic or technical terms, for *habiter* or way of living is a quality of
the person, it is not an accident and links in with actions of building,
thought and speech. *Habiter*, like the processes of dressing, playing,
eating, forms an open sub-system. Lefebvre criticizes the disdain that
the individualistic *pavillon* (detached house) has generated and tries to
understand its problems and contradictions. This form reveals a poetic

[10] The Institut had been set up originally as a non-profitmaking association so that
it needed to obtain contracts in order to retain researchers. Lefebvre, as a
professor, was invited in as director of the Institut and as someone who would
bring to it a strong theoretical line.

[11] Lefebvre lectured and wrote about language and society (1966a; 1971). He was
profoundly hostile to structuralist analyses, including those of Doctor Lacan
whom he accused of performing with stunning virtuosity the formalization of
language and of detaching this form from any support in the movement of the
real. The world of words was thus supposedly creating the world of things. On
the other hand, within its limits, he considered *Mythologies* by Roland Barthes a
brilliant exercise. Barthes and he were both from the Béarn and spent much time
in each other's homes (Hess, 1988). In his American tours, Lefebvre lectured on
Barthes. Though in France this aspect of his work has been forgotten, it is still
highly esteemed in Brazil (comment made by Makan Rafadtjou).

of space and time in which nature is appropriated, that is the transformation of the body and biological life, space and time into human goods. The *pavillon* involves different levels, namely the appropriation of space and a utopia, which is both fiction and reality. He concludes that what people want is to be able to hold onto and combine oppositions, such as inside/outside, intimacy and environment, and thereby reinvent a symbolic dimension.

In the mid 1960s he engaged in a piece of historical research, *La proclamation de la Commune*, that included issues of the use of the city in revolutionary times. History has to be understood as praxis which is the production of people by people, including the production of Paris as an *oeuvre*. The Commune represents a style defined by the fête and drama which introduces sociology into history (1965a, 40). Lefebvre commented that his ideas on the reappropriation of space in this book influenced students, whom he had taught at Nanterre, in their movement through Parisian space in 1968. As we have seen, the Situationists had accused him of plagiarizing their ideas but Lefebvre retorted in the 1970s that although they had been discussing similar ideas in the late 1950s and early 1960s, he had added to the idea of festival and exceptional moments, and the reappropriation of space by workers, who had been thrown out to the periphery by Haussmannian planning (1975b). Furthermore, he never shared the belief in the ability of instantaneous change brought about by spontaneous action; change in everyday life was slow (1959, 613). The theme of exclusion is central to his analysis of urban change in Paris and what the right to the city must combat. As for festivals, whilst they represented a moment in the overthrow of habitual use, they also heightened moments of the everyday, as in peasant communities (see, Notes on a Sunday Afternoon, 1958, 1991, vol. 2); they entailed an expenditure of surplus.

So although *Right to the City* was the first of his major writings on the city, it was preceded by a number of diverse studies on the city in the past, present and future. It took up a series of themes, some of which he had already written about in various essays, and were soon to be assembled in *Du rural à l'urbain* (1970b). The core of his analysis revolves around the deepening contradiction of the destruction of the city and the intensification and extension of the urban (see the section 'Around the critical point'); it is the place of encounter, the assemblage of differences and priority of use over exchange value.

Whilst the crisis of the city is linked to particular forms of rationality (not the application of reason in general), economicism, the State, private sector and bureaucracy, these are not sufficient analyses. The logic of the market has reduced these urban qualities to exchange and suppressed the city as *oeuvre*. In order to understand the nature of the contradiction we have to delve into the dialectical movement between form and content, between thought and reality. Urban form is based on simultaneity (of events, perceptions and elements of the whole in 'reality') which socially involves the bringing together and meeting up of everything in its environs and urban society as the privileged site of the meeting of the *oeuvre* and the product. In modern society simultaneity intensifies and the capacity to meet and gather together have become stronger. The pace of communications has accelerated to the point of becoming quasi-instantaneous. At the same time, dispersal, which must be understood in relation to simultaneity as form, also increases such that the division of labour, social segregation and material and spiritual separations are pushed to the extreme.

Rights were now on the agenda, not just the abstract rights of man and the citizen but concrete rights pertaining to social groups, such as old people and women, conditions of work, culture, housing, amongst others. The right to the city has become more essential than ever, unlike the pseudo right to nature whose resultant occupation of the countryside leads to devastation. It emerges as the highest form of rights: liberty, individualization in socialization, environs (*habitat*) and way of living (*habiter*). It isn't, however, about the simple right to visit the city, more apt we would suggest today than ever, or a return to traditional cities. What is called for is a renewed urban society, a renovated centrality, leaving opportunity for rhythms and use of time that would permit full usage of moments and places, and demanding the mastery of the economic (use value, market and merchandise). The rights not to be excluded from centrality and to participate politically in decision-making were particularly significant for the working class. Centrality of course does not imply the centre of power but the regrouping of differences in relation to each other. Furthermore, the ludic in its fullest sense of theatre, sport, games of all sorts, fairs, more than any other activity restores the sense of *oeuvre* conferred by art and philosophy and prioritizes time over space, appropriation over domination. There is clearly an ambiguity in the book about the role of the working class. Though they had been the most affected by the disintegration of the city and the organization of their daily life by and in the bureaucratic society of directed consumption, their presence, together with other groups that made up the popular classes, was still significant in the centre of major cities in France in the 1960s. On the one hand, the working class is the only one capable of realizing an urban society and which fully knows how and desires to play. On the other hand, it does not have a spontaneous sense of the *oeuvre* from which a sense of totality or unity through difference will be restored.

The right to the *oeuvre* (participation) and appropriation (not to be confused with property but use value) was implied in the right to the city. The *oeuvre* is unique, though it may be copied; it is a totality assembling difference, characterized by formal simultaneity where all parts refer to the whole and vice versa. The city itself is the supreme *oeuvre*, which enters into conflictual, ambiguous and dialectical relationships with its institutional form (1967a, 161). Urbanism was born out of the crisis of the city and referentials in the early twentieth century but the objective of the *oeuvre* is to overcome divisions and restore totality. He develops most fully the implications of the crisis of referentials and the role of the *oeuvre* at length in *La presence et l'absence* (1980b, ch. 4). The crisis in Euclidean and Newtonian space, perspective in painting and architecture, tonal system in music, the city and history (the list is not exhaustive), is due to a number of reasons. These have to do with the multiplication of what had previously been a constrained number of referentials which enabled a 'liberation of the signifier' that were after the First World War often manipulated by State institutions and political powers. The new liberal democracies of the nineteenth century came to be organized around representations which they also extended. To this we must add a very important cause, and that was the automization of different fields such as the economic, the political, technical and scientific. Capitalism and modern statism have both crushed the creative capacity of the *oeuvre*. Taking the *oeuvre* as an objective would provide a new way which will neither fall into dogmatism or scepticism, apocalyptic prophecies or nostalgia (1980b, 186).

He then suggests that we might well want to explore the global as an *oeuvre* whilst keeping in mind its dangers. Hence we should consider the triad of thing (the earth), the product (resulting from the international division of labour, flows of exchange, communications and strategies) and the *oeuvre* (urban centres, architectural and spatial projects, marginal pre- and post-capitalist activities) (192–3). This project does not imply, for example, denial of exchange against use value but rather that the *oeuvre* restores use value. Similarly, we should not reject *savoir* (knowledge) but integrate it into the lived (*vécu*). By no means should we embrace the irrational and archetypes.

To think about alternative possibilities, we need utopias. U-topie, as the search for a place that does not yet exist, plays a major role in Lefebvre's conception of the right to the city, which emerged from a consideration of the possible impossible. Transduction as a method involves developing the theoretical object from the information and problematic posed by reality. It injects rigour into utopian knowledge. Pushing one's ideas to the extreme can help to clarify objectives and the consequences of choices (Lévy, 1994, 15). Alienation for him was not about a distancing from an essence or generic humanity but the loss of the feeling that there is an ability to achieve the possible, make the possible impossible (1970c, 187). Nor is there any thought without u-topie, that is the wish to discover through the process of creation (1970a, 178). Lefebvre would have very much agreed with the comment made in the introduction to Jules Verne's visionary book *Paris au XXe siècle* (1994), written in 1863 but not published until recently, that 'Its strength comes precisely from knowing never to invent, but paying acute, almost hypnotic, attention to the real, so as to get it to yield up its secret and reveal its possibilities' (7).

The extension of processes that he saw in operation in New York and Paris led him to describe the utopia of New Athens where centrality was reserved for the privileged few:

> In this centre occupied by the New Masters, coercion and persuasion converge with the power of decision-making and the capacity to consume. Without necessarily owning it all, the New Masters possess this privileged space, axis of a strict spatial policy. What they especially have is the privilege to possess time . . . There is only for the masses carefully measured space. Time eludes them. (*Right to the City*).

Intellectuals and scientists as secondary elites, he continues, will be organized into competitive laboratories for the greatest good of economic and political Masters. The masses are not called the people or the working class, their daily lives are teledirected, while the permanent threat of unemployment generates latent and generalized terror. As he said one might smile at this scenario, but when it comes true it will be too late!

Today, utopias have been discredited, but they are necessary for thinking about the future and so it is time we rehabilitated them (Latour and Combes, 1991).[12] Although his thinking on the urban demonstrates the qualities of the romantic revolutionary (Löwy, 1991), it should not be dismissed as hopelessly optimistic. Though certainly far more pessimistic about the extension of urban society and the illusions of modernity towards the end of his life (1991a), he wasn't completely unaware in the earlier period of the weakness of political movements in radically challenging urban developments (1970b). He couldn't understand how people could simply accept changes imposed around them (1989)

We have outlined some of the key questions in the *Right to the City*, but he also integrated a number of related themes which are developed elsewhere. These covered the critique of the everyday, the reproduction of objects and social relations (see 1973b), appropriation of space, the relationship between use and exchange value, the role of the philosopher in transcending abstract knowledge aloof from praxis but with a privileged role in thinking about the city as a totality. We see too the application of his method of regression–progression to the changing nature of town–country relations from the ancient Greek period onwards. For Lefebvre, poets have been able to understand the city as the dwelling of man; however, an anti-urban tradition, which goes back a long way and which is clearly present in the Chicago School of Sociology, Judaism and Protestantism and in Marxism, has unfortunately dominated our attitude to it (1986c). Although the Greeks valued the urban core (*cité*) as a place of civilization and the creation of art, they also bequeathed to us an instrumental attitude to the political and military role of the city (1991a). The book was also an attack against the idea that urbanism is a mechanical operation, devoid of ideology, but which had become a sort of catechism for technocrats. This was a theme he would further pursue in *La révolution urbaine* (1970d), which he claims was not the usual history of urbanization.

---

[12] Ruth Levitas (1993) argues for the necessity of utopia because of its potential for social transformation, a really possible world whose emergence from the present state of affairs is credible. It can be defined as the desire for a better way of living expressed in the description of a different kind of society that makes possible that alternative way of life (257). She believes the difficulty in developing utopias arises from the current inability to identify agents and processes of change (265).

Thus urban revolution does not refer to a future stage that has superseded the industrial era. Rather Lefebvre is concerned to explore the possibility of an urban society derived from a radical critique emanating from the Left, that is a utopia in his sense. The other theme of *La révolution urbaine* is the necessity to examine urbanism as a social practice, an ideological practice that contributes in part to the absence of a political critique by *usagers*, the users, which forms the substance of his concluding chapter. Once again he urges the need to analyse the city as totality, which always seems to be elsewhere. Instead we are presented with fragments and vague concepts such as environment and *équipements* (collective services). Despite the failure of 1968 to create an urban society, in which the everyday has been transformed, he still felt that an urban revolution remained a possibility.

In 1970 he founded, with Anatole Kopp, author of books on early Soviet urbanism, the review *Espaces et Sociétés*, but left it due to his disagreement with what he saw as inflexible dogmatism about its views on the spatial and the urban situation (1976–8, vol. 4, 268). 'Why', he asks, 'must Marxism evacuate the symbolic, the dream and the imaginary and systematically eliminate the 'poetic being', the *oeuvre*? (270). During these years he gave numerous conferences and taught courses at the École Spéciale d'Architecture to students who all read the *Right to the City* and *La révolution urbaine*. In addition, until 1968, architectural training was very formalistic and so students, once liberated from this straitjacket, were eager to plunge into the more sociological aspects. He maintained diverse contacts with architects and was sometimes asked to participate as part of the team entering a competition. It is common practice in France to include someone with a broader social science or philosophical approach in such teams, due partly to a conception of architecture derived from its origins within schools of fine arts. Hence he partook in the Galieni renewal project in the north of Paris and that for the New Belgrade in Yugoslavia in the 1980s. He was critical of architectural practice but appreciated architecture and architects. His understanding of space had resonances for their understanding.

Espace et politique, based upon a series of essays and articles, some of which had previously been published in *Espaces et Sociétés*, was an accompanying volume to *Right to the City* and lays the foundation for *Production of Space*. A number of themes come together in this book, reflecting teaching interests, such as courses on alienation, primarily sexual, and nudity in art (1975b, 113–14). It is a book with several centres which he suggests (1974/1986, xi) we re-read using three elements: the individual elements of the analysis, the paradigmatic oppositions that arise from these, such as private/public, use/exchange, space and time; and lastly the dialectization of these elements such as conflicts, social rhythms and times produced by and in this space. Reappropriation of space and the body are equally parts of any revolutionary project (1974, 166–7). Practices and strategy increasingly reproduce spaces according to production relations paralleling biological reproduction and genitality (376).

In effect, he wrote very little on the spatial alone after his retirement from Nanterre in 1973. He published a few short pieces or gave interviews on the nature and future of the city (1986c; 1987; 1989; 1991a; Renaudie, 1988), integrated a chapter on space in his last volume on the State (1976–8, vol. 4, 259–325) and in *Critique de la vie quotidienne* (1981, 128–35). It was primarily the related processes of homogeneity, fragmentation and hierarchization, to which he constantly returned (1980a), and which by the mid 1980s had become even more generalized and penetrated knowledge (*savoir*), culture and the whole of society (1974/1986, viii). He felt that he had said more or less all that was significant on the spatial and that he had to turn his attention to arguing for the retention of Marxism, given the attacks against it from developments in Eastern Europe and French intellectual life (1980a). It was now acceptable to decree Marxism as *passé* and irrelevant to our understanding of the world.

Time, complexity and the city

In the mid 1970s he turned to his earlier, cherished themes of mystification, difference, alienation, fetishism and daily life, and which his analysis of the State (1976–8) enabled him to integrate. He also wanted to return to the concept of modernity sketched out in embryonic form by Nietzsche (1975b, 213). Before looking at these aspects more closely in relation to the everyday and the city, we should note that Lefebvre had published a number of books in the years immediately after 1968, and coterminously with his writing on space and urban society. Difference, the transformation of philosophy (1970a) and the end of history (1970c) were the subject of much general debate of that period. In these books Lefebvre addressed the feeling of malaise and crisis and the transitionary period into a new society, that is a society of difference, of which he saw the dangers and the positive aspects, but also lucidly reminds us that the institutions with homogenizing power, especially the State, are very much with us.

The Nietzschean revival of the 1960s was associated with names such as Deleuze and Foucault, whom Lefebvre called neo-Nietzscheans (1970c). Nietzsche was a thinker Lefebvre felt passionately about and whom he had tried to rescue from misinterpretation in the late 1930s (1939; 1959, section 4, ch. 10). Nietzsche figured in his trinity (1975a). Above all, Lefebvre tried to construct a bridge between Marx and Nietzsche (1970c). It was not just that Marx had not considered a number of later developments, such as the fragmented city, the global (*mondial*), the daily, the repetitive and the differential, the struggle against time within time itself, and the State. Marxism simply is not sufficient as the only theory; a political revolution if it were to happen would not resolve all the problems of love and happiness; what it would do would be to provide the individual with the social conditions which would make any resolution easier (1989, 468). Hegel and Marx focused on mastery of nature and the external world, which for them defined the human being; Nietzsche, on the other hand, turned inwards to the transformation of self through desire and *jouissance*.

Foucault is an obvious though not stated link with Nietzsche, for whom Lefebvre had, on the other hand, little sympathy, calling him, at the height of his invective against structuralism in the 1960s, the ideologue of the system (1971, 297). As with many other Marxists and Sartre, *Les mots et les choses*, published in 1966, was read as a right-wing book, that denied politics and represented a work of Gaullist technocracy (Eribon, 1994, 80, 167). Foucault went even further than Lévi-Strauss in his systematization; he never leaves the terrain of knowledge (*savoir*), theory or the system. *Savoir*, a systematized knowledge, was at the expense of *connaissance*, knowledge produced by the subject and directed towards an object, implicating agency and reflexivity in its production. Subversion must come from the *connaissance* of dominated and marginalized groups. Foucault's explanations too were partial (1980b; 1985a). Lefebvre considered that to achieve an understanding of how workers were progressively made to work from the seventeenth to the nineteenth centuries, necessitated a global analysis. This would encompass not only the role of religion, morality, sexual repression, and asceticism, but also how these modes were initially tried out through military experiments and upon animals. Dressage is also a concept he applies to humans, and has been practised especially on the organs of the senses. It was particularly hard on girls and women of the privileged classes (1992, 59). Foucault explored this process only though the lesser and individual elements such as the institutionalization of the abnormal and anomic, pedagogic pressure and educational institutions and military models (1980b, 158–9). Part of the problem too stemmed from Foucault's refusal to begin with a concept and the fact that he only took account of texts (1980b, 38). It should be noted that Lefebvre did not comment at any length on Foucault's work on space and the urban.[13]

Foucault, together with Deleuze, Derrida and Lyotard contributed to the emergence as from 1960 of a philosophy of difference (Ruby, 1989). Deleuze (1968) argued that a major ontological break had taken place in the replacement of identity, and its negation and contradiction, by difference and repetition. Difference is not about negation nor is repetition a simple recurrence (Huisman, 1993). In *Le manifeste différentialiste*, written against what he saw as the continuing rigidity of homogenizing political systems after 1968 and a malaise which was much debated in France, Lefebvre traced the philosophical genesis and genealogy of the concept of difference and how we might pursue a strategy and method based on difference. He insists that difference is not based on particularity, originality or individualism; it emerges from struggle, conceptual and lived. Despite the different uses to which the idea of difference has been put, Lefebvre defended its relevance to rights associated with difference in-

---

[13] Foucault in the 1960s worked with architects; he undertook a number of research projects for the Ministère de l'Équipement in the 1970s, using a genealogical approach to study the emergence of discourses and practices of collective consumption in health and education in the 18th and 19th centuries. Many well known sociologists and philosophers participated in research financed by this Ministry, such as Deleuze and Guattari who also undertook contract research, for example, on collective services and green spaces, in the same research centre (Centre d'Études de Recherches et de Formation Institutionelle) of which Foucault was director from 1971 to 1975. Indeed Castells (1994, 58) has recently argued that Michel Conan, the administrator-thinker-dispenser of money in the Ministry was the central person in the post-1968 development of the French school of urban sociology. Urban sociology received more money than other social sciences at that time.

scribed in equality. These were a means of concretizing democracy and socialism (1958, 119–22).

The theory of difference implies an increasing complexity of the world and of society (1970a, 171). Its opposite, reduction, appears as a theoretical, practical, strategic and ideological instrument of power that seeks to dominate. Difference is a way of linking that which is near and far, here and there, actual and utopian, possible and impossible. That is why we must struggle against a society of 'indifference', not just by producing discourses but also in the way we live 'differentially' (185). And this is the meaning of urban society and the importance of the notion and practice of centrality.

Urban society was one of plural and differential times. In traditional metaphysics, real and mental time bear no relationship to each other and history is thus dispensed with (1970c, 190–1). Structuralism too expunged history, the conjunctural from the structural; it reflected the current middle-class fear of history. The fetishism of culture blocks history but uses it as a product of consumption (182). Whilst opposed to historicism, interpreted both as a predetermined sense of history and excessive detail to boring minutiae without any overall conceptualization (Hess, 1988, ch. 17), he desired a renewal of *historicité*. Historicity too has several related meanings. In philosophy and history it refers to the situation in which people define their existence. In sociology, it covers the manner in which works are produced, distributed and consumed, and the capacity of a society to act upon itself (Grawitz, 1994). It wasn't any longer a matter of transcending a particular historical moment through history, but of overcoming (*surmonter*) nihilism which arises from the fact that history has not transcended anything (1970c, 73). Becoming continues, in contrast to Heidegger's conception of history as that of being, traced in its passage through forests, paths and clearings. There is no end to history as Hegel and Marx hoped for; it was Nietzsche who had the courage to proclaim that man and culture could not be complete and this was a good thing (121). If modernity, on the other hand, claims it has liquidated history, it is an abusive pretension, which simply masks what has not actually changed (183). He concludes that it is no longer possible to conceive of a historical totality as that which transcends all separations, but we need to think of history as a totality that overcomes the fragmentation of history and society (190).

However, during this period he only devoted a few pages to the plurality of times. Within the philosophical tradition, one can distinguish three approaches to time – firstly, the cosmological or the time of nature, secondly, the lived or phenomenological, concerned with duration or the individual time- consciousness, and thirdly, the inter-subjective or social perspective, dealing with multiplicity of time-consciousness and its social composition through struggle over conflicting rhythms (Osborne, 1994, 4–5).[14] Unlike his lengthy analysis of the production of space he only sketches out a periodization of the significance of time in society. In pre-historic societies (not to be taken as prehistoric or pre-writing), continuity dominates and time does not figure in consciousness. In historic societies, history is credited with great significance, while homogeneous time, which engenders a unitary history, moves to the centre of consciousness. This is a period associated with industrialization and the destruction of nature. The contradictions between homogeneity and difference become apparent, leading to a transitional period, into which society is now entering. The next stage is post-or transhistory when unitary history is finally abandoned and multiple codes are invented such that they may give an impression of endless disorder (1970c, 203–4). Such a period emerges in urban society, but it has so far been very unequally developed. It by no means signals an end to conflict and violence for these may break out without 'historical reason', nor does it entail the disappearance of ghettos and violence in cities (214).

Borrowing from Gurvitch,[15] time is not only a mental time, it is also social, biological, physical, cosmic, linear and cyclical. Linear time, in the same way as abstract space increasingly displaces the absolute, takes over the cyclical, though the latter never disappears. The second major source on time is George Bachelard (1950),[16] who treated *durées*

---

[14] For a wide-ranging discussion of history temporality and narration, see Ricoeur (1985).

[15] George Gurvitch (1896–1965) was a highly influential sociologist in France who brought Lefebvre into the CNRS. He founded the *Cahiers Internationaux de Sociologie*. Lefebvre often refers to him. He was not only interested in time and causality, but also the *oeuvre* which was a crucial component of society.

[16] Lefebvre notes that philosophers (including Nietzsche) have only vaguely understood the importance of rhythms. Bachelard (1884–1962) wrote a number of books on the imagination in contact with nature and on time (1931; 1938). Whilst borrowing the term *rythmanalyse*, Bachelard did not develop it in *Psychanalyse du feu*. However in *La dialectique de la durée*, Bachelard sees its psycho-analytic and therapeutic potential, whereby it could be a means of temporal dislocation and disorganization that would get rid of false permanences. It is not

(time periods) as essentially dialectical and built upon undulations and rhythms; they were material, biological and psychological. His objective was to understand the complexity of life through a plurality of *durées*, each of which has its own specific rhythm, solidity of linkages and strength of continuity. There is an alternation between rest and action producing discontinuities in psychic production; the continuity of the psyche is not given but an *oeuvre*. Paradoxically the *durées* that appear the most stable owe their stability to rhythmic discordance. Therefore to treat time as uniform was to forget a fundamental principle.

Bachelard traced the origins of rhythmanalysis to a Brazilian philosopher, Peinheiro dos Santos writing in 1931. It was an idea Lefebvre begins to envisage in *Production of Space* (1974, 205–7) and announced as a project in *Critique de la vie quotidienne* (1981), and for which he held high hopes as complementary to or as a replacement for psychoanalysis, to which he had become vehemently opposed since its adoption and popularization by some Parisian intellectuals in the 1960s.[17] The other source of inspiration for the theory of rhythm-

enough to bring the past to consciousness, as psychoanalysis has done. We have to ensure that we do not continue to give the same form to that which is without form. In the conclusion he outlines the material and biological aspects of rhythmanalysis. It is however Lefebvre who takes apart the different rhythms and applies them to the everyday.

[17] There is much to say about Lefebvre's relationship and critique of psychoanalysis and psychoanalysts which we cannot undertake in this introduction. Early on he was attracted to the surrealists by their interest in psychoanalysis (Jay, 1984, 293) but he became sceptical about it (1975b, 166–7). Lefebvre's attitude towards psychoanalysis markedly hardened in the 1960s, if we compare his two autobiographies. By this time it had become an established ideology in the United States and was taken up by a number of Parisian intellectuals. In 1960 a conference was held at Bonneval on the unconscious, at which Henri Lefebvre and Jacques Lacan participated. Lefebvre considered that for the most part the concept of the unconscious had been manipulated and reduced to a fetishized species (Bonnafé, 1991, 22). In his view, Freud had conceptualized sexuality and brought to light sexual misery, but psychoanalysis had in turn generated an ideology of normality and mythology of desire. Without making capitalism the sole reason for sexual misery, psychoanalysis has a tendency to ignore it and the State. Furthermore, for Freud like Heidegger, difference disappears in such a way that the masculine represents the universal (1980b, 166–8).

In particular he poured scorn on Lacan whom he called an *escroc* (swindler) and a *fumiste* (not serious) (1975b, 174) because he dared speak about women, sex and the libido without knowing what he was talking about! The dislike of Lacan is also likely to have stemmed from his psychoanalytical practices and relationship to his analysands.

analysis can be seen in his theory of moments, which goes back to 1925, before his adherence to Marxism (Hess, 1994; Lefebvre, 1959, part 3, ch. 1). It was also in the mid 1920s that the discontinuity generated by the First World War made him aware of the significance of plebeian romanticism and the rehabilitation of everyday life. Modernity and its critique, epitomized by the most acerbic one of all, surrealism, made considerable advances as from this period (1985a, 145).

Time itself seemed not to be exhausted by concepts such as evolution, revolution or growth, while the *durée* was not solely defined by linearity but was also characterized by discontinuity. These moments, or internal *durées* (love, play, rest, poetry), were modes of communication, communicable and communicating, or modes of presence. Although he discarded these ideas in the late 1920s, partly because he felt it tended to eliminate the historicity that he was discovering in Marx, he nevertheless did not dispense with the idea that the non-linearity of time was important. He later linked moments with the idea of creating new situations (1975b, 109–10). Indeed Debord created situations out of moments which he deemed too abstract (Hess, 1988, 215). The moments that an individual can experience are elaborated by the society in which the individual participates or the practices which a social group diffuses more widely (1959, 651). A moment defines a form and is defined by one (648). The everyday is composed of a multiplicity of moments, such as games, love, work, rest, struggle, knowledge, poetry and justice, and links professional life, direct social life, leisure and culture. If we take the case of play, as a moment in advanced societies, it has its specific categories of rules, partners, stakes, risk, bets and luck. An important aspect of the temporality of a moment is its repetition. So when playing, one accepts the rules of the game and each time recreates and reinvents the usage of the game.

Thus sixty years later (1985a, 142–60) he was turning full circle to his preoccupations as a member of the new philosophers group in the 1920s and concentrating on philosophical issues of representation and a phenomenological description of the relationship between the body, its rhythms and surrounding space, which remained a virtuality. These ideas were dropped, as we have seen because of his turn to Marxism. However, *Éléments de rythmanalyse* (1992), in which the latter theme is taken up, was not published until after his death. Whilst written in the early 1980s and announced in the special issue on time and space of *Communications* in 1985, practical problems and the feeling that it was not of the stature befitting a thinker of Lefebvre's calibre, meant that a publisher couldn't be found for several years. The series of essays brings together themes of rhythms, temporalities, music, poetry, philosophy, everyday life and the city.

Rhythmanalysis is a concept that interweaves cyclical and linear rhythms in the everyday. The linear, which can be made totally uniform and quantifiable, has more and more eliminated the qualitative from time and space. The disappearance of rhythms and cycles engenders in turn a need for rhythms, exemplified by the growing significance of music in social life or the commercialized and recuperated fête (1981, 134–5). Although time and space are intimately linked and measured in terms of one another, time can never be reversed. Time is projected onto space through measures, uniformizing it and emerging in things and products. The apparent reversibility of time through products in the everyday gives us a feeling of contentedness, constructing a rampart against the tragic and death. The tragic exists outside dailyness but it irrupts within it, for example, through aggression, violence and crime (1981, 169). As we can see in *Right to the City*, time in particular was increasingly measured out and rationed. Certainly any political project will entail a revaluation of time since use value based on 'appropriation itself implies time (or times), rhythm (or rhythms), symbols and practices' (1974, 356). 'The buyer of space or property acquires time.' New struggles, both visible and invisible, were forming around time and its uses (1985b, 192).

Rhythmanalysis is the means by which we understand the struggle against time within time itself (1986a). The body represents the surmounting of the mental and the sensory, whilst differences emerge from the repetitions of gesture (linear), rhythms (cyclical) that the body generates (1974, 385). It is the most basic form of production of time; in itself is engraved the passage from immaturity to maturity and the supreme difference, that of old age and death. The study of rhythmanalysis was intended to be pluridisciplinary, integrating chronobiology, living rhythms, rhythms of speech, thought, music and the city, and of which each city has its own. Starting from the everyday rhythms of the body and its subjection to training and rules (*dressage*), he proceeds to analyse capitalism as not only the production of classes, but also as a system that is built upon contempt of the body and its life times. The rhythms of capital have displaced the major historical rhythms, such as affirmation and negation of the body, and now on a planetary scale both produce all things and destroy them through war, progress and speculation (1992, 72–7).

He argued that Western philosophy had abandoned the living body as the store of non-formal knowledge (*non-savoir*) which constitutes a source of potential knowledge (*connaissance*) (1974, 407). The placing of the body and its creation of a differential field runs throughout *Production of Space*. The eye, the ear and the hand, for example, are not passive components of the body; each has their own rhythm in a body which is the place of interaction between the biological, the physical and the social (1985b, 197). Merleau-Ponty (1945) too had placed the body in a field of time and space, but Lefebvre criticized phenomenology for positing an absolute conscience, with no relation to social practice or influenced by nature, the body and the external world, and eliminating mediations, becoming, time and history, and substituting substances for them (1957, 38–41). What is the act of thinking, he asks. It is to think the relationships between human beings and the universe. It is the separation and conjoining of forms and content (1985a, 123–4). Phenomenology also refused the concept as a means of investigation and limited itself to the immediacy of the lived. Modern physics has taught us that things which appear inert are not, so that we need to go beyond appearances (1985b, 198). In effect, rhythmanalysis translates socially and philosophically Einsteinian notions of space–time relativity. Although the world has become more complex, and the mechanisms seemingly require experts to analyse them, we can still grasp the significance of rhythms of daily life through looking and using our intellect (1992, 21). And one of the aims of complex thought (*la pensée complexe*) has been to reflect on epistemological and social consequences of changes in scientific ideas (Barreau, 1985; Béchillon, 1994; Morin, 1994).

Lefebvre uses phenomenological concepts but deploys them differently as in 'Seen from the Window' where, starting from the subject and its different corporeal senses, he attempts to counteract the dominance of the visual which accompanies an abstract, violent and phallic space. This was a theme he had discussed in *Production of Space*. Scattered throughout Lefebvre's writings are numerous references to male sexuality and its production of spaces, feminism and gender relations (1980b), exploitation of women in daily life (1970b), the subjection and control of the body as in *dressage* (breaking in and

training) (1992). That feminitude will revolt against phallic dominance is inevitable, but it would be regrettable if it were to substitute a
uterine space (1974, 410). He does not however elaborate at length
what would be a dialectical relationship between the production of the
sexualized body and its relationship to and positioning in lived and
conceived spaces.

Yet using and applying rhythmanalysis will develop the analysis, as
he begins to do with a study of Mediterranean cities in the last
selection in this book, drawing together the scientific and the poetic,
and breaking down separations between space and time, private and
public, State-political and the intimate. A somewhat different application, though also referring to different rhythms and closely associating
spatial and temporal strategies, is the examination by Pierre George of
fifty years of changing relationships with space at different scales,
including neighbourhoods, new towns and regions. Thus: 'The space
which is no longer mobilized by individual times passes into the
jurisdiction of the local authority, region or State . . . It is recuperated
in administrative programmes of "territorial planning". These spatial
programmes have as an indirect, if not direct, objective, to reproject
individual and collective slices of time, (1985, 167).

In the 1980s too Lefebvre turned to an examination of rights within
a new political culture (1986b). In 1978 he had launched with Victor
Faye[18] a group called *Autogestion*, initially concerned with self-management in the workplace and, from 1981 to 1985, local democracy.
Within this context, the idea of the new citizenship as a social project
crystallized and led to the formation of the Groupe de Navarrenx,
consisting of about a dozen people who met regularly until 1989. The
objective was to set out a global vision linking the political, the
productive citizen and the user. For 200 years the rights of the citizen
had hardly changed from that of the right to express an opinion and
vote. However, citizenship should aim to create a different social life,
a more direct democracy, and a civil society based not on an abstraction but on space and time as they are lived (1986a, 173). Furthermore, given the situation of the suburbs and peripheral zones, the right
to the city was obviously important. Lefebvre was also intensely

---

[18] Victor Faye was a member of the Parti Socialiste Unifié, a group to the left of the
Socialist Party. He left the PSU before 1981 and headed the Socialist Commission
on Self-Management in the workplace.

interested, after his visit to California in 1983, by the treatment of space and time in information technology[19] (1991b). In large modern cities, one also has to take into account the internationalization of social relations, not just because of migration but also due to the multiplication of the technical means of communication and globalization of knowledge (1991a):

> The right to the city, complemented by the right to difference and the right to information, should modify, concretize and make more practical the rights of the citizen as an urban dweller (*citadin*) and user of multiple services. It would affirm, on the one hand, the right of users to make known their ideas on the space and time of their activities in the urban area; it would also cover the right to the use of the centre, a privileged place, instead of being dispersed and stuck into ghettos (for workers, immigrants, the 'marginal' and even for the 'privileged').

The hopes he had held out for urbanization could not furnish the basis for the values of a new civilization, and were vanishing together with the last illusions of modernity. The expansion of existing cities and creation of new ones has continued to support relationships of dependence, domination, exclusion and exploitation. The form of everyday life and information has changed but not the content. His critique continues with the disappearance of the historic centre such that those who were deported to the suburbs now return as dispossessed tourists. Nor has urban sociology lived up to its promises, giving rise to constraining urbanism which has become a sort of catechism for technocrats. His conclusion, in the light of the series of transformations, and especially in the everyday riven by contradictions in social practice, is that we must reformulate the framework of citizenship such that the right to the city brings together the urban dweller (*citadin*) and the citizen (1991a).

What therefore Lefebvre encourages us to do is to think critically about the myths and rhetoric of contemporary urbanism, and recog-

---

[19] Lefebvre stated in an interview in 1989 that technology and communications were the themes that interested him the most. This interest goes back to the 1950s in relation to language (1971) and in *Vers le cybernanthrope* he highlighted the growing importance of information and knowledge. Today information technology is the theatre and stake of a gigantic conflict which is being used by the capitalist mode of production to get out of a crisis (1986a, 56). There is some interest in extending Lefebvrian ideas on rights and appropriation to information technology (Couvidat, 1994).

nize the tensions between unity and difference as an integral movement of dialectical materialism, the necessity for thinking about the
city as a totality, that is as a concept to be reconstituted, a procedure
that does not ignore the importance of the parts. He also champions
the possibility of progressive political projects and the continuing
necessity for utopias as the basis for action. One of his oft repeated
aphorisms was '*demander l'impossible pour avoir tout le possible*'
(demand the impossible in order to get all that is possible).

French Context and Influence

His books on the city and urbanism, *Le droit à la ville* and *La révolution
urbaine* reached a wide public, including the much despised technocrats.
The new urban policy that germinated under Olivier Guichard in the
early 1970s and was finally implemented under Giscard d'Estaing after
1974, echoed many of the themes of Lefebvre's writing (Garnier and
Goldschmidt, 1978, ch. 2).[20] These included the urban, conceived in
social as well as spatial terms, and the revival of the city as a collective
entity and its quality of life. Architects on the other hand had traditionally adopted a spatial treatment of the city. Both Right and Left lamented
the lack of the *fête*, around which inhabitants could unify, and the
disappearance of the ludic element (Garnier and Goldschmidt, 321).

The Left in the 1970s spoke of democratic participation, self-management (*autogestion*) and urban change, expressed in slogans such as
changer la ville, changer la vie (change the city, change life). This was
a period of the *programme commun* between the Socialist and Communist Parties when they took over a large number of muncipalities.
With the Socialists in power after 1981, the urban question began to
turn its attention more to the suburbs (*banlieues*) and not focus to
the same degree on historic centres and medium-sized towns. Effectively, the programme known as Banlieue 89 launched by Michel
Cantal-Dupart and Roland Castro in 1983 implemented a number of

---

[20] Garnier and Goldschmidt argue that the new urban policy prioritized the urban
because of fears by the bourgeoisie of both discontent about quality of life and a
connection between workplace and residential struggles. It all sought to incorporate the nouvelle petite bourgeoisie which had not had a political voice in the
1960s, some of whom had been implicated in the turbulence of the late 1960s. The
latter sentiments were clearly expressed by Giscard d'Estaing (1976).

principles recognizable to any Lefevbrian – the introduction of centrality into the peripheral zones and the transformation of suburbs
into real cities, the right to the city, the struggle against exclusion, and
a renewed sense of urbanity (Kofman, 1994). Although Castro (1994)
cites Lefebvre as the only major post-war intellectual to have taken the
city seriously, unlike Merleau-Ponty or Sartre, he nevertheless remains
silent on the debt owed to his urban writing, despite Lefebvre's influence
amongst radical architects through his teaching in the early 1970s. It
should be said that Banlieue 89 tended to focus on the more physical
elements and minimize the economic and social processes at play. So too
did the policy *politique de la ville* launched in 1988 under Yves Dauges,
which owed much to a Lefebvrian sensibility. Occasionally his work, and
in particular *Right to the City* was brandished in front of the media for
example by Michel Delebarre, the first *Ministre de la ville* during the
Socialist years (Garnier, 1994). Lefebvre himself ironically complained
that 'his writings on space and the urban were deemed scandalous until
these "truths" were proclaimed obvious and trivial, that is taken up by
politicians without the least polite formula, but then that was how it is'
(1976–8, vol. 4, 324). Was this all that different from the earlier experiences, such as the concept of mystification, developed in *La conscience
mystifiée*, which was used and abused polemically by politicians and then
passed into general usage (1959, 462). Over the years, the more his work
was plundered, the less it was cited (Garnier, 1994, 131).

On the whole Lefebvre has tended to be marginalized in France and
his work undervalued. He remained faithful to a living and constantly
renewed Marxism (Anderson, 1983; Löwy, 1991) and this had not
helped his reputation. After all his book *Le marxisme*, first published
in 1948, and now in its 21st edition, is the bestseller of the small and
cheap paperback series Que Sais-Je published by Presses Universitaires
de France. Neither did the conflictual relationship with the Communist
Party, which he joined in 1928, help. Partly, too, he suffered from being
the person who throughout his career always maintained a critical
stance. Was he not thinking of himself when he wrote (1980b, 202):

> It is correct that in the conditions of the modern world, only the man
> apart, the marginal, the peripheral, the anomic, those excluded from
> the horde (Gurvitch) has a creative capacity . . . the greatest chances of
> creating: isn't it the man of frontiers? . . . (who) bears a tension that
> would kill others: he is both inside and outside, included and excluded,

yet without being for that matter torn asunder . . . He passes alongside-promised lands, but he doesn't enter. . . . Discovery, that's his passion.

Whilst he was the guru of 1968, the attraction of structural Marxism in the early 1970s, to which he was profoundly hostile, supplanted him to some extent (Davidson, 1993). Structural Marxism had a strong hold in the urban sociology of the early 1970s (see Castells, 1972). The waning of structuralist positions in the late 1970s still left Lefebvre marginalized in these circles. Perhaps his critical stance was too difficult to face from those who now wanted to shake off the intellectual rigidity of structural Marxism. Marxism more generally was out of fashion, and certainly this is the reason many would put forward for his marginal status in the 1980s; intellectuals were more concerned with the *l'ère du vide* (the era of emptiness) (Lipovetsky, 1983) and the abolition of the subject.

Unlike the situation in Anglo-American geography, a Marxist inspired geography was never adopted, not even by members of the Communist Party. Geography in general tended to be empiricist and with little contact with developments in sociology, except for those (e.g. Kayser, Rochefort) who had been taught by Pierre George, one of the leading French geographers of this century, and a Marxist like Lefebvre. In the 1950s the two had worked together, organizing a conference on Villes et Campagnes. George also at times deployed the regression–progression method (conversation with Antoine Haumont). On the whole, geographers were concerned with concrete space, while much sociology has spoken of social space in metaphorical terms. So neither were preoccupied with the production of space as such. Nor did a Marxist urban sociology, tending to reduce the city to various functions of capitalism, embrace his ideas.[21] Some Marxist sociologists, on the other hand, turned to social history. As for philosophers, despite the recent interest in the city (Ansay and Schoonbrodt, 1989; Cahiers de Philosophie, 1993), they have not recognized the significance of Lefebvre's thinking on the various dimensions of the philosopher in, of and on the city.[22] Finally, he was barely taken

---

[21] For example, Michel Amiot (1986), an orthodox Marxist, simply writes out Lefebvre from his otherwise interesting history of urban sociology in France.

[22] Ansay and Schoonbrodt's collection of philosophical texts on the city reprints two short extracts from *Right to the City* but in a lengthy section on the right to the city omits any mention of Lefebvre as the instigator of the concept. Paquot (1993) refers very briefly to the concept of everyday life in his article on civility, urbanity and urban citizenship.

into account by Marxist economists, despite his acute insights into the reproduction and survival of capitalism. In part this was due to Lefebvre's disdain for economics as the privileged discipline of the Communist Party, the influence of Althusserianism and his weakly structured discourse (Dieuaide and Motamed-Nejad, 1994).

His sharp critique, especially of technocrats (1967a), whether of the Left or the Right, was also accompanied by an unwillingness to compromise. It was as if he was telling them they might as well commit suicide (interview with Henri Raymond). After 1974, the technocrats, in particular from the Ministère de l'Équipement, thought they had found solutions to urban problems. They read Lefebvre and distilled a number of his ideas, not in the way he approved and against which he fulminated. Above all he fought against falsehoods, and this stance too served to marginalize him. At the same time, he didn't make a pedagogic effort to ensure his succession, although he did have a large number of postgraduate students, not exclusively in urban sociology, during his later years at Nanterre. On the one hand, he did not produce, and indeed was totally antagonistic to a closed and tightly knit systematic approach, which would have also been more easily reproducible, theoretically and empirically. On the other hand, a series of aphorisms could be derived from his analysis of urban society and everyday life. Indeed, in an imaginary conversation between Lefebvre and Herbert Marcuse, Charlotte Delbo (1969), his secretary for many years, distilled the best known sayings from the events of 1968.

Thus his critics in the 1970s levelled the charge of recuperation (Castells, 1972; Garnier and Goldschmidt, 1978).[23] His reponse to those he called his hypercritics did not really confront them head on

---

[23] Lefebvre points out that recuperation has taken a specific form in the years after 1968 in that technocrats got the critics themselves to work out what would be applicable out of the radical critiques (1981, 107). Many Marxist sociologists at this time accepted contracts from State ministries. Marxists were not the only ones subjected to recuperation although they offered the richest pickings. The notion of 'changer la vie' (changing life) was exemplary. It was originally subversive and fluid, but was transformed into quality of life and reduced to the signs and discourses of transformation (108). It is interesting that Vaneigem (1992, 10) specifically notes the lack of understanding of his ideas on the quality of life, transparency, participation and creativity in the original text published in 1967, and its later official integration.

(1981, 104–9). Any innovative idea was capable of being recuperated and since the French Revolution the Left had constantly come up with ideas which were adopted and adapted by the Right (1975b, 98, 155). 'There is no gesture so radical that ideology will not try to recuperate.' So thought Guy Debord (quoted in Plant, 1992, 188). Lefebvre also asked what was the point of hammering the innovator who was not necessarily the person involved in recuperation? However, Garnier and Goldschmidt argue that this does not address the question of why the bourgeoisie specifically needed to prioritize the urban and pursue a policy based on quality rather than quantity.

It is quite easy now to highlight the outdatedness of a number of his concrete analyses, for example, the reign of the quantitative or the statement that the housing question was occluding issues about the city. Instead the *Politique de la ville* pushed housing into the background, although in the past few years it has come back with a vengeance.[24] We should not forget that Lefebvre's critique was made in a different context of shortage in the post-war period and, later on, rapid urban growth. Garnier (1994) suggests we might want to explain his current marginalization by pointing out that Lefebvre is tarred with unfashionable positions. Only a few social scientists are still concerned with a sociology of demystification (*dévoilement*); the others are content to embrace the world as it is. However, after showing the ways in which his ideas have been appropriated and often inverted, Garnier concludes on a positive note, highlighting the durable aspects of his thinking on the urban, and his reminder to us of the illusions of urban thinking – avoiding social relations in the production of the city and its exclusions, treating the city in pathological terms and as essence and spirit, using alienation to treat a product of human activity as an autonomous entity. As long as relations of production and ownership are not altered, centrality will be the preserve of those who use and benefit from these relations. At best it will be elitist, at worst military and policed. On the periphery he was

---

[24] In the few past years associations calling for the requisition of vacant housing and representing the homeless, such as DAL (*Droit au logement*) have been created. They have been active in Paris with a spectacular coup in December 1994 when they occupied with tactical precision an uninhabited building in the fashionable 6th arrondissement belonging to a large development company under investigation. It has been commented that in France right to housing, unlike the right to education and health, does not exist.

extremely lucid when he wrote in the 1980s, that whilst they were threatening, nothing would be born out of these disturbances except for the possibility of blood being spilt (1986a, 167). And rare, he concludes are those today who are audacious enough to maintain a theoretical and political vision and a critique of the existing state of affairs, that is, want the impossible to realize the possible (Garnier, 1994, 143).

Now several years after his death, we can detect signs of his return as an appreciated thinker on the city. A conference on Lefebvre's work, 'Henri Lefebvre Traces de futurs, held in Paris in June 1994, brought together those who, with different political and ideological positions, have been influenced by Lefebvre. Topics as varied as ecology, the city (Courbon, 1994; Jehl, 1994), informational society (Couvidat, 1994; Lacroix, 1994), differentialism (Michaux, 1994), theory of moments and education (Hess, 1994), and modernity (Schnaidt, 1994) were discussed. A special issue of *Espaces et Sociétés* (no. 76, 1994) was devoted to a critical appraisal of his writing on modernity, urban and the city (Garnier, 1994), architecture (Pellegrino and Neves, 1994), relevance to economic thinking (Dieuaide and Motamed-Nejad, 1994) and as a precursor of postmodernism (Dear, 1994; Hamel and Poitras, 1994). The issue of *Annales de la Recherche Urbaine* (1994), though not specially devoted to Lefebvre, also recognizes his contribution to thinking about the city and urbanity as totality, the significance of the concept of the everyday (Joseph, 1994), the continuing relevance of the right to the city in Europe (Ostrowestsky, 1994). and utopian thinking (Lévy, 1994). It is clear that the themes with which he was absorbed and his methodology still retain much of relevance for the present and the future.

We would suggest that the deepening polarization of urban life may well be a catalyst for a more penetrating, integrative and totalizing (in the Lefebvrian sense) thought about the city. Visions of the city in terms of alienation and *déracinement* are still employed in the French programme on urban research (Joseph, 1994). Too many reiterate the impossibility of thinking beyond the fragments (Castro, 1994), and the fear that if everything is linked, or what may be called the holistic syndrome, then it will be impossible to gain control of processes (Joseph, 1994). There is however a need to think the city as a totality, not in the sense of an inventory but as a concept to be constituted, as a whole that articulates relationship between elements. Centrality is not fixed but liable to dispersal and movement (1974, 399). We see too that Lefebvrian notions of appropriation, recognition of difference assembled together, the user, who is both a conservative and a subversive figure in the reproduction of social relations, and the theory of moments, in which social links are constructed and torn asunder, are all themes relevant to an understanding of the city (Joseph, 1994). Some are also trying to bring together different paradigms of the city – alienation and uprootedness in the city and different approaches to the everyday.[25] An example of the latter would be the juxtaposition of Lefebvre and Goffmann (1969) for both of whom the everyday was not the dark side of history. Goffmann devoted much attention to the everyday, derived from an initial and detailed analysis of life in institutions, and which can be extended to the institutionalization of society (discussion with Antoine Haumont). Others consider that a revival in Lefebvre's fortunes will come primarily from a wider reading of and reflection upon his thought, especially notions of dailyness and alienation, rather than specifically urban notions (Garnier, 1994). A more social analysis of the economic (Dieuaide and Motamed-Nejad, 1994) might emerge from an institutional and social application of regulation theory which would also seem to be a fruitful path towards exploring Lefebvrian insights in relation to urban policies. Finally, the interaction of temporalities and spatialities will surely be an area worthy of the application of Lefebvrian concepts and dialectical reasoning.

More than ever it is necessary in the context of urban transformation to affirm rights against exclusion from the city, but not in the sense of treating the city as autonomous and pathological. Today, rights are increasingly questioned, granted more and more conditionally and delivered at lower standards. How, we must ask, can we conjoin abstract and concrete rights? At the same time we should not forget that for Lefebvre rights are not simply derived from the politico-State level but are also anchored in civil society.

---

[25] For Michel de Certeau (1994, xi) the study of the everyday and the art of doing are to reveal the subterranean forms of dispersed creativity in the everyday, a tactic of bricolage adopted in the face of networks of surveillance. He poses both similar and contrary questions to those of Foucault. The procedures and ruses of consumers are an anti-discipline, for which he states in a footnote, that Lefebvre's work is a fundamental source.

When Lefebvre wrote *Right to the City*, the popular classes had already begun to be pushed out of central Paris by processes of State and market-led redevelopment. However, in the intervening years not only have vast tracts of the centre been dramatically transformed, but the Eastern sector of Paris, the most working-class area, has been turned into an extensive building site. This is part of Paris's continued transformation into a global city (Sassens, 1994). The domination of a culture of the same and the exclusion of the more marginal, is most evident under the Chirac regime that has tightened its domination since winning power in 1977 (*Le Nouvel Observateur*, 23 September 1994). Specific rights, such as those of housing, thus conjoin with the more abstract and generalized calls for the right to the city for those whom the market and the State have expelled from centrality.

At the same time the metropolitization of the suburban municipalities (Genestier, 1994), following principles of creating multiple centres, is producing its own pattern of exclusion. Communes such as Saint-Denis and Bobigny, through a programme of redevelopment of their centres and the extension of existing transport lines, are now an integral part of Paris. This is in turn generating a strengthened core and periphery in these municipalities.

Anglo-American Reception

The present esteem in which Lefebvre is held in Anglo-Saxon countries has been spearheaded by geographers (Gregory, 1994; Harvey, 1993; Merrifield, 1993; Smith 1984, 1993a; Soja 1985, 1989a, b)[26] and those arguing that space has become more important in social theory and postmodernism (Jameson, 1991). Other concepts are made to revolve around space such that it is seen as a recoding of everyday life,

---

[26] Gottdeiner (1985) was one of the few to take account of the variety of Lefebvre's urban and spatial corpus and not treat it as a unity (Katznelson, 1992). Since the publication of *Production of Space*, Lefebvre's breadth and depth has been increasingly recognized (Gregory, 1994: Merrifield, 1993: Soja, Forthcoming), especially with an eye for the richness of his reflection on the body, the everyday, especially its colonization, and utopias (Gregory, 1994). Of all those striving to extract a geographical legacy or relevance from Lefebvre's writing, Shields (1994) has explored in greatest depth the concepts and methods which wove their way through his work, including a recognition of the significance of history as virtuality.

itself primarily a spatial concept (Ross, 1988, 9). However, it would be unfortunate if *Production of Space* were to be treated as the core of his work and other writing subordinated to it, for, as we have amply seen, his own production after the mid 1970s remained massive and, most significantly, represented a return to earlier passions and concepts which had in some cases lain dormant, though not forgotten (1988, 78).

We can trace Lefebvre's influence on Marxist geography to Harvey (1973) in *Social Justice and the City*, which was based primarily on his reading of *La révolution urbaine*. He commented that he had no one else to turn to for a Marxist analysis of the city. Harvey uses him to construct a grid of changing functions, forms and structures and circulation of capital. Harvey's (1989) analysis of changing modes of capital accumulation, flexibility, new cultural forms and space-time compression is also heavily influenced by the historically evolving forms of spatial representations and representations of space deli-neated by Lefebvre. In particular, the consequences of the breakup of Euclidean space and pictorial representation as from 1910 are em-phasized. Harvey (1993) has recently suggested combining Lefebvre and Heidegger in the dialectical interplay of experience, perception and imagination in the construction of place.[27] Lefebvre, however, warns us against falling too easily into eclecticism with Heidegger (as occurred with the combination of Freud and Marx). The only way out is to define convergences and divergences outside of the philosophical arena (1965b, 133).

Soja refers extensively to his writing and, unlike Harvey, deploys a socio-spatial dialectic within a postmodernist perspective. Yet, whilst Soja refers to the critique of everyday life, repetition and difference, he does not show its relevance to the production of space which is simplified to capitalist spatiality, dialectics and reproduction through occupance of space and production of space. This reading gives the impression that Lefebvre thinks about space politically and ideologic-ally, certainly more subtly than structural Marxism, but nevertheless

---

[27] Massey (1993, 62) notes that notions derived from Heidegger are problematic in that he sees places as having single essential identities stemming out of an inward-looking history. It is not surprising since Heidegger looked back to a rural world in which the philosopher could meditate undisturbed by the trivialities and banalities of urban life and conviviality.

well within the concepts of early Marx. The crying absence is Nietzsche who of course constitutes the break in historical thinking.

The problem is that Lefebvre has basically been read as a Marxist
urban geographer by his Anglo-Saxon admirers, as Shields (1994)
comments. This is somewhat ironic given his constant castigation of
disciplinary fragmentation without autocritique. If any label were to
be affixed, it would be as a philosopher/sociologist, which is how he
described himself. As he often said, death to philosophy, long live
philosophical thinking. In *Right to the City* he devotes much attention
to the emergence of philosophy in the city and the failings of contemporary philosophy, whether it be in relation to the city or everyday
life. Sociology constitutes one of the fragmentary sciences contributing
to an understanding of the city, although this has to be related to the
historical which is often forgotten.

There seems currently to be an attempt amongst those labelling
themselves postmodern geographers to appropriate any thinker who
'prioritizes' space, as if this accolade automatically makes a geographer.[28] Maybe this could be a means of gluing together the fragments! Indeed, Lefebvre has been seen as a latent postmodernist
(Dear, 1994) and as a precursor (Hamel and Poitras, 1994), and who
by the end of the latter article becomes a postmodernist without
qualification. In both cases, and for Soja (1989b), it is the attention to
and primacy of space in social theory and life that qualifies him
admirably. In addition Hamel and Poitras highlight Lefebvre's critique
of modernist urbanism and what it supposedly shares with postmodernist critiques in terms of difference, anti-positivism and anti-techni-
cism. Postmodernism is not of course a unified body of thought but
the problem shared by the various attempts at appropriation is that
fundamental differences are collapsed and glued together in a reduc-
tionist fashion. Shared concerns do not mean shared analyses or
conclusions, as was the situation with Lefebvre's engagement with
Heidegger and phenomenological concepts (1965b).

Jameson (1991, 364), who knew Lefebvre and took him around Los
Angeles in 1983–4, rightly notes that the idea of a postmodern period

---

[28] This is not to say that all geographers are involved in this enterprise. Harvey, for
example, who periodizes postmodernism and retains a critical distance, does not.
There is also an interest in geography in the historical geography of modernity,
more closely aligned to a reading of Habermas, who calls for a renewal of
modernity.

or stage was alien to Lefebvre, because his experiential framework was largely shaped by the modernization of France, primarily in the Gaullist period. This, however, was not the principal reason for his rejection of postmodernism.

Lefebvre was a philosopher and critic of modernity which he contrasted with modernism. Modernism for him meant the exaltation of the new, often with lots of illusions and little perspicacity. It was the consciousness of a period, which he loosely said might have gone back centuries. Modernity, on the other hand, an unfinished concept, is critique and autocritique, an attempt at knowledge. Modernism and modernity are inseparable and together constitute two aspects of the modern world; the former is certitude and arrogance, the latter is questioning and reflection (1962, 9–10). Later on, Lefebvre situated the beginning of modernity in the silent catastrophe when a whole series of referentials of social practice (time, space, representation and reality) in Europe collapsed (1980b). From 1886 to 1924, from symbolism to surrealism, 51 isms were thrown up (Meschonnic, 1988, 59–60). Daily life however remained generally aloof from these discontinuities; one continued to live in Euclidean space and the homogeneous time of clocks, and sing tonal melodies. Thought took the audacious path and daily life prudence. Out of this breakup, three values of modernity – technique, work, language – emerge. It promised happiness through the satisfaction of needs in the everyday. Yet the illusion of a rupture with the past has been dissolved and so discussions about its essence have lost some of their interest. Today this modernity has come to an end but modernism as technological practice remains strong and it is this which is effectively transforming daily life. However, the critics of modernity have, in clamouring for the immediate, opted for the retro. And in proclaiming the end of all ideologies, together with the advent of the myth of transparency in society, the State and political action, they have left the field clear for technological deployment. This is where the real question lies and one which is not answered by the false dichotomy of modernity or postmodernity (1981, 47–52).

The nature and status of the term 'post' in relation to the modern and modernity is unclear: continuity or rupture (Meschonnic, 1988, 218). Is it a total rejection of all the modern or a particular crisis within it, emphasizing the ephemeral and chaotic (Harvey, 1989, 113). There is a tendency to expel the critique, complexity, and contradictions within modernity and to focus on one element of modernity. Too frequently modernism and modernity are used indiscriminately.

In France, on the whole, the term 'postmodernism' tends to be reserved for those who fall into the apocalyptic group (Ruby, 1990), including those who perceive a social void, for example Lipovetsky, (1983) and the impossibility of any project for change. Any whiff of the dialectical, unity or totality is immediately lambasted and rejected. So for Lyotard, any sense of hidden values must be abandoned and reality is that which appears in discourse. Baudrillard takes spectacle for what it appears. It is world in which everything has been done so nothing remains but to play with the fragments. Postmodernism is a game with the vestiges of what has been destroyed (Plant, 1992, 155). At the same time, there is much less interest in France in periodizations of postmodernism as a cultural logic of late capitalism or space–time compression. For example, neither Jameson nor Harvey have been translated. In relation to a politics of difference, there is little evidence of any real practice of difference in a country still strongly attached to the highly unitary Republican tradition, which is capable, if attacked, of producing strong resistance, as for example in the recent very heated debates over the wearing of headscarves by Muslim girls at secondary schools.

Certainly Lefebvre acknowledged one was living in a time of malaise and that there was uncertitude about where urban society was going, but he frequently referred scathingly to the nihilists or hyperrealists. He considered the announcement of posthistory, post-industrialism or postmodernism to be premature and that we remained in a transitional period (1986a, 47–8). History certainly had not ended. Indeed we must expect history to continue (1985a, 113). Would the current disorder contain a virtual order? This is a question he says postmodernism posses but does not answer. All they can do, obsessed as they are by nostalgia, is to construct neo-villages.

> As with so many other denominations proposed in the name of social transformation (post-industrial society, consumer society etc.) the post-modern has a sense but not that which the words say; these words are intended to designate something precise, an intuition if not a project. However they only express a backward move faced with the errors and the false audacities of 'modernism'. . . . Industry, work and industrial workers are not disappearing and will not disappear immediately. Similarly for material production, exchange, merchandise, the market,

money and systems of equivalences, even if they have ceased to appear to be the dominant tendency characteristic of our era. (1986a, 167).

At the same time, he did not share the total disparagement of the eighteenth century which, though it had many faults, had also led to the emergence of civil society, civility and urbanity. He still believed to the end in the possibility of creating something new, of the necessity of a project reconstructed out of new ideas and old materials, but not one which would lay down the details. This project he concluded would be 'inspired principally by a "Marxist" tradition (not without critiques) but could not afford not to borrow some elements from other currents: for example, ecology and neo-Ricardism' (1986a, 176).

More specifically, it is worth examining the presences and absences that have been alluded to in the geographical appropriation. The first of these is the relationship between space and time. For Jameson (1991), whose work has been influential amongst postmodern geographers, the spatial is predominant in the post-contemporary period (whatever that may mean); postmodern culture is spatial. Time is pressed into the service of space. The first casualty of the postmodernist period is 'modernist history', deep memory and temporality. If temporality has any place, it is only in writing about it rather than as lived experience. Jameson feels totally lost in this world[29] where the insertion of the individual into multidimensional sets of radically discontinuous realities, in which all intervening mediations between the barrage of immediacy have been removed (411–13).[30] For Soja (1989, 15) too, it is history which must be dethroned. To the various definitions of historicism he adds as the following characteristic 'an overdeveloped historical contextualization of social life and social theory that actively submerges and peripheralizes the geographical imagination'.

What we end up with is the crowning of space at the expense of an impoverished historical understanding and simplification of the rich-

[29] Sadie Plant (1992, 7) shows too the complexity of the relationship between the Situationist International and postmodernism. Postmodernism stems from the same social and cultural context and is underwritten by Situationist theory which, unlike postmodernism, subjects the world of spectacle to passionate critique.

[30] 'Postmodernism is a manual for survival in a capitalist world which seems immune to transformation. It is natural to feel lost, confused and uncertain of the solidity of the ground beneath one's feet' (Plant, 1992).

ness of temporalities and their significance for lived experience in different places and by different social groups.[31] It is a pity that Lefebvre effectively did not produce a sustained analysis of the production of time, although his analysis of the everyday and rhythmanalysis certainly yield significant insights on presence and absence, multiple temporalities and the interplay of time and space.

Time and space have ontologically the same status. Methodologically, they are subjected to the same form of analysis of homogeneity, fragmentation and hierarchization. Each is measured by and inscribed in the other. The everyday is the weaving of cyclical and linear time and of moments, while the urban is duration and passage. Although linear time has encroached on the cyclical, the latter never fully disappeared. The right to the city includes the struggle for the appropriation of lived time. As we have seen in his New Athens, the Masters who live in the centre not only possess a privileged space but above all time. For the masses living in programmed suburbs and residential ghettos, they have carefully measured space but time eludes them (1968a, ch. 15).

If we examine more carefully what he says about the emergence of space as a privileged concept, we see that he traces it to just before the First World War when attempts were made to resolve the crisis, in the firm and globally, through organizational methods. It is then that space consigns time and becoming to the shadows. Urbanistic ideology formulates problems of society and turns what emanates from history and consciousness into spatial terms. Worse still, spaces are pathologized into healthy and unhealthy spaces that are thereby normalized (1968a, ch. 6). This reads like a paraphrasing of Jameson for an earlier period, but with the recognition that the spatialization of society and history are ideological; it belongs to the realm of conceived and not lived space.

---

[31] Why, Doreen Massey asks pertinently, does the new mobility generate such feelings of vulnerability and insecurity given that it is those who are in relative control of this mobility who agonize over these feelings? This is most applicable to Jameson. It raises questions of differing perceptions of postmodernity and the distinct ways in which different groups relate to flows and interconnections. What is the meaning of simultaneity for different groups? Reading Jameson one might think late capitalism and postmodernism had wiped out any different experiences. But as with many postmodernist writers there is a tendency to postulate a scenario and merrily assume it has come to pass, without much attention to the restricted and privileged world they live in.

So too is the global as the replacement of history by a system of states ideological. History no longer holds the pre-eminence it had; it has tended to become no more than representation whose obliteration has been pursued by states who nonchantly use the products of the past and territorial resources as memories and folklore. Historical images are turned into political icons. In elevating the global against historical knowledge, it draws up planetary contours on the basis of new factors, such as energy, techniques, strategies and productive forces. Certainly space is decisive as product and *oeuvre* in the opening onto the global (1976–8, vol. 4, 94–6). 'Qui dit "mondialité" dit spatialité et non temporalité' ('Who speaks "of the world" speaks of space and not time') (326).

However, the status of time in relation to abstract space is uncertain and raises problems. Spatial practices tend to restrict time to the time of productive work and reduce lived rhythms to rationalist and localized gestures in the division of labour. The potential of altering existing spatial morphologies as a means of emancipating time is questionable (1974, 408). These increasingly important questions were not fully taken up by Lefebvre for several possible reasons. Firstly, although a philosopher of becoming (*devenir*), the shadow of historicism lurks in the background, and this makes him reluctant to project history into the future and separate temporality from it, so as to incorporate the former into an opening onto the world (*mondialité*). Secondly, it might be related to the fact that although he analysed concepts, such as exchange, he didn't pay much attention to the economic as a system as such. It should be noted that the practices of flexible accumulation as an element in the reproduction of capitalism were less evident in France in the early to mid 1980s than in the United States and Britain. Furthermore, his attention first and foremost to the consciousness of temporalities and attendant social practices in everyday life, reflected his initial interests. In effect, Lefebvre tended to associate temporality with the city and the everyday, on the one hand, and space with globalization and opening onto the world.

However, his outline of a theory of rhythms clearly suggests a multitude of directions in which we could develop an analysis of time and space, from the positioning of the body to the nature of changes in the world brought about by the changing rhythms of capitalism in relation to the body, nature and the planet. Historically, he showed how rhythms, gestures and behaviour altered between 1789 and 1830, that is, how the everyday altered. Today, the reproduction of capitalism clearly has a major effect on restructuring temporalities as an integral part of regionalization and globalization of the world and on new temporal relations in the division of labour and the everyday. It is partly for this reason that there has been a renewed interest in time, social policy and citizenship, the generalized reduction of working hours and diversification of labour contracts ranging from part-time work to temporary and fixed contracts. What we have yet to follow through is the dialectic between phenomenological and social perspective times.

The second aspect of the the postmodernist appropriation is an indifference to differences in the definition and use of concepts and how they fit into the overall conceptualization of a particular writer. As Jameson himself has remarked, postmodernist theory tends to digest all, flattening it out and translating it into its own terms. The same words do not necessarily mean the same thing or have the same resonances. The concept of difference provides an exemplary case. Difference in Lefebvrian terms is not at all the *différance* of Anglo-Saxon critical social theorists (Soja 1989b, 49–50). The latter comes from Derrida who sought to convey a different kind of difference, through using in French a term that looked different but sounded the same (Ree, 1994, 42). It derives principally from one of the meanings of *différer* which means to defer, put off or distance the realization of something, hence its use in a radical move of alterity. While Lefebvre shares a Nietzschean heritage with the philosophers of difference, their thinking and objectives are quite distinctive, not to say very different. Their aim was to produce a thinking that completely disengaged itself from Hegel as they read him (Ruby, 1989, ch. 4). Repetition as movement (divergence, displacement, decentering) replaced history; dialectical reasoning, contradictions and identity, amongst a litany of taboos, were to be banished in a quest for constant displacement and resistance to any form of reduction or reintegration of otherness to the same. It is therefore a world in which differences are juxtaposed and coexist within non-stable networks, that cannot be mediated or synthesized. A far cry from a recognizably Lefebvrian conceptualization. For Lefebvre, identity (and not difference) is the form from which other forms such as the contractual, equivalence and simultaneity are derived.

Nor for Lefebvre is difference, as we have seen, about particularity, originality or distinctiveness; difference arises out of struggle. Differentialist thinking is a method that seeks to regroup in order to situate, to bring together that which is separate. This is the sense of urban centrality, of differences assembled through unity. It is not at all clear that postmodernist planning, in which cities and companies seek to distinguish or differentiate themselves through their architecture, especially the selling of their image, responds to social needs in an increasingly neo-liberal society (Jehl, 1994). Does the attention to diversity of façades belie the same attention to content, to the way we inhabit? Does the inclusion of difference as particularity in postmodern planning challenge the ideology and myth of technocracy which were Lefebvre's critique of urbanism? These are just some of the questions we need to ask of postmodern planning. Postmodernizing Lefebvre thus imposes an undifferentiated and homogenizing thought.

Lefebvre, as many others in the French New Left[32] of the 1960s, was interested in complex thought and determination without determinism. In the 1980s he was keen to develop the concept of complex thinking but nothing came of it (comment by Serge Renaudie). For example, Edgar Morin[33] has sought since 1973 to construct a theory of complexity in an open world which spans the physical, biological and social sciences. Complex thinking, he notes, has existed for a long time (Heraclitus, Descartes, Kant, Hegel) but it has only become conscious with the present crisis in philosophy (1994, 315–17). Calling then any contemporary thinker of complexity a postmodernist arises because some have all too easily presented a caricature of modernity, its critiques and complexities. Never mind if in addition the thinker does not posit a threshold that has already been crossed, as postmodernism tends to do.

---

[32] Lefebvre was involved in and the pivot between a number of the non-institutional Marxist currents, such as *Arguments*, dissolved in 1962, Socialisme ou Barbarie and Situationist International.

[33] Edgar Morin, a sociologist with many diverse interests, was the editor of *Arguments* from 1956 to 1962. He left the Communist Party in 1951. Rhythmanalysis too, as we have seen, straddles different disciplines. Nor should it be forgotten that Lefebvre began as a mathematician and followed developments in various sciences.

It is possible to pick out the same trend, but diverge in the nature of the theoretical and political analysis, for example, the consumer society analysed by Lefebvre, the Situationists and Baudrillard, who was a lecturer at Nanterre in the department headed by Lefebvre. In relation to a very intelligent person (no prizes for guessing who), he ironically comments that, since there exists nothing but signs, given that objects and their usage have disappeared, that means we no longer have an economy in the traditional sense, but "an empire of signs" (1985a, 18). We tend, he continues, to focus on something and then extrapolate to produce a world that consists of nothing else, or the opposite, which is to discern a trend, such as the reduction of the social to specific 'social questions', such as the poor, the handicapped etc., and then decide that the social has come to an end.

Conclusion

Reading Lefebvre diachronically and synchronically enables us to enter into the dialogues and autocritiques that he engaged in throughout his writing. This is not to say that we have been able to encompass the depth and breadth of his interests. Yet, without a degree of appreciation and understanding of how his thinking unfolded, we lose the richness, the density and historical depth of his analysis. Though associated with the spatial in Anglo-American circles, he was better known in France for his involvement and writings on urbanism and the city. As much today as then, his vision reminds us of the need for imagination and intellectual rigour in thinking about the city. In translating his writings on the city, we have tried to show the significance of the interplay of time – space and the everyday in the city. We hope too that in our transposition, that we have been able to give a feel, not just of the varied nature of his thinking, but how he responded to others in his adventure through the second half of the century. The philosopher is not detached from the world; his theories speak of himself in the world and the form of Marxism which was profoundly marked by surrealism (1988, 75–6; Jay, 1984, ch. 9). The desire to create lucidly his own life as *oeuvre*, and not as the prose of the world (incidentally, the title of a book by Merleau-Ponty), troubled him profoundly from the 1920s (1985a, 146).

Lefebvre's conceptualization is dynamic, stressing dialectical movement, complexity, conflicts and contradictions. Concepts from the past are not discarded, they can be rethought creatively. He applies an open and non-teleological dialectic (Ruby, 1990) that is eminently suitable for thinking through the transformations taking place in cities and their relationships with the wider world. These relationships start with the urban as the everyday and the lived, from which we must construct our utopias to clarify the possible-impossible, not as fixed ideas and projects, but responsive to changing conjunctures and structures. Understanding is not however closed or exhausted by analysis, there is always an opening.

Let us end in Lefebvre's own words about his thinking on the city and what might lie ahead (1985a, 110):

> To think about the city is to hold and maintain its conflictual aspects: constraints and possibilities, peacefulness and violence, meetings and solitude, gatherings and separation, the trivial and the poetic, brutal functionalism and surprising improvization. The dialectic of the urban cannot be limited to the opposition centre–periphery, although it implies and contains it . . . Thinking the city moves towards thinking the world (thought as a relationship to the world) . . . globality as totality ·. . . the universe, space-time, energies, information, but without valuing one rather than another . . . One can hope that it will turn out well but the urban can become the centre of barbarity, domination, dependence and exploitation . . . In thinking about these perspectives, let us leave a place for events, initiatives, decisions. All the hands have not been played. The sense of history does not suppose any historic determinism, any destiny.

References

Works by Henri Lefebvre

La conscience mystifiée, with Norbert Guterman, 1936, new edn Sycomore, 1979.
Nietzsche, Éditions Sociales, 1939.
Le matérialisme dialectique, PUF, 1940, reprinted in Quadrige series, 1990.
Logique formelle, logique dialectique, Éditions Sociales, 1947, 3rd edn, 1982.
Le marxisme, PUF, 1948 (constantly reprinted).
M. Merleau-Ponty et la philosophie de l'ambiguité, *La Pensée* 73, 1957, pp. 37–52.

Critique de la vie quotidienne, vol. 1, 2nd edn, L'Arche, 1958; English translation *Critique of Everyday Life*, Verso, 1991.

La somme et le reste, 1959; 3rd edn 1989, Méridiens- Klincksieck with a preface by René Louraun page numbers refer to 3rd edn.

Introduction à la modernité, Éditions de Minuit, 1962.

La proclamation de la Commune, Gallimard, 1965a.

Métaphilosophie, Éditions du Minuit, 1965b.

La langage et la société, Gallimard, 1966a.

Introduction, in H. Raymond, M. G. Raymond, N. Haumont and M. Coornaert, *L'Habitat pavillonaire*, Centre de Recherche d'Urbanisme, 1966b.

Position. Contre les technocrates, Gonthier, 1967, reprinted with short foreword as *Vers le cybernanthrope*, 1971; references taken from 1971 version.

'Quartier et ville de quartier', *Cahiers de l'Institut d'Aménagement et d'Urbanisme de la Région parisienne*, 7, 1967b.

'L'Urbanisme aujourd'hui. Mythes et réalités' *Les Cahiers du Centre d'Études Socialistes*, 72–3, 1967c. (debate between Henri Lefebvre, Jean Balladur and Michel Ecochard, but Lefebvre's talk alone is reprinted in *Du rural à l'urbain*, 1970).

Le droit à la ville, Anthropos, 1968a.

La vie quotidienne dans le monde moderne, 1968b.

L'Irruption à Nanterre au sommet, Anthropos, 1968c.

Le manifeste différentialiste, Gallimard, 1970a.

Du rural à l'urbain, Anthropos, 1970b.

La fin de l'histoire, Anthropos, 1970c.

La révolution urbaine, Gallimard, 1970d.

Au delà du structuralisme, Anthropos, 1971 (a series of essays from the 1950s of which the later ones are reprinted in *Idéologie structuraliste*, Seuil, 1975; page references are to 1971 version.

La pensée marxiste et la ville, Casterman, 1972.

Espace et politique, 2nd part of *Le droit à la ville*, Anthropos, 1973a.

La survie du capitalisme, Anthropos, 1973b (a collection of essays written between 1968 and 1972). The English translation *The Survival of Capitalism*, Allison and Busby, 1976, leaves out most of the 1968 essays as well as the footnotes. Hence all references are to the original French.

'Les autres Paris', *Espaces et Sociétés*, 13–14, 1973, pp.185–92 (text used for a film called *Le droit à la ville*, 26 mins).

La production de l'espace, Anthropos 1974, 3rd edn, 1986, with preface by Lefebvre; English translation *Production of Space*, Blackwell, 1991, is of the 1st edition. Page references are to the English translation except for preface in 3rd edn.

Hegel, Marx, Nietzsche ou le royaume des ombres, Casterman, 1975a.

Le temps des méprises, Stock, 1975b.
De l'état, 4 vols, Union Générale d'Éditions, 1976–8.
Une pensée devenue monde. Faut-il abandonner Marx?, Fayard, 1980a.
La présence et l'absence, Casterman, 1980b.
Critique de la vie quotidienne, vol. 3, L'Arche, 1981.
Qu'est-que penser?, Publisud, 1985a.
'Le projet rythmanalytique', with Catherine Régulier, *Communications*, 41, 1985b, pp. 191–9.
Le retour de la dialectique. 12 mots clés, Messidor Éditions Sociales, 1986a.
'Pour une nouvelle culture politique', *M. Mensuel, Marxisme, mouvement*, 1, 1986b.
'Hors du centre, point de salut?' *Espaces Temps*, 33, 1986, pp. 17–19.
'An interview with Henri Lefebvre', *Environment and Planning: Society and Space*, 5, 1987, pp. 27–38.
'Toward a leftist cultural politics: remarks occasioned by the centenary of Marx's death', in C. Nelson and L. Grossman (eds), *Marxism and the Interpretation of Culture*, Macmillan, 1988.
'L'Urbain en question', *Société Française*, 33, 1989, pp. 44–7.
'Les illusions de la modernité', *Manières de voir* 13, Le Monde Diplomatique, 1991a, pp. 14–17.
'Une intervention inédite', *M. Mensuel, marxisme, mouvement*, 50, 1991b, pp. 32–3.
Éléments de rythmanalyse. Introduction à la connaissance des rythmes, Syllepse-Périscope, 1992.

Other References

Ajzenberg, A. 'Toujours engagé' *M. Mensuel, marxisme, mouvement*, 50, 1991, pp. 30–1.
Ajzenberg, A. 'A partir d'Henri Lefebvre. Vers un mode de production écologique', in *Traces de futurs. Henri Lefebvre, le possible et le quotidien*, La Société Française, Paris, pp. 1–5, 1994.
Amiot, M. *Contre l'État, les sociologues*, Maison des Sciences de l'Homme, Paris, 1986.
Anderson, P. *On the Tracks of Western Marxism*, New Left Books, 1976.
Anderson, P. *Historical Materialism*, Verso, 1983.
Ansay, P. and Schoonbrodt, R. (eds), *Penser la ville, choix de textes philosophiques*, Aux Archives de l'Architecture Moderne, Brussels, 1989.
Bachelard, G. *L'Intuition de l'instant*, Stock, Paris, 1931, 1992.
Bachelard, G. *La psychanalyse du feu*, Stock, Paris, 1938, 1992.
Bachelard, G. *La dialectique de la durée*, PUF 1950, 1993.
Bachelard, G. *La poétique de l'espace*, PUF, 1957, 1993.
Barreau, H. 'Les théories philosophiques de la connaissance face à la relativité Einstein', *Communications*, 41, 1985, pp. 95–109.

Béchillon, D. de (ed.). Les défis de la complexité, Vers un nouveau paradigme de la connaissance?, Harmattan, Paris, 1994.

Bellos, D. *Georges Perec. Une vie dans les mots*, Éditions du Seuil, Paris, 1994 (original English *Georges Perec. A Life in Words*, HarperCollins, 1993).

Benjamin, W. *Paris, capitale du XIXe siècle, le livre des passages*, Éditions du Cerf, Paris, 1993.

Bernié-Boissard, C. 'Henri Lefebvre, sociologue du quotidien, philosophe de la modernité', *Espaces et Sociétés*, 76 (1), 1994, pp. 13–29.

Blanchot, M. *L'Amitié*, Gallimard, Paris, 1971.

Body-Gendrot, S. *Ville et violence. L'Irruption de nouveaux acteurs*, PUF, Paris, 1993.

Bonnafé, L. 'Sur l'audience d'Henri Lefebvre', *M. Mensuel, marxisme, mouvement*, 50, 1991, pp. 20–2.

Braidotti, R. 'Foucault. La convergence avec le féminisme', *Magazine Littéraire*, 325, 1994, pp. 68–70.

Cahiers de Philosophie Les (*Le philosophe dans la cité*, 17, 1993.

Castells, M. *La question urbaine*, Maspero, 1972, trans. A. Sheridan, *The Urban Question: a Marxist approach*, Edward Arnold, 1977.

Castells, M. 'L'École française de sociologie vingt ans après. Retour au futur?', *Les Annales de la Recherche Urbaine*, 64, 1994, pp. 58–60.

Castro, R. *Civilisation urbaine ou barbarie?*, Plon, Paris, 1994.

Certeaun, M. de *L'Invention du quotidien, I. Arts de faire*, 2nd edn Gallimard, Paris, 1994.

Chemetov, P. 'Henri Lefebvre nous parle' *M. Mensuel, marxisme, mouvement*, 50, 1991, pp. 40–1.

Courbon, J. 'Pour une définition du concept d'écologie politique et urbaine *Traces de futurs. Henri Lefebvre, le possible et le quotidien*, Société Française, Paris, 1994.

Couvelakis, E. 'L'Espace entre philosophie de l'histoire et pratique politique' *Espaces et Sociétés*, 76 (1), 1994, pp 99–122.

Couvidat, Y. 'L'Anthrope, le cybernanthrope et les technopoles', *Traces de futurs, Henri Lefebvre, le possible et le quotidien*, La Société Française, Paris, 1994.

Davidson, A. 'Henri Lefebvre' *Thesis 11*, 33, 1993, pp. 152–5.

Dear, M., 'Les Aspects post modernes de Henri Lefebvre *Espaces et Sociétés*, 76 (1), 1994, pp. 31–40.

Debord, G. *La société du spectacle*, Buchet-Castel, Paris, 1967 (translated *Society of the Spectacle*, Black and Red, 1977).

Debord, G. 'Guide de psychogéographie de Paris. Discours sur les passions de l'amour', in *Asger Jorn Exhibition*, Stedlijk Museum, Amsterdam, 1994.

Delbo, C. *La théorie et la pratique. Dialogue imaginaire mais non tout à fait apocryphe entre Henri Marcuse et Henri Lefebvre*, Anthropos, Paris, 1969.

Deleuze, G. *Différence et répétition*, PUF, Paris, 1968.

Dieuaide, P. and Motamed-Nejad, R. 'Méthodologie et hétérodoxie en économie: retours sur Henri Lefebvre', *Espaces et Sociétés*, 76 (1), 1994, pp. 69–98.

Eribon, D. *Michel Foucault et ses contemporains*, Fayard, Paris, 1994.

Foucault, M. (ed. P. Rabinon) *The Foucault Reader*, Penguin Books, 1984.

Foucault, M. (ed. C. Gordon). *Michel Foucault. Power/Knowledge*, Harvester, Brighton, 1986.

Garnier, J. P. 'La vision urbaine de Henri Lefebvre: des previsions aux révisions', *Espaces et Sociétés*, 76 (1), 1994, pp. 123–45.

Garnier, J. P. and Goldschmidt, D. *La comédie urbaine*, Maspero, Paris, 1978.

Gaudin, J. P. 'La ségrégation et la recherche urbaine. Chassés-croisés entre chercheurs et décideurs', *Les Annales de la Recherche Urbaine*, 64, 1994, pp. 28–33.

Genestier, P. 'La banlieue au risque de la métropolitisation', *Le Débat*, 80, 1994, pp. 192–218.

George, P. 'Cinquante ans qui ont transformé les rapports avec l'espace', *Communications*, 41, 1985, pp. 159–67.

Giard, L. and Mayol, P. *L'Invention du quotidien. II. Habiter, cuisiner*, Gallimard, Paris, 1994.

Giscard d'Estaing, V. *La démocratie française*, Fayard, Paris, 1976.

Goffman, E. *The Presentation of Self in Everyday Life*, Allen and Unwin, 1969.

Gottdiener, M. *Social Production of Urban Space*, University of Texas, 1985.

Grawitz, M. *Lexique des sciences sociales*, 6th edn, Dalloz, 1994.

Gregory, D. *Geographical Imaginations*, Blackwell, Oxford, 1994.

Hamel, P. and Poitras, C. 'Henri Lefebvre, penseur de la postmodernité *Espaces et Societés*, 76 (1), 1994, pp. 41–58.

Harvey, D. *Social Justice and the City*, Edward Arnold, 1973.

Harvey, D. *The Condition of Postmodernity*, Blackwell, Oxford, 1989.

Harvey, D. 'From space to place and back again: Reflections on the condition of postmodernity', in J. Bird, B. Curtis, T. Putnam, G. Robertson, L. Tickner (eds), *Mapping Futures: Local cultures, global change*, Routledge, 1993, pp. 3–29.

Hess, R. *Henri Lefebvre et l'aventure du siècle*, Éditions A. M. Métailié, Paris, 1988.

Hess, R. 'La théorie des moments, ce qu'elle pourrait apporter à un dépassement de l'interactionnisme', *Traces de futurs. Henri Lefebvre, le possible et le quotidien*, La Société Française, Paris, 1994.

Hoffman, E. *Lost in Translation*, 1990.

Huisman, D. *Dictionnaire des mille oeuvres clés de la philosophie*, Nathan, Paris, 1993.

Jameson, F. *Postmodernism or, the cultural logic of late capitalism*, Verso, London, 1991.

Jay, M. *Marxism and Totality – the adventures of a concept from Lukacs to Habermas*, University of California Press, 1984.

Jehl, B. 'La ville-image', in *Traces de futurs. Henri Lefebvre, le possible et le quotidien*, La Société Française, Paris, 1994.

Joseph, I. 'Le droit à la ville, la ville à l'oeuvre. Deux paradigmes de la recherche urbaine', *Les Annales de la Recherche Urbaine*, 64, 1994, pp. 4–10.

Katznelson, I. *Marxism and the City*, Clarendon Press, Oxford, 1992.

Kofman, E. 'La politique de la ville', *Modern and Contemporary France*, 1, 4, 1993, pp. 379–83.

Kofman, M. *Edgar Morin: From Big Brother to Fraternity*, Pluto, 1995.

Lacroix, G. 'Autour de cybernantrope. Informatique et identité', *La Traces de futurs, Henri Lefebvre, le possible et le quotidien*, in Société Française, Paris, 1994.

Latour, P. and Combes, F. *Conversation avec Henri Lefebvre*, Messidor, Paris, 1991.

Lebas, E. 'The state in British and French urban research, or the crisis of the urban question', in V. Pons and R. Francis (eds), *Urban Social Research: problems and prospects*, Routledge and Kegan Paul, London, 1983.

Levitas, R. 'The future of thinking about the future', in J. Bird et al. (eds), Routledge, *Mapping Futures*, 1993, pp. 257–66.

Lévy, J. 'Urbanité: à inventer. Villes: à décrire', *Annales de la Recherche Urbaine*, 64, 1994, pp. 10–15.

Lipovetsky, G. *L'Ère du vide. Essais sur l'individualisme contemporain*, Gallimard, Paris, 1983.

Löwy, M. 'Le marxisme romantique', *M. Mensuel, marxisme, mouvement*, 50, 1991, pp. 6–8.

Lufti, B., Sochaczweski, S. and Janel, T. 'Henri Lefebvre et la critique de la représentation' *Traces de futurs. Henri Lefebvre, le possible et le quotidien*, La Société Française, Paris, 1994.

Macey, D. 'Review. Everything is dangerous', *Radical Philosophy*, 65, 1993, pp. 45–6.

Martins, M. 'The theory of social space in the work of Henri Lefebvre', in R. Forrest, J. Henderson and P. Williams (eds), *Urban Political Economy and Social Theory: critical essays in urban studies*, Gower, 1983, pp. 160–85.

Massey, D. 'Politics and space/time', *New Left Review*, 196, 1992, pp. 65–84.

Massey, D. 'Power-geometry and a progressive sense of place', in J. Bird et al. (eds), Routledge, *Mapping Futures*, 1993, pp. 58–68.

Melly, G. and Woods, M. *Paris and the Surrealists*, Thames and Hudson, 1991.

Merleau-Ponty, M. *Phénoménologie de la perception*, Gallimard, 1945.

Merrifield, A. 'Space and place: a Lefebvrian reconciliation', *Trans. IBG*, 18, 4, 1993, pp. 516–31.

Meschonnic, H. *Modernité modernité*, Gallimard, Paris, 1988.

Michaux, B. 'Le manifeste différentialiste et après? Quelques considérations sur le métissage et l'autoproduction de l'espèce humaine', in *Traces de futurs. Henri Lefebvre, le possible et le quotidien*, La Société Française, Paris, 1994.

Morin, E. *La complexité humaine*, Flammarion, 1994.

Osborne, P., 'The Politics of Time', *Radical Philosophy*, 68, 1994, pp. 3–9.

Ostrowetsky, S. 'L'urbain comme acte de langage espace et sociologie' *Annales de la Recherche Urbaine*, 64, 1994, pp. 39–45.

Pacquot, T. 'Civilité, urbanité et citadinité', *Les Cahiers de Philosophie*, 17, 1993, pp. 121–48.

Pellegrino, P. and Neves, J. 'L'architecture et la projection des rapports sociaux sur le sol: effet, représentation ou production de l'espace', *Espaces et Sociétés*, 76 (1), 1994, pp. 59–68.

Perec, G. *Les choses. Chronique des années soixante*, Les Lettres Nouvelles, Paris (trans. D. Bellos, *Things, a Chronicle of the Sixties*), 1965.

Perec, G. *Espèces d'espaces*, Éditions Galilée, 1974.

Perec, G. *La vie mode d'emploi*, Hachette, Paris trans. D. Bellos, *A User's Manual*, 1978.

Petitjean, G. 'Le Paris secret de Jacques Chirac', *Le Nouvel Observateur*, 22–8 septembre, 1994, pp. 90–3.

Plant, S. 'The Situationist International: a case of spectacular neglect', *Radical Philosophy*, 55, 1990, pp. 3–10.

Plant, S. *Most Radical Gesture: Situationist International in a Postmodern Age*, Routledge, 1992.

Rée, J. 'Return of the translator', *Radical Philosophy*, 67, 1994, pp. 41–3.

Renaudie, S. 'Henri Lefebvre. Une nouvelle positivité de l'urbain' *M. Mensuel, marxisme, mouvement*, 17, 1988, pp. 62–6.

Ricoeur, P. *Temps et récit*, 3 vols Seuil, Paris, 1985. English translation K. Balmey and D. Pellauer, *Time and Narrative*, 3rd vol. University of Chicago Press, 1988.

Ross, K. *The Emergence of Social Space: Rimbaud and the Paris Commune*, Macmillan, 1988.

Ruby, C. *Les archipels de la différence. Foucault, Derrida, Deleuze, Lyotard*, Éditions du Félin, Paris, 1989.

Ruby, C. *Le champ de bataille. Post-moderne/neo-moderne*, Harmattan, Paris, 1990.

Sassen, S. 'La ville globale. Éléments pour une lecture de Paris', *Le Débat*, 80, 1994, pp. 146–64.

Schnaidt, C. 'Fragments pour penser le moderne. Complément tardif à l'introduction à la modernité de Henri Lefebvre', in *Traces de futurs. Henri Lefebvre, le possible et le quotidien*, La Société Française, Paris, 1994.

Shields, R. 'Body, spirit and production: the geographical legacies of Henri Lefebvre', unpublished paper, Association of American Geographers Conference, San Francisco, 1994.

Sintomer, Y. 'Le soleil crucifié', M. *Mensuel, marxisme, mouvement*, 50, 1994, 12–15.

Smith, N. *Uneven Development; Nature, Capital and the Production of Space*, Blackwell, 1984.

Smith, N. 'Homeless/global: scaling places' in J. Bird et al., *Mapping Futures*, Routledge, 1993a.

Smith, N. 'Grounding metaphor', in M. Keith and S. Pile (eds), *Place and the Politics of Identity*, Routledge, 1993b.

Société Française, *Traces de futurs. Henri Lefebvre, le possible et le quotidien*, papers for conference held 3–5 June. 1994.

Soja, E. 'The spatiality of social life: towards a transformative retheorisation', in D. Gregory and J. Urry (eds), *Social Relations and Spatial Structures*, Macmillan, 1985, pp. 90–127.

Soja, E. 'Modern geography, Western Marxism, and the restructuring of critical social theory', in R. Peet and N. Thrift (eds), *New Models in Geography. The political-economy perspective*, Unwin Hyman, 1989a, 318–47.

Soja, E. *Postmodern Geographies*, the reassertion of space in critical social theory Verso, 1989b.

Soja, E. *Third space* (forthcoming) Blackwell Publishers Ltd.

Stokvis, W. *Cobra. An international movement in art after the Second World War*, Ediciones Poligrafa, Barcelona, 1987.

Vaneigem, R. *Traité de savoir-vivre à l'usage des jeunes générations*, Gallimard, Paris, 1967, 1992; trans. *Revolution of Everyday Life*, Rebel Press, 1994.

Vernes, J. *Paris au XXe siècle*, Hachette, Paris (with an introduction by P. Gondolo della Riva), 1994.

Wacquant, L. 'Bourdieu in America: notes on the transatlantic interpretation of social theory', in C. Calhoun, E. Lipuma and M. Postone (eds), *Bourdieu: Critical Perspectives*, Polity, Cambridge, 1993, pp. 235–55.

Wollen, P. *Bitter Victory. The Situationist International in A Situationist Scrapbook. An endless passion . . . an endless banquet*, ICA/Verso, 1990.

PART II

Right to the City

2

Preface

Great things must be silenced or talked about with grandeur, that is, with cynicism and innocence . . .
I would claim as property and product of man all the beauty, nobility, which we have given to real or imaginary things . . .

Frederic Nietzsche

This work will take an offensive form (that some will perhaps find offending). Why?

Because conceivably each reader will already have in mind a set of ideas systematized or in the process of being systematized. Conceivably, each reader is looking for a 'system' or has found his 'system'. The System is fashionable, as much in thought as in terminologies and language.

Now all systems tend to *close off* reflection, to block off horizon. This work wants to break up systems, not to substitute another system, but to *open up* through thought and action towards *possibilities* by showing the horizon and the road. Against a form of reflection which tends towards formalism, a thought which tends towards an opening leads the struggle.

Urbanism, almost as much as the system, is fashionable. Urbanistic questions and reflections are coming out of circles of technicians, specialists, intellectuals who see themselves as at the 'avant-garde'. They enter the public domain through newspaper articles and writings of diverse import and ambitions. At one and the same time urbanism becomes ideology and practice. Meanwhile, questions relative to the city and to urban reality are not fully known and recognized, they have not yet acquired *politically* the importance and the meaning that they have in *thought* (in ideology) and in *practice* (we shall show an urban strategy already at work and in action). This little book does not only propose to critically analyse thoughts and activities related to urbanism. Its aim is to allow its problems to enter into consciousness and political policies.

From the theoretical and practical situation of problems (from the problematic) concerning the city, reality and possibilities of urban life, let us begin by taking what used to the called a 'cavalier attitude'.

3

Industrialization and Urbanization

To present and give an account of the 'urban problematic', the point of departure must be the process of industrialization. Beyond any doubt this process has been the dynamic of transformations in society for the last century and a half. If one distinguishes between the *inductor* and the *induced*, one can say that the process of industrialization is inductive and that one can count among the induced, problems related to growth and planning, questions concerning the city and the development of the urban reality, without omitting the growing importance of leisure activities and questions related to 'culture'. Industrialization characterizes modern society. This does not inevitably carry with it terms of 'industrial society', if we want to define it. Although urbanization and the problematic of the urban figure among the induced effects and not among the causes or inductive reason, the preoccupation these words signify accentuate themselves in such a way that one can define as an urban society the social reality which arises around us. This definition retains a feature which becomes capital.

Industrialization provides the point of departure for reflection upon our time. Now the city existed prior to industrialization. A remark banal in itself but whose implications have not been fully formulated. The most eminent urban creations, the most 'beautiful' *oeuvres* of urban life (we say '*beautiful*', because they are *oeuvres* rather than products) date from epochs previous to that of industrialization. There was the oriental city (linked to the Asiatic mode of production), the antique city (Greek and Roman associated with the possession of slaves) and then the medieval city (in a complex situation embedded in feudal relations but struggling against a landed feudalism). The oriental and antique city was essentially political; the medieval city, without losing its political character, was principally related to commerce, crafts and banking. It absorbed merchants, who had previously been quasi nomadic and relegated outside the city.

When industrialization begins, and capitalism in competition with a specifically industrial bourgeoisie is born, the city is already a powerful reality. In Western Europe, after the virtual disappearance of the antique city, the decay of Roman influence, the city took off again. More or less nomadic merchants elected as centre of their activities what remained of the antique urban cores. Conversely, one can suppose that these degraded cores functioned as accelerators for what remained of exchange economies maintained by wandering merchants. From the growing surplus product of agriculture, to the detriment of feudal lords, cities accumulate riches: objects, treasures, virtual capitals. There already existed in these urban centres a great monetary wealth, acquired through usury and and commerce. Crafts prosper there, a production clearly distinct from agriculture. Cities support peasant communities and the enfranchisement of the peasants, not without benefit for themselves. In short, they are centres of social and political life where not only wealth is accumulated, but knowledge (*connaissances*), techniques, and *oeuvres* (works of art, monuments). This city is itself '*oeuvre*', a feature which contrasts with the irreversible tendency towards money and commerce, towards exchange and *products*. Indeed, the *oeuvre* is use value and the product is exchange value. The eminent use of the city, that is, of its streets and squares, edifices and monuments, is *la Fête* (a celebration which consumes unproductively, without other advantage but pleasure and prestige and enormous riches in money and objects).

A complex, but contradictory, reality. Medieval cities at the height of their development centralize wealth: powerful groups invest unproductively a large part of their wealth in the cities they dominate. At the same time, banking and commercial capital have already made wealth *mobile* and has established exchange networks enabling the transfer of money. When industrialization begins with the pre-eminence of a specific bourgeoisie (the entrepreneurs), wealth has ceased to be mainly in real estate. Agricultural production is no longer dominant and nor is landed property. Estates are lost to the feudal lords and pass into the hands of urban capitalists enriched by commerce, banking, usury. The outcome is that 'society' as a whole, made up of the city, the country and the institutions which regulate their relations, tend to constitute themselves as a *network of cities*, with a certain division of labour (technically, socially, politically) between cities linked together by road, river and seaways and by commercial and banking relations. One can think that the division of labour between cities was neither sufficiently advanced nor sufficiently aware to determine stable associations and put an end to to rivalries and competition. This urban system was not able to establish itself. What is erected on this base is the State, or centralized power. Cause and effect of this particular centrality, that of power, one city wins over the others: the capital.

Such a process takes place very unevenly, very differently in Italy, Germany, France, Flanders, England, and Spain. The city predominates and yet it is no longer the City-State of antiquity. There are three different terms: society, State and city. In this urban system each city tends to constitute itself as an enclosed self-contained, self-functioning system. The city preserves the organic character of community which comes from the village and which translates itself into a corporate organization (or guild). Community life (comprising general or partial assemblies) does not prohibit class struggle. On the contrary. Violent contrasts between wealth and poverty, conflicts between the powerful and the oppressed, do not prevent either attachment to the city nor an active contribution to the beauty of the *oeuvre*. In the urban context, struggles between fractions, groups and classes strengthen the feeling of belonging. Political confrontations between the 'minuto popolo' the 'popolo grosso', the aristocracy and the oligarchy, have the city as their battle ground, their stake. These groups are rivals in their love of the city. As for the rich and powerful, they always feel threatened. They justify their privilege in the community by somptuously spending their fortune: buildings, foundations, palaces, embellishments, festivities. It is important to emphasize this paradox, for it is not a well understood historical fact: very oppressive societies were very creative and rich in producing *oeuvres*. Later, the production of products replaced the production of *oeuvres* and the social relations attached to them, notably the city. When exploitation replaces oppression, creative capacity disappears. The very notion of 'creation' is blurred or degenerates by miniaturizing itself into 'making' and 'creativity' (the 'do-it-yourself', etc.). Which brings forth arguments to back up a thesis: *city and urban reality are related to use value. Exchange value and the generalization of commodities by industrialization tend to destroy it by subordinating the city and urban reality* which are

refuges of use value, the origins of a virtual predominance and reva-
lorization of use.

In the urban system we are attempting to analyse, action is exercized
over specific conflicts: between use value and exchange value, between
mobilization of wealth (in silver and in money) and unproductive
investment in the city, between accumulation of capital and its squan-
dering on festivities, between the extension of the dominated territory
and the demands of a strict organization of this territory around the
dominating city. The latter protects itself against all eventualities by a
corporate organization which paralyses the initiatives of banking and
commercial capitalism. The coporation does not only regulate a craft.
Each enters into an organic whole: the corporate system regulates the
distribution of actions and activities over urban space (streets and
neighbourhoods) and urban time (timetables and festivities). This
whole tends to congeal itself into an immutable structure. The outcome of which is that industrialization supposes the destructuration
of existing structures. Historians (since Marx) have showed the
fixed nature of guilds. What perhaps remains to be shown is the
tendency of the whole urban system towards a sort of crystallization
and fixation. Where this system consolidated itself, capitalism and
industrialization came late: in Germany, in Italy, a delay full of
consequences.

There is therefore a certain discontinuity between an emerging
industry and its historical conditions. They are neither the same thing
nor the same people. The prodigious growth of exchanges, of a
monetary economy, of merchant production, of the 'world of commodities' which will result from industrialization, implies a radical
change. The passage of commercial and banking capitalism as well as
craft production to industrial production and competitive capitalism
is accompanied by a gigantic crisis, well studied by historians, except
for what relates to the city and the 'urban system'.

Emerging industry tends to establish itself outside cities. Not that it
is an absolute law. No law can be totally general and absolute. This
setting up of industrial enterprises, at first sporadic and dispersed,
depended on multiple local regional and national circumstances. For
example, *printing* seems to have been able in an urban context to go
from a craft to the private enterprise stage. It was otherwise for the
textile industry, for mining, for *metallurgy*. The new industry establishes itself near energy sources (rivers, woods then charcoal), means

of transport (rivers and canals, then railways), raw materials (minerals), pools of labour power (peasant craftmen, weavers and blacksmiths already providing skilled labour).

There still exist today in France numerous small textile centres (valleys in Normandy and the Vosges, etc.) which survive sometimes with difficulty. Is it not remarkable that a part of the heavy metallurgical industry was established in the valley of the Moselle, between two old cities, Nancy and Metz, the only real urban centres of this industrial region? At the same time old cities are markets, sources of available capital, the place where these capitals are managed (banks), the residences of economic and political leaders, reservoirs of labour (that is, the places where can subsist 'the reserve army of labour' as Marx calls it, which weighs on wages and enables the growth of surplus value). Moreover, the city, as workshop, allows the concentration over a limited space of the means of production: tools, raw materials, labour.

Since settlement outside of cities is not satisfactory for 'entrepreneurs', as soon as it is possible industry comes closer to urban centres. Inversely, the city prior to industrialization accelerates the process (in particular, it enables the rapid growth of productivity). The city has therefore played an important role in the *take-off* of industry. As Marx explained, urban concentrations have accompanied the concentration of capital. Industry was to produce its own urban centres, sometimes small cities and industrial agglomerations (Le Creusot), at times medium-sized (Saint-Etienne) or gigantic (the Ruhr, considered as a 'conurbation'). We shall come back to the deterioration of the centrality and urban character in these cities.

This process appears, in analysis, in all its complexity, which the word 'industrialization' represents badly. This complexity becomes apparent as soon as one ceases to think in terms of private *enterprise* on the one hand and global production statistics (so many tons of coal, steel) on the other – as soon as one reflects upon the distinction between the *inductor* and the *induced*, by observing the importance of the phenomena induced and their interaction with the inductors. Industry can do without the old city (pre-industrial, precapitalist) but does so by constituting agglomerations in which urban features are deteriorating. Is this not the case in North America where 'cities' in the way they are understood in France and in Europe, are few: New York, Montreal, San Francisco? Nevertheless, where there is a pre-existent network of old cities, industry assails it. It appropriates this network and refashions it according to its needs. It also attacks the city (each city), assaults it, takes it, ravages it. It tends to break up the old cores by taking them over. This does not prevent the extension of urban phenomena, cities and agglomerations, industrial towns and suburbs (with the addition of shanty towns where industrialization is unable to employ and fix available labour).

We have before us a *double process* or more precisely, a process with two aspects: industrialization and urbanization, growth and development, economic production and social life. The two 'aspects' of this inseparable process have a unity, and yet it is a conflictual process. Historically there is a violent clash between urban reality and industrial reality. As for the complexity of the process, it reveals itself more and more difficult to grasp, given that industrialization does not only produce firms (workers and leaders of private enterprises), but various *offices* – banking, financial, technical and political.

This *dialectical* process, far from being clear, is also far from over. Today it still provokes 'problematic' situations. A few examples would be sufficient here. In Venice, the active population leaves the city for the industrial agglomeration which parallels it on the mainland: Mestre. This city among the most beautiful cities bequeathed to us from pre-industrial times is threatened not so much by physical deterioration due to the sea or to its subsidence, as by the exodus of its inhabitants. In Athens a quite considerable industrialization has attracted to the capital people from small towns and peasants. Modern Athens has nothing more in common with the antique city covered over, absorbed, extended beyond measure. The monuments and sites (agora, Acropolis) which enable to locate ancient Greece are only places of tourist consumption and aesthetic pilgrimage. Yet the organizational core of the city remains very strong. Its surroundings of new neighbourhoods and semi-shanty towns inhabited by uprooted and disorganized people confer it an exorbitant power. This almost shapeless gigantic agglomeration enables the holders of decision-making centres to carry out the worst political ventures. All the more so that the economy of the country closely depends on this network: property speculation, the 'creation' of capitals by this means, investments of these capitals into construction and so on and so forth. It is this fragile network, always in danger of breaking, which defines a *type* of urbanization, without or with a weak industrialization, but with a rapid extension of the agglomeration, of property and speculation; a prosperity falsely maintained by the network.

We could in France cite many cities which have been recently submerged by industrialization: Grenoble, Dunkirk, etc. In other cases, such as Toulouse, there has been a massive extension of the city and urbanization (understood in the widest sense of the term) with little industrialization. Such is also the general case of Latin American and African cities encircled by shanty towns. In these regions and countries old agrarian structures are dissolving: dispossessed or ruined peasants crowd into these cities to find work and subsistence. Now these peasants come from farms destined to disappear because of world commodity prices, these being closely linked to industrialized countries and 'growth poles'. These phenomena are still dependent on industrialization.

An induced process which one could call the 'implosion–explosion' of the city is at present deepening. The urban phenomenon extends itself over a very large part of the territory of great industrial countries. It happily crosses national boundaries: the Megalopolis of Northern Europe extends from the Ruhr to the sea and even to English cities, and from the Paris region to the Scandinavian countries. The *urban fabric* of this territory becomes increasingly tight, although not without its local differentiations and extension of the (technical and social) division of labour to the regions, agglomerations and cities. At the same time, there and even elsewhere, urban concentrations become gigantic: populations are heaped together reaching worrying densities (in surface and housing units). Again at the same time many old urban cores are deteriorating or exploding. People move to distant residential or productive peripheries. Offices replace housing in urban centres. Sometimes (in the United States) these centres are abandoned to the 'poor' and become ghettos for the underprivileged. Sometimes on the contrary, the most affluent people retain their strong positions at the heart of the city (around Central Park in New York, the Marais in Paris).

Let us now examine the *urban fabric*. This metaphor is not clear. More than a fabric thrown over a territory, these words designate a kind of biological proliferation of a net of uneven mesh, allowing more or less extended sectors to escape: hamlets or villages, entire regions. If these phenomena are placed into the perspective of the countryside and old agrarian structures, one can analyse a general movement of concentration: from populations in boroughs and small and large towns – of property and exploitation – of the organization of transports and commercial exchanges, etc. This leads at the same time to the depopulation and the 'loss of the peasantry' from the villages which remain rural while losing what was peasant life: crafts, small local shops. Old 'ways of life' become folklore. If the same phenomena are analysed from the perspective of cities, one can observe not only the extension of highly populated peripheries but also of banking, commercial and industrial networks and of housing (second homes, places and spaces of leisure, etc.).

The urban fabric can be described by using the concept of *ecosystem*, a coherent unity constituted around one or several cities, old and recent. Such a description may lose what is essential. Indeed, the significance of the urban fabric is not limited to its morphology. It is the support of a more or less intense, more or less degraded, 'way of life': *urban society*. On the economic base of the *urban fabric* appear phenomena of another order, that of social and 'cultural' life. Carried by the *urban fabric*, urban society and life penetrate the countryside. Such a way of living entails systems of objects and of values. The best known elements of the urban system of objects include water, electricity, gas (butane in the countryside), not to mention the car, the television, plastic utensils, 'modern' furniture, which entail new demands with regard to 'services'. Among the elements of the system of values we can note urban leisure (dance and song), suits, the rapid adoption of fashions from the city. And also, preoccupations with security, the need to predict the future, in brief, a rationality communicated by the city. Generally youth, as an age group, actively contributes to this rapid assimilation of things and representations coming from the city. These are sociological trivialities which are useful to remember to show their implications. Within the mesh of the urban fabric survive islets and islands of 'pure' *rurality*, often (but not always) poor areas peopled with ageing peasants, badly 'integrated', stripped of what had been the nobility of peasant life in times of greatest misery and of oppression. The 'urban–rural' relation does not disappear. On the contrary, it intensifies itself down to the most industrialized countries. It interferes with other representations and other real relations: town and country, nature and artifice, etc. Here and there tensions become conflicts, latent conflicts are accentuated, and then what was hidden under the *urban fabric* appears in the open.

Moreover, urban cores do not disappear. The fabric erodes them or integrates them to its web. These cores survive by transforming themselves. There are still centres of intense urban life such as the Latin Quarter in Paris. The aesthetic qualities of these urban cores play an important role in their maintenance. They do not only contain monuments and institutional headquarters, but also spaces appropriated for entertainments, parades, promenades, festivities. In this way the urban core becomes a high quality consumption product for foreigners, tourists, people from the outskirts and suburbanites. It survives because of this double role: as place of consumption and consumption of place. Thus centres enter more completely into exchange and exchange value, not without retaining their use value due to spaces provided for specific activities. They become centres of consumption. The architectural and urbanistic resurgence of the *commercial* centre only gives a dull and mutilated version of what was the core of the old city, at one and the same time commercial, religious, intellectual, political and economic (productive). The notion and image of the commercial centre in fact date from the Middle Ages. It corresponds to the small and medium-sized medieval city. But today exchange value is so dominant over use and use value that it more or less suppresses it. There is nothing original in this notion. The creation which corresponds to our times, to their tendencies and (threatening) horizonss is it not the *centre of decision-making*? This centre, gathering together training and information, capacities of organization and institutional decision-making, appears as a project in the making of a new centrality, that of *power*. The greatest attention must be paid to this concept, the practice which it denotes and justifies.

We have in fact a number of terms (at least three) in complex relations with each other, definable by oppositions each on their own terms, although not exhausted by these oppositions. There is the rural and the urban (urban society). There is the urban fabric which carries this 'urbanness' and centrality, old, renovated, new. Hence a disquieting problematic, particularly if one wishes to go from analysis to synthesis, from observations to a project (the 'normative'). Must one allow the urban fabric (what does this word mean?) to proliferate spontaneously? Is it appropriate to capture this force, direct this strange life, savage and artificial at the same time? How can one strengthen the centres? Is it useful or necessary? And which centres, which centralities? Finally, what is to be done about islands of ru-ralism?

Thus the *crisis* of the city can be perceived through distinct problems and problematical whole. This is a theoretical and practical crisis. In theory, the *concept of the city* (of urban reality) is made up of facts, representations and images borrowed from the ancient pre-industrial and precapitalist city, but in a process of transformation and new elaboration. In practice the *urban core* (an essential part of the image and the concept of the city) splits open and yet maintains itself: overrun, often deteriorated, sometimes rotting, the urban core does not disappear. If someone proclaims its end and its reabsorption into the fabric, this is a postulate, a statement without proof. In the same way, if someone proclaims the urgency of a restitution or reconstitution of urban cores, it is again a postulate, a statement without proof. The urban core has not given way to a new and well-defined 'reality', as the village allowed the city to be born. And yet its reign seems to be ending. Unless it asserts itself again even more strongly as centre of power . . .

Until now we have shown how the city has been attacked by industrialization, giving a dramatic and globally considered picture of this process. This analytical attempt could lead us to believe that it is a natural process, without intentions or volitions. There is something like this, but that vision would be truncated. The ruling classes or fractions of the ruling classes intervene actively and voluntarily in this process, possessing capital (the means of production) and managing not only the economic use of capital and productive investments, but also the whole society, using part of the wealth produced in 'culture', art, knowledge, ideology. Beside, or rather, in opposition to, dominant social groups (classes and class fractions), there is the working class: the proletariat, itself divided into strata, partial groups, various tendencies, according to industrial sectors and local and national traditions.

In the middle of the nineteenth century in Paris the situation was somewhat like this. The ruling bourgeoisie, a non-homogenous class, after a hard-fought struggle, has conquered the capital. Today the Marais is still a visible witness to this: before the Revolution it is an aristocratic quarter (despite the tendency of the capital and the wealthy to drift towards the west), an area of gardens and private mansions. It took but a few years, during the 1830s, for the Third

Estate to appropriate it. A number of magnificent houses disappear, workshops and shops occupy others, tenements, stores, depots and warehouses, firms replace parks and gardens. Bourgeois ugliness, the greed for gain visible and legible in the streets takes the place of a somewhat cold beauty and aristocratic luxury. On the walls of the Marais can be read class struggle and the hatred between classes, a victorious meanness. It is impossible to make more perceptible this paradox of history which partially escaped Marx. The 'progressive' bourgeoisie, taking charge of economic growth, endowed with ideological instruments suited to rational growth, moves towards democracy and replaces oppression by exploitation, this class as such no longer creates – it replaces the *œuvre*, by the product. Those who retain this sense of the *œuvre*, including writers and painters, think and see themselves as 'non bourgeois'. As for oppressors, the masters of societies previous to the democratic bourgeoisie – princes, kings, lords, emperors – they had a sense and a taste of the *œuvre*, especially in architecture and urban design. In fact the *œuvre* is more closely related to use value than to exchange value.

After 1848, the French bourgeoisie solidly entrenched in the city (Paris) possesses considerable influence, but it sees itself hemmed in by the working class. Peasants flock in, settling around the 'barriers' and entrances of the fortifications, the immediate periphery. Former craftsmen and new proletarians penetrate right up to the heart of the city. They live in slums but also in tenements, where the better-off live on the ground floors and the workers on the upper ones. In this 'disorder' the workers threaten the '*parvenus*', a danger which became obvious during the days of June 1848 and which the Commune was to confirm. *A class strategy* is elaborated, aimed at the replanning of the city, without any regard for reality, for its own life.

The life of Paris reaches its greatest intensity between 1848 and the Haussmann period – not what is understood by 'la vie parisienne', but the urban life of the capital. It engages itself into literature and poetry with great vigour and power. Then it will be over. Urban life suggests meetings, the confrontation of differences, reciprocal knowledge and acknowledgement (including ideological and political confrontation), ways of living, 'patterns' which coexist in the city. During the nineteenth century, a democracy of peasant origins which drove the revolutionaries could have transformed itself into an urban democracy. It was and it is still for history one of the beliefs of the

Commune. As urban democracy threatened the privileges of the new ⁻ ruling class, that class prevented it from being born. How? By expelling from the urban centre and the city itself the proletariat, by destroying 'urbanity'.

Act One. Baron Haussmann, man of this Bonapartist State which erects itself over society to treat it cynically as the booty (and not only the stake) of the struggles for power. Haussmann replaces winding but lively streets by long avenues, sordid but animated 'quartiers' by bourgeois ones. If he forces through boulevards and plans open spaces, it is not for the beauty of views. It is to 'comb Paris with machine guns'. The famous Baron makes no secret of it. Later we will be greateful to him for having opened up Paris to traffic. This was not the aim, the finality of Haussmann 'planning'. The voids have a meaning: they cry out loud and clear the glory and power of the State which plans them, the violence which could occur. Later transfers towards other finalities take place which justify in another way these gashes into urban life. It should be noted that Haussmann did not achieve his goal. One strong aspect of the Paris Commune (1871) is the strength of the return towards the urban centre of workers pushed out towards the outskirts and peripheries, their reconquest of the city, this belonging among other belongings, this value, this *œuvre* which had been torn from them.

Act Two. The goal was to be attained by a much vaster manoeuvre and with more important results. In the second half of the century, influential people, that is rich or powerful, or both, sometimes ideologues (Le Play) with ideas strongly marked by religions (Catholic and Protestant), sometimes informed politicians (belonging to the centre right) and who moreover do not constitute a coherent and unique group, in brief, a few notables, discover a new notion. The Third Republic will insure its fortune, that is, its realization on the ground. It will conceive the notion of *habitat*. Until then, 'to inhabit' meant to take part in a social life, a community, village or city. Urban life had, among other qualities, this attribute. It gave the right to inhabit, it allowed townsmen-citizens to inhabit. It is thus that 'mortals inhabit while they save the earth, while they wait for the gods . . . while they conduct their lives in preservation and use'. Thus speaks the poet and philosopher Heidegger of the concept *to inhabit*. Outside philosophy and poetry the same things have been said sociologically in prose. At the end of the nineteenth century the notables isolate a function, detach it from a very complex whole which was and remains the city, to project it over the ground, not without showing and signifying in this manner the society for which they provide an ideology and a practice. Certainly suburbs were created under the pressure of circumstances to respond to the blind (although motivated and directed) growth of industrialization, the massive arrival of peasants led to the urban centres by 'rural exodus'. The process has none the less been oriented by a strategy.

A typical *class strategy*, does that mean a series of concerted actions, planned with a single aim? No. Class character seems that much deeper than several concerted actions, centered around several objectives, has nevertheless converged towards a final result. It goes without saying that all these notables were not proposing to open up a means to speculation: some of them, men of good will, philanthropists, humanists, seem even to wish the opposite. They have none the less mobilized property wealth around the city, the entrance without restriction into exchange and exchange value of the ground and housing. This had speculative implications. They were not proposing to demoralize the working classes, but on the contrary, to moralize it. They considered it beneficial to involve the workers (individuals and families) into a hierarchy clearly distinct from that which rules in the firm, that of property and landlords, houses and neighbourhoods. They wanted to give them another function, another status, other roles than those attached to the condition of the salaried producers. They meant in this way to give them a better everyday life than that of work. In this way they conceived the role of owner-occupied housing. A remarkably successful operation (although its political consequences were not always those anticipated by its promoters). Nevertheless, a result was achieved, predicted or otherwise, conscious or unconscious. Society orients itself ideologically and practically towards other problems than that of production. Little by little social consciousness ceased to refer to production and to focus on everyday life and consumption. With 'suburbanization' a process is set into motion which decentres the city. Isolated from the city, the proletariat will end its sense of the *oeuvre*. Isolated from places of production, available from a sector of habitation for scattered firms, the proletariat will allow its creative capacity to diminish in its conscience. Urban consciousness will vanish.

In France the beginnings of the suburb are also the beginnings of a violently anti-urban planning approach; a singular paradox. For

decades during the Third Republic appeared documents authorizing
and regulating owner-occupied suburbs and plots. What could be
more accurately referred to here is the *banlieue pavillonaire*, a type of
suburbanization begun in this period in France characterized by small
owner-occupied houing whose nearest Anglo-Saxon equivalent in
terms of typology and social relations is the '*bungalow*'.

A de-urbanized, yet dependent periphery is established around the
city. Effectively, these new suburban dwellers are still urban even
though they are unaware of it and believe themselves to be close to
nature, to the sun and to greenery. One could call it a de-urbanizing
and de-urbanized urbanization to emphasize the paradox.

Its excesses will slow this extension down. The movement it engenders
will carry along the bourgeoisie and the well-off who will establish
residential suburbs. City centres empty themselves for offices. The whole
then begins to struggle with the inextricable. But it is not finished. .

Act Three. After the Second World War it becomes evident that the
picture changes according to various emergencies and constraints
related to demographic and industrial growth and the influx of people
from the provinces to Paris. The housing crisis, acknowledged and
proven, turns into a catastrophe and threatens to worsen the political
situation which is still unstable. 'Emergencies' overwhelm the initiatives of capitalism and 'private' enterprise, especially as the latter is not
interested in construction, considered to be insufficiently profitable.
The State can no longer be content with simply regulating land plots
and the construction of informal suburban housing or fighting (badly)
property speculation. By means of intermediary organisms it takes
charge of housing construction and an era of "*nouveaux ensembles*'
(large-scale housing estates) and 'new towns' begins.

It could be said that public powers take charge of what hitherto was
part of a market economy. Undoubtedly. But housing does not necessarily become a public service. It surfaces into social consciousness as
a right. It is acknowledged in fact by the indignation raised by
dramatic cases and by the discontent engendered by the crisis. Yet it is
not formally or practically acknowledged except as an appendix to the
'rights of man'. Construction taken in charge by the State does not
change the orientations and conceptions adopted by the market economy. As Engels had predicted, the housing question, even aggra-
vated, has politically played only a minor role. Groups and parties on
the Left will be satisfied with demanding 'more housing'. Moreover,

what guides public and semi-public initiatives is not a conception of urban planning, it is simply the goal of providing as quickly as possible at the least cost, the greatest possible number of housing units. The new housing estates will be characterized by an abstract and functional character: the concept of *habitat* brought to its purest form by a State bureaucracy.

This notion of *habitat* is still somewhat 'uncertain'. Individual owner-occupation will enable variations, particular or individual interpretations of *habitat*. There is a sort of plasticity which allows for modifications and appropriations. The space of the house – fence, garden, various and available corners – leaves a margin of initiative and freedom to *inhabit*, limited but real. State rationality is pushed to the limit. In the new housing estate *habitat* is established in its purest form, as a burden of constraints. Certain philosophers will say that large housing estates achieve the concept of *habitat*, by excluding the notion of *inhabit*, that is, the plasticity of space, its modelling and the appropriation by groups and individuals of the conditions of their existence. It is also a complete way of living (functions, prescriptions, daily routine) which is inscribed and signifies itself in this *habitat*.

The villa *habitat* has proliferated in the suburban communes around Paris, by extending the built environment in a disorderly fashion. This urban, and at the same time non-urban, growth has only one law: speculation on plots and property. The interstices left by this growth have been filled by large social housing estates. To the speculation on plots, badly opposed, was added speculation in apartments when these were in co-ownership. Thus housing entered into property wealth and urban land into exchange value. Restrictions were disappearing.

If one defines urban reality by dependency *vis-à-vis* the centre, suburbs are urban. If one defines urban order by a perceptible (legible) relationship between centrality and periphery, suburbs are de-urbanized. And one can say that the 'planning thought' of large social housing estates has literally set itself against the city and the urban to eradicate them. All perceptible, legible urban reality has disappeared: streets, squares, monuments, meeting places. Even the café (the bistro) has encountered the resentment of the builders of those large housing estates, their taste for asceticism, the reduction of '*to inhabit*' to *habitat*. They had to go to the end of their destruction of palpable urban reality before there could appear the demand for a restitution.

Then one saw the timid, slow reappearance of the cafe, the commercial, centre, the street, 'cultural' amenities, in brief, a few elements of urban reality.

Urban order thus decomposes into two stages: individual and owner-occupied houses and housing estates. But there is no society without order, signified, perceptible, legible on the ground. Suburban disorder harbours an order: a glaring opposition of individually owner-occupied detached houses and housing estates. This opposition tends to constitute a *system* of *significations* still urban even into de-urbanization. Each sector defines itself (by and in the consciousness of the inhabitants) in relation to the other, against the other. The inhabitants themselves have little consciousness of the internal order of their sector, but the people from the housing estates see and perceive themselves as not being villa dwellers. This is reciprocal. At the heart of this opposition the people of the housing estates entrench themselves into the *logic of the habitat* and the people of owner-occupied houses entrench themselves into the *make-believe of habitat*. For some it is the rational organization (in appearance) of space. For others it is the presence of the dream, of nature, health, apart from the bad and unhealthy city. But the logic of the *habitat* is only perceived in relation to make-believe, and make-believe in relation to logic. People represent themselves to themselves by what they are lacking or believe to be lacking. In this relationship, the imaginary has more power. It over-determines logic: the fact of *inhabiting* is perceived by reference to the owner-occupation of detached dwellings. These dwellers regret the absence of a spatial logic while the people of the housing estates regret not knowing the joys of living in a detached house. Hence the surprising results of surveys. More than 80 per cent of French people aspire to be owner-occupiers of a house, while a strong majority also declare themselves to be 'satisfied' with social housing estates. The outcome is not important here. What should be noted is that *consciousness of the city and of urban reality is dulled* for one or the other, so as to disappear. The practical and theoretical (ideological) destruction of the city cannot but leave an enormous emptiness, not including administrative and other problems increasingly difficult to resolve. This emptiness is less important for a critical analysis than the source of conflict expressed by the end of the city and by the extension of a mutilated and deteriorated, but real, urban society. The suburbs are urban, within a dissociated morphology, the empire of separation and scission between the elements of what had been created as unity and simultaneity.

Within this perspective critical analysis can distinguish three periods (which do not exactly correspond to the distinctions previously made in three acts of the drama of the city).

First period. Industry and the process of industrialization assault and ravage pre-existing urban reality, destroying it through practice and ideology, to the point of extirpating it from reality and consciousness. Led by a class strategy, industrialization acts as a *negative* force over urban reality: the urban social is denied by the industrial economic.

Second period (in part juxtaposed to the first). Urbanization spreads and urban society becomes general. Urban reality, in and by its own destruction makes itself acknowledged as socio-economic reality. One discovers that the whole society is liable to fall apart if it lacks the city and centrality: an essential means for the planned organization of production and consumption has disappeared.

Third period. One finds or reinvents urban reality, but not without suffering from its destruction in practice or in thinking. One attempts to restitute centrality. Would this suggest that class strategy has disappeared? This is not certain. It has changed. To the old centralities, to the decomposition of centres, it substitutes the *centre of decision-making.*

Thus is born or reborn urban thought. It follows an urbanism without thought. The masters of old had no need for an urban theory to embellish their cities. What sufficed was the pressure exercised by the people on their masters and the presence of a civilization and style which enabled the wealth derived from the labour of the people to be invested into '*œuvres*'. The bourgeois period puts an end to this age-old tradition. At the same time this period brings a new *rationality*, different from the rationality elaborated by philosophers since ancient Greece.

Philosophical Reason proposed definitions of man, the world, history and society which were questionable but also underpinned by reasonings which had been given shape. Its democratic generalizations later gave way to a rationalism of opinions and attitudes. Each citizen was expected to have a reasoned opinion on every fact and problem concerning him, this wisdom spurning the irrational. From the confrontation of ideas and opinions, a superior reason was to emerge, a general wisdom inciting the general will. It is fruitless to insist upon the difficulties of this classical rationalism, linked to the political difficulties of democracy, and to the practical difficulties of humanism. In the nineteenth and especially in the twentieth century, organizing rationality, operation at various levels of social reality, takes shape. Is it coming from the capitalist firm and the management of units of production? Is it born at the level of the State and planning? What is important is that it is an *analytical reason* pushed to its extreme consequences. It begins from a most detailed methodical analysis of elements – productive operation, social and economic organization, structure and function. It then subordinates these elements to a finality. Where does this finality come from? Who formulates it and stipulates it? How and why? This is the gap and the failure of this operational rationalism. Its tenets purport to extract finality from the sequence of operations. Now, this is not so. Finality, that is, the whole and the orientation of the whole, decides itself. To say that it comes from the operations themselves, is to be locked into a vicious circle: the analysis giving itself as its own aim, for its own meaning. Finality is an object of decision. It is a *strategy*, more or less justified by an *ideology*. Rationalism which purports to extract from its own analyses the aim pursued by these analyses is itself an *ideology*. The notion of *system* overlays that of strategy. To critical analysis the system reveals itself as strategy, is unveiled as decision, that is, as decided finality. It has been shown above how a *class strategy* has oriented the analysis and division of urban reality, its destruction and restitution; and projections on the society where such strategic decisions have been taken.

However, from the point of view of a technicist rationalism, the results on the ground of the processes examined above represent only chaos. In the 'reality', which they critically observe – suburbs, urban fabric and surviving cores – these rationalists do not recognize the conditions of their own existence. What is before them is only contradiction and disorder. Only, in fact, *dialectical* reason can master (by reflective thought, by practice) multiple and paradoxically contradictory processes.

How to impose order in this chaotic confusion? It is in this way that organizational rationalism poses its problem. This is not a normal disorder. How can it be established as norm and normality? This is unconceivable. This disorder is unhealthy. The physician of modern society see himself as the physician of a sick social space. Finality? The cure? It is *coherence*. The rationalist will establish or re-establish coherence into a chaotic reality which he observes and which offers itself up to his action. This rationalist may not realize that coherence is a form, therefore a means rather than an end, and that he will systematize the *logic of the habitat* underlying the disorder and apparent incoherence, that he will take as point of departure towards the coherence of the real, his coherent approaches. There is in fact no single or unitary approach in planning thought, but several tendencies identifiable according to this operational rationalism. Among these tendencies, some assert themselves *against*, others *for* rationalism by leading it to extreme formulations. What interferes with the general tendencies of those involved with planning is understanding only what they can translate in terms of graphic operations: seeing, feeling at the end of a pencil, drawing.

One can therefore identify the following:

(1) The planning of men of good will (architects and writers). Their thinking and projects imply a certain philosophy. Generally they associate themselves to an old classical and liberal humanism. This not without a good dose of nostalgia. One wishes to build to the 'human scale', for 'people'. These humanists present themselves at one and the same time as doctors of society and creators of new social relations. Their ideology, or rather, their idealism often come from agrarian models, adopted without reflection: the village, the community, the neighbourhood, the townsman-citizen who will be endowed with civic buildings, etc. They want to build buildings and cities to the 'human scale', 'to its measure', without conceiving that in the modern world 'man' has changed scale and the measure of yesteryear (village and city) has been transformed beyond measure. At best, this tradition leads to a *formalism* (the adoption of models which had neither content or meaning), or to an *aestheticism*, that is, the adoption for their beauty of ancient models which are then thrown as fodder to feed the appetites of consumers.

(2) The planning of these administrators linked to the public (State) sector. It sees itself as scientific. It relies sometimes on a science, sometimes on studies which call themselves synthetic (pluri or multi-disciplinary). This scientism, which accompanies the deliberate forms of operational rationalism, tends to neglect the so-called 'human factor'. It divides itself into tendencies. Sometimes through a particu-

lar science, a technique takes over and becomes the point of departure; it is generally a technique of communication and circulation. One extrapolates from a science, from a fragmentary analysis of the reality considered. One optimizes information and communication into a model. This technocratic and systematized planning, with its myths and its ideology (namely, the primacy of technique), would not hesitate to raze to the ground what is left of the city to leave way for cars, ascendant and descendant networks of communication and information. The models elaborated can only be put into practice by eradicating from social existence the very ruins of what was the city.

Sometimes, on the contrary, information and analytical knowledge coming from different sciences are oriented towards a synthetic finality. *For all that, one should not conceive an urban life having at its disposal information provided by the sciences of society.* These two aspects are confounded in the conception of *centres of decision-making*, a global vision, planning already unitary in its own way, linked to a philosophy, to a conception of society, a political strategy, that is, a global and total system.

(3) The planning of developers. They conceive and realize without hiding it, for the market, with profit in mind. What is new and recent is that they are no longer selling housing or buildings, but *planning*. With or without ideology, planning becomes an exchange value. The project of developers presents itself as opportunity and place of privilege: the place of happiness in a daily life miraculously and marvellously transformed. The make-believe world of *habitat* is inscribed in the logic of *habitat* and their unity provides a social practice which does not need a system. Hence these advertisements, which are already famous and which deserve posterity because publicity itself becomes ideology. Parly II (a new development) 'gives birth to a new art of living', a 'new lifestyle'. Daily life resembles a fairy tale. 'Leave your coat in the cloakroom and feeling lighter, do your shopping after having left the children in the nurseries of the shopping mall, meet your friends, have a drink together at the drugstore . . .' Here is the fulfilled make-believe of the joy of living. Consumer society is expressed by orders: the order of these elements on the ground, the order to be happy. Here is the context, the setting, the means of your happiness. If you do not know how to grasp the happiness offered so as to make it your own – don't insist!

A *global strategy*, that is, what is already an unitary system and total planning, is outlined through these various tendencies. Some will put into practice and will concretize a directed consumer society. They will build not only commercial centres, but also centres of privileged consumption: the renewed city. They will by making 'legible' an ideology of happiness through consumption, joy by planning adapted to its new mission. This planning programmes a daily life generating satisfactions – (especially for receptive and participating women). A programmed and computerized consumption will become the rule and norm for the whole society. Others will erect *decision-making* centres, concentrating the means of power: information, training, organization, operation. And still: repression (constraints, including violence) and persuasion (ideology and advertising). Around these centres will be apportioned on the ground, in a dispersed order, according to the norms of foreseen constraints, the peripheries, de-urbanized urbanization. All the conditions come together thus for a perfect domination, for a refined exploitation of people as producers, consumers of products, consumers of space.

The convergence of these projects therefore entails the greatest dangers, for it raises *politically* the problem of urban society. It is possible that new contradictions will arise from these projects, impeding convergence. If a unitary strategy was to be successfully constituted, it might prove irretrievable.

4

Philosophy and the City

Having contextualized the 'cavalier' attitude mentioned at the beginning, particular aspects and problems concerning the urban can now be emphasized. In order to take up a radically critical analysis and to deepen the urban problematic, philosophy will be the starting point. This will come as a surprise. And yet, has not frequent reference to philosophy been made in the preceding pages? The purpose is not to present a *philosophy of the city*, but on the contrary, to refute such an approach by giving back to the whole of philosophy its place in history: that of a *project* of synthesis and totality which philosophy as such cannot accomplish. After which the *analytical* will be examined, that is, the ways fragmentary sciences have highlighted or partitioned urban reality. The rejection of the synthetic propositions of these specialized, fragmentary, and particular sciences will enable us – to pose better – in *political* terms – the problem of synthesis. During the course of this progress one will find again features and problems which will reappear more clearly. In particular, the opposition between *use value* (the city and urban life) and *exchange value* (spaces bought and sold, the consumption of products, goods, places and signs) will be highlighted.

  For philosophical meditation aiming at a totality through speculative systematization, that is, classical philosophy from Plato to Hegel, the city was much more than a secondary theme, an object among others. The links between philosophical thought and urban life appear clearly upon reflection, although they need to be made explicit. The city and the town were not for philosophers and philosophy a simple objective condition, a sociological context, an exterior element. Philosophers have thought the city: they have brought to language and concept urban life.

Let us leave aside questions posed by the oriental city, the Asiatic mode of production, 'town and country' relations in this mode of production, and lastly the formation of ideologies (philosophies) on this base. Only the Greek and Roman antique city from which are derived societies and civilizations known as 'Western' will be considered. This city is generally the outcome of a *synoecism*, the coming together of several villages and tribes established on this territory. This unit allows the development of division of labour and landed property (money) without however destroying the collective, or rather 'communal' property of the land. In this way a community is constituted at the heart of which is a minority of free citizens who exercise power over other members of the city: women, children, slaves, foreigners. The city links its elements associated with the form of the communal property ('common private property', or 'privatized appropriation') of the active citizens, who are in opposition to the slaves. This form of association constitutes a democracy, the elements, of which are strictly hierarchical and submitted to the demands of the oneness of the city itself. It is the democracy of non-freedom (Marx). During the course of the history of the antique city, private property pure and simple (of money, land and slaves) hardens, concentrates, without abolishing the rights of the city over its territory.

The separation between town and country takes place among the first and fundamental divisions of labour, with the distribution of tasks according to age and sex (the biological division of labour), with the organization of labour according to tools and skills (technical division). The social division of labour between town and country corresponds to the separation between material and intellectual labour, and consequently, between the natural and the spiritual. Intellectual labour is incumbent upon the city: functions of organization and direction, political and military activities, elaboration of theoretical knowledge (philosophy and sciences). The whole divides itself, separations are established, including the separation between the *Physics* and the *Logos*, between theory and practice, and in practice, the separations between between *praxis* (action on human groups), *poiesis* (creation of 'oeuvres'), *techne* (activities endowed with techniques and directed towards product). The countryside, both practical reality and representation, will carry images of nature, of being, of the innate. The city will carry images of effort, of will, of subjectivity, of contemplation, without these representations becoming disjointed from real activities. From these images confronted against each other great symbolisms will emerge. Around the Greek city, above it, there is the *cosmos*, luminous and ordered spaces, the apogee of place. The city has as centre a hole which is sacred and damned, inhabited by the forces of death and life, times dark with effort and ordeals, the *world*. The Apollonian spirit triumphs in the Greek city, although not without struggle, as the luminous symbol of reason which regulates, while in the Etruscan-Roman city what governs is the demonic side of the urban. But the philosopher and philosophy attempt to reclaim or create totality. The philosopher does not acknowledge separation, he does not conceive that the world, life, society, the cosmos (and later, history) can no longer make a Whole.

Philosophy is thus born from the city, with its division of labour and multiple modalities. It becomes itself a specialized activity in its own right. But it does not become fragmentary, for otherwise it would blend with science and the sciences, themselves in a process of emerging. Just as philosophy refuses to engage in the opinions of craftsmen, soldiers and politicians, it refutes the reasons and arguments of specialists. It has totality as fundamental interest for its own sake, which is recovered or created by the system, that is, the oneness of thought and being, of discourse and act, of nature and contemplation, of the world (or the cosmos) and human reality. This does not exclude but includes meditation on *differences* (between Being and thought, between what comes from nature and what comes from the city, etc.). As Heidegger expressed it, the logos (element, context, mediation and end for philosophers and urban life) was simultaneously the following: to put forward, gather together and collect, then to recollect and collect oneself, speak and say, disclose. This gathering is the harvest and even its conclusion. 'One goes to collect things and brings them back. Here sheltering dominates and with it in turn dominates the wish to preserve . . . The harvest is in itself a choice of what needs a shelter.' Thus, the harvest is already *thought out*. That which is gathered is put in reserve. To say is the act of collection which gathers together. This assumes the presence of 'somebody' before which, for whom and by whom is expressed the being of what is thus successful. This presence is produced with clarity (or as Heidegger says, with 'non-mystery'). The city linked to philosophy thus gathers by and in its logos the wealth of the territory, dispersed activities and people, the spoken and the written (of which each assumes already its collection and recollection). It makes *simultaneous* what in the countryside and according to nature takes place and passes, and is distributed according to cycles and rhythms. It grasps and defends 'everything'. If philosophy and the city are thus associated in the dawning logos (reason), it is not within a subjectivity akin to the Cartesian '*cogito*'. If they constitute a system, it is not in the usual way and in the current meaning of the term.

To the organization of the city itself can be linked the primordial whole of urban form and its content, of philosophical form and its meaning: a privileged centre, the core of a political space, the seat of the logos governed by the logos before which citizens are 'equal', the regions and distributions of space having a rationality justified before the logos (for it and by it).

The logos of the Greek city cannot be separated from the philosophical logos. The *œuvre* of the city continues and is focused in the work of philosophers, who gather opinions and viewpoints, various *œuvres*, and think them simultaneously and collect differences into a totality: urban places in the cosmos, times and rhythms of the city and that of the world (and inversely). It is therefore only for a superficial historicity that philosophy brings to language and concept urban life, that of the city. In truth, the city as emergence, language, meditation comes to theoretical light by means of the philosopher and philosophy.

After this first interpretation of the internal link between the city and philosophy, let us go to the European Middle Ages. *It begins from the countryside.* The Roman city and the Empire have been destroyed by Germanic tribes which are both primitive communities and military organizations. The feudal property of land is the outcome of the dissolution of this sovereignty (city, property, relations of production). Serfs replace slaves. With the rebirth of cities there is on the one hand the feudal organization of property and possession of land (peasant communities having a customary possession and lords having an 'eminent' domain as it will later be called), and on the other hand, a corporate organization of crafts and urban property. Although at the beginning seigneurial tenure of land dominates it, this double hierarchy contains the demise of this form of property and the supremacy of wealth in urban property from which arises a deep conflict, basic to medieval society. 'The necessity to ally themselves against the plunderer lords associated themselves together; the need for common market halls at a time when industry was craft, when serfs in breach

of their bondage and in competition with each other were flooding to
the increasingly rich cities, the whole of feudal organization was giving
birth to the corporations (or guilds). Small capitals, slowly saved by
isolated craftsmen, their numbers stable in the middle of a growing
population, developed a system of journeymen and apprentices which
established in the cities a hierarchy similar to that of the countryside'
(Marx). In these conditions theology subordinates philosophy. The
latter no longer meditates on the city. The philosopher (the theolo-
gian) deliberates upon the *double hierarchy*. He gives it shape, with or
without taking conflicts into account. The symbols and notions
relative to the *cosmos* (spaces, the hierarchy of matter in that space)
and to the *world* (the actualization of finished matter, hierarchies in
time, descent or fall, ascension and redemption) erase the consciousness of the city. From the moment when there are not two but three
hierarchies (feudal landed property, guild organization, the king and
his State apparatus), thought takes again a critical dimension. The
philosopher and philosophy find themselves again, no longer having
to choose between the Devil and the Lord. Philosophy will not however recognize its link to the city, although the rise of rationalism
accompanies the rise of capitalism (commercial and banking, then
industrial), and the development of cities. This rationalism is attached
either to the State or to the individual.

For Hegel, at the height of speculative, systematic and contemplative
philosophy, the unity between the perfect Thing, that is, the Greek
city, and the Idea, which animates society and the State, this admirable
whole, has been irremediably broken by historic becoming. In modern
society, the State subordinates these elements and materials, including
the city. The latter, however remains as a sort of subsystem in the total
philosophico-political system, with the system of needs, that of rights
and obligations, and that of the family and estates (crafts and guilds),
that of art and aesthetics, etc.

For Hegel, philosophy and the 'real' (practical and social) are not, or
rather, are no longer external to each other. Separations disappear.
Philosophy is not satisfied to meditate upon the real, to attempt the
link up of the real and the ideal: it fulfills itself by achieving the ideal:
the rational. The real is not satisfied with giving excuse to reflection,
to knowledge, to consciousness. During a history which has a meaning
– which has this meaning – it becomes rational. Thus the real and the
rational tend towards each other; each from their own side moves

towards an identity thus acknowledged. The rational is basically philosophy, the philosophical system. The real is society and law and the State which cements the edifice by crowning it. Consequently, in the modern State, the philosophical system, becomes real: in Hegel's philosophy, the real acknowledge the rational. The system has a double side, philosophical and political. Hegel discovers the historical moment of this shift from the rational into the real and vice versa. He brings to light identity at the moment when history produces it. *Philosophy achieves itself*. There is for Hegel, as Marx will articulate it, at one and the same time a becoming of a philosophy of the world and a becoming of the world of philosophy. An initial repercussion: there can no longer be a divide between philosophy and reality (historical, social, political). A second repercussion: the philosopher no longer has independence: he accomplishes a public function, as do other officials. Philosophy and the philosopher integrate themselves (by mediation of the body of civil servants and the middle class) in this rational reality of the State – no longer in the city, which was only a thing (perfect, it is true, but only thing), denied by a higher and more inclusive rationality.

One knows that Marx neither refuted nor refused the essential Hegelian affirmation: *Philosophy achieves itself*. The philosopher no longer has a right to independence *vis-à- vis* social practice. Philosophy inserts itself into it. There is indeed a simultaneous becoming-philosophy of the world and a becoming-world of philosophy, and therefore a tendency towards wholeness (knowledge and acknowledgement of non-separation). And yet Marx thrusts Hegelianism aside. History does not achieve itself. Wholeness is not reached, nor are contradictions resolved. It is not by and in the State, with bureaucracy as social support, that philosophy can be realized. The proletariat has this historic mission: only it can put an end to separations (alienations). Its mission has a double facet: to destroy bourgeois society by building another society – abolish philosophical speculation and abstraction, the alienating contemplation and systematization, to accomplish the philosophical project of the human being. It is from industry, from industrial production, from its relation with productive forces and labour, not from a moral or philosophical judgement, that the working class gets its possibilities. One must turn this world upside down: the meeting of the rational and the real will happen in another society.

The history of philosophy in relation to the city is far from being accomplished within this perspective. Indeed, this history would also suggest the analysis of themes whose emergence are linked to the representation of nature and the earth, to agriculture, to the sacraliza-tion of the land (and to its desacralization). Such themes, once born, are displaced and represented sometimes far from their starting points in time and space. The points of imputation and impact, conditions, implications, consequences do not coincide. The themes are enunci-ated and inserted into social contexts and categories different from those which distinguish their emergence, inasmuch as one can speak of 'categories'. The urban problematic, for example that which refers to the destiny of the Greek city, used to disengage itself or hide itself, cosmic themes anterior or exterior to this city; the visions of a cyclical becoming or of the hidden immobility of the human being. The purpose of these remarks is to show that the relation considered has yet to receive an explicit formulation.

What relation is there today between philosophy and the city? An ambiguous one. The most emminent contemporary philosophers do not borrow their themes from the city. Bachelard has left wonderful pages on the house. Heidegger has meditated on the Greek city and the logos, and on the Greek temple. Nevertheless the metaphors which resume Heideggerian thought do not come from the city but from a primary and earlier life: the 'shepherds of being', the 'forest paths'. It seems that it is from the Dwelling and the opposition between *Dwell-ing* and *Wandering* that Heidegger borrows his themes. As for so-called 'existential' thought, it is based on individual consciousness, on the subject and the ordeals of subjectivity, rather than on a practical, historical and social reality.

However, it is not proven that philosophy has said its last word on the city. For example, one can perfectly conceive of a *phenomenolo-gical* description of urban life. Or construct a *semiology* of urban reality which would correspond for the present city to what was the logos in the Greek city. Only philosophy and the philosopher propose a *totality*, the search for a global conception or vision. To consider 'the city' is it not already to extend philosophy, to reintroduce philosophy into the city or the city into philosophy? It is true that the concept of *totality* is in danger of remaining empty if it is only philosophical. Thus is formulated a problematic which does not reduce itself to the city but which concerns the world, history, 'man'.

Moreover, a certain number of contemporary thinkers have pondered on the city. They see themselves, more or less clearly, as philosophers of the city. For this reason these thinkers want to inspire architects and planners, and make the link between urban preoccupations and the old humanism. But these philosophers lack breadth. The philosophers who claim to think the city and put forward a philosophy of the city by extending traditional philosophy, discourse on the 'essence' of the city or on the city as 'spirit', as 'life' or 'life force', as being or 'organic whole'. In brief, sometime as subject, sometime as abstract system. This leads to nothing, thus a double conclusion. Firstly, the history of philosophical thought can and must reclaim itself from its relation with the city (the condition and content of this thought). It is a way of putting this history into perspective. Secondly, this articulation figures in the problematic of philosophy and the city (knowledge, the formulation of the urban problematic, a notion of this context, a strategy to envisage). Philosophical concepts are not operative and yet they situate the city and the urban – and the whole of society – as a totality, over and above analytical fragmentations. What is proclaimed here of philosophy and its history could equally be asserted for art and its history.

5

Fragmentary Sciences and Urban Reality

During the course of the nineteenth century, the sciences of social reality are constituted against philosophy which strives to grasp the global (by enclosing a real totality into a rational systematization). These sciences fragment reality in order to analyse it, each having their method or methods, their sector or domain. After a century, it is still under discussion whether these sciences bring distinct enlightenment to a unitary reality, or whether the analytical fragmentation that they use corresponds to objective differences, articulations, levels and dimensions.

One cannot claim that the city has escaped the researches of historians, economists, demographers and sociologists. Each of these specialities contributes to a science of the city. It has already been ascertained and corroborated that history elucidates better the genesis of the city, and especially identifies better than any other science, the problematic of urban society. Inversely, there is also no doubt that the knowledge of urban reality can relate to the possible (or possibilities) and not only to what is finished or from the past. If one wishes to build a commercial or cultural centre, taking into account functional and functioning needs, the economist has his word to say. In the analysis of urban reality, the geographer, the climatologist, the botanist also intervene. The environment, global and confused concept, fragments itself according to these specialities. In relation to the future and the conditions of the future, mathematical calculations provide essential evidence. Yet, what gathers these facts together? A project, or in other words, a strategy. On the other hand, a doubt remains and is even confirmed. Is the city the sum of indices and facts, of variables and parameters, of correlations, this collection of facts, of descriptions, of fragmentary analyses, because it is fragmentary? These analytical divisions do not lack rigour, but as has already been said, rigour is uninhabitable. The problem coincides with the general questioning of the specialist sciences. On the one hand, the only approach which seeks to find the global reminds us strangely of philosophy when it is not openly philosophical. On the other hand, the partial offers more positive but scattered facts. Is it possible to extract from fragmentary sciences a science of the city? No more than a holistic science of society, or of 'man', or of human and social reality. On the one hand, a concept without content, on the other, content or contents without concept. Either one declares that the 'city', the urban reality as such, does not exist but is only a series of correlations. The 'subject' is suppressed. Or the continues to assert the existence of the global: one approaches and locates it, either by extrapolations in the name of a discipline, or by wagering on an 'interdisciplinary' tactic. One does not grasp it except by an approach which transcends divisions.

Upon closer examination, one realizes that specialists who have studied urban reality have almost always (except in the case of a logically extremist positivism) introduced a global representation. They can hardly go without a synthesis, settling for a quantity of knowledge, of dividing and splitting urban reality. As specialists, they then claim to be able to go legitimately from their analyses to a final synthesis whose principle is borrowed from their speciality. By means of a discipline or interdisciplinary endeavour, they see themselves as 'men of synthesis'. More often, they conceptualize the city (and society) as an *organism*. Historians have frequently linked these entities to an 'evolution' or to an 'historical development': cities. Sociologists have conceptualized them as a 'collective being', as a 'social organism'. Organicism, evolutionism, continuism, have therefore dominated representations of the city elaborated by specialists who believed themselves to be scholars and only scholars. Philosophers without knowing it, they leapt, without legitimizing their approach, from the partial to the global as well as from fact to right.

Is there a dilemma? An impasse? Yes and no. Yes, there is an obstacle, or if one wants another metaphor, a hole is dug. No. One should be able to cross the obstacle because there is a quite recent *practice* which already spills over the speculative problem, or the partial facts of the real problem, and which tends to become global by gathering all the facts of experience and knowledge, namely, *planning*.

What is involved here is not a philosophical view on *praxis*, but the fact that so-called planning thought becomes practice at a global level. For a few years now planning has gone beyond partial techniques and applications (regulation and administration of built space) to become a social practice concerning and of interest to the whole of society. *The critical examination of this social practice (the focus being on critique) cannot not allow theory to resolve a theoretical difficulty arising from a theory which has separated itself from practice.*

As *social practice*, planning (which it becomes without having reached a level of elaboration and action, which indeed it can only reach through confrontation with *political* strategies) has already crossed the initial stage, namely, the confrontation and communication of experts, and the gathering of fragmentary analyses, in brief, what is called the *interdisciplinary.* Either the planner is inspired by the practice of partial knowledge which he applies, or he puts into action hypotheses or projects at the level of a global reality. In the first case, the application of partial knowledge gives results which can determine the relative importance of this knowledge: these results, experimentally revealing absences and lacunae, enable us to specify on the ground what is lacking. In the second case, the failure (or success) allows the discernment of what is ideological in the presuppositions, and to identify what they define at the global level. Thus, what is effectively involved is a *critical examination* of the activity called 'planning', and not a belief in the word of planners or the unchallenged acceptance of their propositions and decisions. In particular, the displacements and distortions between practice and theory (ideology), between partial knowledge and results, come to the fore instead of being hidden. As does the questioning over *use* and *users*.

6

Philosophy of the City and Planning Ideology

In order to formulate the problematic of the city (to articulate problems by linking them), the following must be clearly distinguished:

1　The philosophers and philosophies of the city who define it speculatively as whole by defining the 'homo urbanicus' as man in general, the world or the cosmos, society, history.
2　Partial knowledge concerning the city (its elements, functions, structures).
3　The technical application of this knowledge (in a particular context defined by strategic and political decisions).
4　Planning as doctrine, that is, as ideology, interpreting partial knowledge, justifying its application and raising these (by extrapolation) to a poorly based or legitimated totality.

The aspects or elements which this analysis distinguishes do not appear separately in various works; they interest, reiforcing or neutralizing each other. Plato proposes a concept of the city and ideal town in *Critias*. In *The Republic* and *The Laws*, Platonic utopia is tempered by very concrete analyses. It is the same for Aristotle's political writings which study the constitution of Athens and other Greek cities.

Today, Lewis Mumford and G. Bardet among others still imagine a city made up not of townspeople, but of free citizens, free from the division of labour, social classes and class struggles, making up a community, freely associated for the management of this community. As philosophers, they make up a model of the ideal city. They conceive freedom in the twentieth century according to the freedom of the Greek city (this is an ideological travesty: only the city as such possessed freedom and not individuals and groups). Thus they think of the modern city according to a model of the antique city, which is at the same time identified with the ideal and rational city. The agora, place and symbol of a democracy limited to its citizens, and excluding women, slaves and foreigners, remains for a particular philosophy of the city the symbol of urban society in general. This is a typically ideological extrapolation. To this ideology these philosophers add partial knowledge, this purely ideological operation consisting in a passage (a leap), from the partial to the whole, from the elementary to the total, from the relative to the absolute. As for Le Corbusier, as philosopher of the city he describes the relationship between the urban dweller and dwelling with nature, air, sun, and trees, with cyclical time and the rhythms of the cosmos. To this metaphysical vision, he adds an unquestionable knowledge of the real problems of the modern city, a knowledge which gives rise to a planning practice and an ideology, a functionalism which reduces urban society to the achievement of a few predictable and prescribed functions laid out on the ground by the architecture. Such an architect sees himself as a 'man of synthesis', thinker and practitioner. He believes in and wants to create human relations by defining them, by creating their environment and décor. Within this well- worn perspective, the architect perceives and imagines himself as architect of the world, human image of God the Creator.

Philosophy of the city (or if one wants, urban ideology), was born as a superstructure of society into which structures entered a certain type of city. This philosophy, precious heritage of the past, extends itself into speculations which often are travesties of science just because they integrate a few bits of real knowledge.

Planning as ideology has acquired more and more precise definitions. To study the problems of circulation, of the conveying of orders and information in the great modern city, leads to real knowledge and to technical applications. To claim that the city is defined as a network of circulation and communication, as a centre of information and decision-making, is an absolute ideology; this ideology proceeding from a particularly arbitrary and dangerous reduction-extrapolation and using terrorist means, see itself as total truth and dogma. It leads to a planning of pipes, of roadworks and accounting, which one claims to impose in the name of science and scientific rigour. Or even worse!

This ideology has two interdependent aspects, mental and social. Mentally, it implies a theory of rationality and organization whose expression date from around 1910, a transformation in contemporary society (characterized by the beginning of a deep crisis and attempts to resolve it by organizational methods, firstly the scale of the firm, and then on a global scale). It is then that socially the notion of space comes to the fore, relegating into shadow time and becoming. Planning as ideology formulates all the problems of society into questions of space and transposes all that comes from history and consciousness into spatial terms. It is an ideology which immediately divides up. Since society does not function in a satisfactory manner, could there not be a pathology of space? Within this perspective, the virtually official recognition of the priority of space over time is not conceived of as indication of social pathology, as symptom among others of a reality which engenders social disease. On the contrary, what are represented are healthy and diseased spaces. The planner should be able to distinguish between sick spaces and spaces linked to mental and social health which are generators of this health. As physician of space, he should have the capacity to conceive of an harmonious social space, normal and normalizing. Its function would then be to grant to this space (perchance identical to geometrical space, that of abstract topologies) preexisting social realities.

The radical critique of philosophies of the city as well as of ideology is vital, as much on the theoretical as on the practical level. It can be made in the name of public health. However, it cannot be carried out without extensive research, rigorous analyses and the patient study of texts and contexts.

7

The Specificity of the City

A philosophy of the city answered questions raised by social practice in precapitalist societies (or if one prefers this terminology, in pre-industrial societies). Planning as technique and ideology responds to demands arising from this vast crisis of the city already referred to, which starts with the rise of competitive and industrial capitalism and which has never stopped getting deeper. This *world* crisis gives rise to new aspects of urban reality. It sheds light on what was little or poorly understood; it unveils what had been badly perceived. It forces the reconsideration of not only the history of the city and knowledge of the city, but also of the history of philosophy and that of art. Until recently, theoretical thinking conceived the city as an entity, as an organism and a whole among others, and this in the best of cases when it was not being reduced to a partial phenomenon, to a secondary, elementary or accidental aspect, of evolution and history. One would thus see in it a simple result, a local effect reflecting purely and simply general history. These representations, which are classified and are given well-known terms (organicism, evolutionism, continuism), have been previously criticized. They did not contain theoretical knowledge of the city and did not lead to this knowledge; moreover, they blocked at a quite basic level the enquiry; they were ideologies rather than concepts and theories.

Only now are we beginning to grasp the *specificity* of the city (of urban phenomena). The city always had relations with society as a whole, with its constituting elements (countryside and agriculture, offensive and defensive force, political power, States, etc.), and with its history. It changes when society as a whole changes. Yet, the city's transformations are not the passive outcomes of changes in the social whole. The city also depends as essentially on relations of immediacy, of direct relations between persons and groups which make up society (families, organized bodies, crafts and guilds, etc.). Furthermore, it is not reduced to the organization of these immediate and direct relations, nor its metamorphoses to their changes. It is situated at an interface, half-way between what is called the *near order* (relations of individuals in groups of variable size, more or less organized and structured and the relations of these groups among themselves), and the *far order*, that of society, regulated by large and powerful institutions (Church and State), by a legal code formalized or not, by a 'culture' and significant ensembles endowed with powers, by which the *far order* projects itself at this 'higher' level and imposes itself. Abstract, formal, supra-sensible and transcending in appearances, it is not conceptualized beyond ideologies (religious and political). It includes moral and legal principles. This *far order* projects itself into the practico-material reality and becomes visible by writing itself within this reality. It persuades through and by the *near order*, which confirms its compelling power. It becomes apparent by and in immediacy. The city is a *mediation* among mediations. Containing the *near order*, it supports it; it maintains relations of production and property; it is the place of their reproduction. Contained in the *far order*, it supports it; it incarnates it; it projects it over a terrain (the site) and on a plan, that of immediate life; it inscribes it, prescribes it, *writes* it. A text in a context so vast and ungraspable as such except by reflection.

And thus the city is an *oeuvre*, closer to a work of art than to a simple material product. If there is production of the city, and social relations in the city, it is a production and reproduction of human beings by human beings, rather than a production of objects. The city has a history; it is the work of a history, that is, of clearly defined people and groups who accomplish this *oeuvre*, in historical conditions. Conditions which simultaneously enable and limit possibilities, are never sufficient to explain what was born of them, in them, by them. It was in this way that the city created by the Western Middle Ages was animated and dominated by merchants and bankers, this city was their *oeuvre*. Can the historian consider it as a simple object of commerce, a simple opportunity for lucre? Absolutely not, precisely not. These merchants and bankers acted to promote exchange and generalize it, to extend the domain of exchange value; and yet for them the city was much more use value than exchange value. These merchants of Italian, Flemish, English and French cities loved their cities like a work of art and adorned them with every kind of works of art. So that, paradoxically, the city of merchants and bankers remains for us the type and model of an urban reality whereby *use* (pleasure, beauty, ornamentation of meeting places) still wins over lucre and profit, exchange value, the requirements and constraints of markets. At the same time, wealth arising from commerce in goods and money, the power of gold, the cynicism of this power, are also inscribed in this city and in it prescribe an order. So that, as such it still remains for some model and prototype.

By taking 'production' in its widest sense (the production of *oeuvres* and of social relations), there has been in history the production of cities as there has been production of knowledge, culture, works of art and civilization, and there also has been, of course, production of material goods and practico-material objects. These modalities of production cannot be disjointed unless one has the right to confuse them by reducing differences. The city was and remains *object*, but not in the way of particular, pliable and instrumental object: such as a pencil or a sheet of paper. Its objectivity, or 'objectality', might rather be closer to that of the *language* which individuals and groups receive before modifying it, or of *language* (a particular language, the work of a particular society, spoken by particular groups). One could also compare this 'objectality' to that of a cultural reality, such as the *written book*, instead of the old abstract object of the philosophers or the immediate and everyday object. Moreover, one must take precautions. If I compare the city to a book, to a writing (a semiological system), I do not have the right to forget the aspect of mediation. I can separate it neither from what it contains nor from what contains it, by isolating it as a complete system. Moreover, at best, the city constitutes a sub-system, a sub-whole. On this book, with this writing, are projected mental and social forms and structures. Now, analysis can achieve this context from the text, but it is not given. Intellectual operations and reflective approaches are necessary to achieve it (deduction, induction, translation and transduction). The whole is not immediately present in this written text, the city. There are other levels of reality which do not become *transparent* by definition. The city *writes* and *assigns*, that is, it signifies, orders, stipulates. What? That is to be discovered by reflection. This text has passed through ideologies, as it also 'reflects' them. The *far order* projects itself in/on the *near order*. However, the *near order* does not *reflect* transparently the *far order*. The later subordinates the immediate through mediations.

It does not yield itself up. Moreover, it hides itself without discovering itself. This is how it acts without one having the right to speak of a transcendence of order, the Global or the Total.

If one considers the city as *oeuvre* of certain historical and social 'agents', the action and the result, the group (or groups) and their 'product' can be clearly identified without separating them. There is no *oeuvre* without a regulated succession of acts and actions, of decisions and conducts, messages and codes. Nor can an *oeuvre* exist without things, without something to shape, without practico-material reality, without a site, without a 'nature', a countryside, an environment. Social relations are achieved from the sensible. They cannot be reduced to this sensible world, and yet they do not float in air, they do not disappear into transcendence. If social reality suggests forms and relations, if it cannot be conceived in a way homologous to the isolated, sensible or technical object, it does not survive without ties, without attachment to objects and things. We must insist on this methodologically and theoretically important point. There is cause and reason to distinguish between material and social morphologies. We should perhaps here introduce a distinction between the *city*, a present and immediate reality, a practico-material and architectural fact, and the *urban*, a social reality made up of relations which are to be conceived of, constructed or reconstructed by thought. This distinction none the less reveals itself to be dangerous and the designation proposed cannot be handled without risk. Thus designated, the *urban* seems not to need land and material morphology and is outlined according to a speculative mode of existence of entities, spirits and souls, freed from attachments and inscriptions; a kind of imaginary transcendence. If one adopts this terminology, the relations between the *city* and the *urban* will have to be determined with the greatest care, by avoiding separation as well as confusion, and metaphysics as well as reduction to the immediate and tangible. Urban life, urban society, in a word, the *urban*, cannot go without a practico-material base, a morphology. They have it and do not have it. If they do not have it, if the *urban* and urban society are conceived without this basis, it is that they are perceived as possibilities, it is that the virtualities of actual society are seeking, so to speak, their incorporation and incarnation through knowledge and planning thought: through our 'reflections'. If they do not find them, these possibilities go into decline and are bound to disappear. The *urban* is not a soul, a spirit, a philosophical entity.

8

Continuities and Discontinuities

Organicism and its implications, namely the simplifying evolutionism of many historians and the naïve continuism of many sociologists, has disguised the specific features of urban reality. The acts or events 'producers' of this reality as formation and social *oeuvre* escaped knowledge. In this sense, to produce is to create: to bring into being 'something' which did not exist before the productive activity. For a long time knowledge has hesitated in the face of creation. Either creation appears to be irrational, spontaneity swelling up from the unknown and the unknowable. Or else it is denied and what comes to be is reduced to what was already existing. Science wants itself to be a science of determinisms, a knowledge of constraints. It abandons to philosophers the exploration of births, of decline, transitions, disappearances. In this, those who challenge philosophy abandon the idea of creation. The study of urban phenomena is linked to overcoming these obstacles and dilemmas, to the solution of these internal conflicts by reason which knows.

As much in the past as now, history and sociology conceived as an organicist model have not known better how to apprehend *differences*. Abusive reductions take place to the detriment of these differences and to the detriment of creation. It is quite easy to grasp the link between these reductive operations. The *specific* flees before simplifying schematas. In the rather troubled light shed by many confused crises (such as the city and the urban), among the crevices of a 'reality' which too often one believes to be as full as an egg or as a entirely written page, analysis can now perceive why and how global processes (economic, social, political, cultural) have formed urban space and shaped the city, without creative action arising instantaneously and deductively from these processes. Indeed, if they have influenced urban rhythms and spaces, it is by enabling groups to insert themselves, to take charge of them, to *appropriate* them; and this by inventing, by sculpting space (to use a metaphor), by giving themselves rhythms. Such groups have also been innovative in how to live, to have a family, to raise and educate children, to leave a greater or lesser place to women, to use and transmit wealth. These transformations of everyday life modified urban reality, not without having from it their motivations. The city was at one and the same time the place and the milieu, the theatre and the stake of these complex interactions.

The introduction of temporal and spatial discontinuities in the theory of the city (and the urban), in history and sociology, does not give one the right to abuse it. Separations must not be substituted for organicism and continuism by consecrating them by theory. If the city appears as a *specific level* of social reality, general processes (of which the most important and accessible were the generalization of commercial exchanges, industrialization in such a global context, the formation of competitive capitalism), did not take place above this specific mediation. Moreover, the level of immediate relations, personal and interpersonal (the family, the neighbourhood, crafts and guilds, the division of labour between crafts, etc.) is only separated from urban reality through an abstraction: the correct approach of knowledge cannot change this abstraction into separation. Reflection emphasizes articulations so that delineations do not disarticulate the real but follow articulations. The methodological rule is to avoid confusion in an illusory continuity as well as separations or absolute discontinuities. Consequently, the study of articulations between the levels of reality enables us to demonstrate the distortions and discrepancies between levels rather than to blurr them.

The city is transformed not only because of relatively continuous 'global processes' (such as the growth of material production over a long period of time with its consequences for exchanges, or the development of rationality) but also in relation to profound transformations in the mode of production, in the relations between 'town and country', in the relations of class and property. The correct approach consists in going from the most general knowledge to that which concerns historical processes and discontinuities, their projection or refraction onto the city and conversely, particular and specific knowledge of urban reality to its global context.

The city and the urban cannot be understood without *institutions* springing from relations of class and property. The city itself, perpetual *oeuvre* and act, gives rise to specific institutions: that is, municipal institutions. The most general institutions, those which belong to the State, to the dominant religion and ideology have their seat in the political, military and religious city. They coexist with properly urban, administrative, and cultural institutions. Hence a number of remarkable continuities through changes in society.

One knows that there was and there still is the oriental city, expression and projection on the ground, effect and cause, of the Asiatic mode of production; in this mode of production State power, resting on the city, organizes economically a more or less extensive agrarian zone, regulates and controls water, irrigation and drainage, the use of land, in brief, agricultural production. There was in the era of slavery, a city which organized its agricultural zone through violence and by juridical rationality, but which undermined its own base by replacing free peasants (landowners) with latifundial type properties. In the West there was also the medieval city, rooted in a feudal mode of production where agriculture was predominant, but which was also place of commerce, theatre of class struggle between an emerging bourgeoisie and territorial feudalism, the point of impact and lever of royal State action. Finally, in the West, and in North America, there has been the capitalist, commercial and industrial city, more or less delimited by the political State whose formation accompanied the rise of capitalism and whose bourgeoisie knew how to appropriate the management of the whole of society.

Discontinuities are not only situated between urban formations, but also between the most general of social relations, and the immediate relations of individuals and groups (between codes and sub-codes). The medieval city has however lasted for almost eight centuries. The rupture of the big city tends to disintegrate urban cores of medieval origins, although these persist in many small or medium-sized towns. Many urban centres, which today perpetuate or protect the image of *centrality* (which might have disappeared without them) are of very ancient origins. This can explain without inasmuch legitimizing the illusion of continuism and evolutionary ideology. This illusion and this ideology have disguised the dialectical movement in the metamorphoses of cities and the urban, and particularly in the relations of 'continuity–discontinuity'. In the course of development some *forms* change themselves into *functions* and enter structures *which take them back and transform them. Thus the extension of commercial exchanges from the European Middle Ages* onwards, contributes to this extraordinary formation, the merchant city (integrating completely the merchants established around the market square and market hall). Since industrialization these local and localized markets have only one function in urban life, in the relations of the city with the surrounding countryside. *A form which has become function enters into new structures.* And yet, planners have recently come to believe that they have invented the commercial centre. Their thinking progressed from that of a denuded space, reduced to a residential function, to that of a commercial centrality which brought a difference, an enrichment. But planners were only rediscovering the medieval city laid bare of its historical relation to the countryside, of the struggle between the bourgeoisie and feudalism, of the political relation with a royal and despotic State, and as a consequence reduced to the unifunctionality of local exchanges.

Forms, structures, urban functions (in the city, in the relations of the city to the territory influenced or managed by it, in the relations with society and State) acted upon each other modifying themselves, a movement which thought can now reconstruct and master. Each urban formation knew an ascent, an apogee, a decline. Its fragments and debris were later used for/in other formations. Considered in its historical movement, at its specific level (above and beyond global transformations, but above immediate and locally rooted relations, often linked to the consecration of the ground, and therefore durable and quasi-permanent in appearance), the city has gone through critical periods. Destructurations and restructurations are followed in time and space, always translated on the ground, inscribed in the practico-material, written in the urban text, but coming from elsewhere: from history and becoming. Not from the supersensible, but from another level. Local acts and agents left their mark on cities, but also impersonal relations of production and property, and consequently, of classes and class struggles, that is, ideologies (religious and philosophical, that is, ethical, a esthetical, legal, etc.). The projection of the global on the ground and on the specific plane of the city were accomplished only through mediations. In itself mediation, the city was the place, the product of mediations, the terrain of their activities, the object and objective of their propositions. Global processes, general relations inscribed themselves in the urban text only as transcribed by ideologies, interpreted by tendencies and political strategies. It is this difficulty upon which one must now insist, that of conceiving the city as a semantic system, semiotic or semiological system arising from linguistics, urban language or urban reality considered as grouping of signs. In the course of its projection on a specific level, the general code of society is modified: the specific code of the urban is an incomprehensible modulation, a version, a translation without the original or origins. Yes, the city can be read because it writes, because it was writing. However, it is not enough to examine this without recourse to context. To write on this writing or language, to elaborate the *metalanguage of the city* is not to know the city and the urban. The context, what is *below* the text to decipher (daily life, immediate relations, the *unconscious* of the urban, what is little said and of which even less is written), hides itself in the inhabited spaces – sexual and family life – and rarely confronts itself, and what is *above* this urban text (institutions, ideologies), cannot be neglected in the deciphering. A book is not enough. That one reads and re-reads it, well enough. That one goes as far as to undertake a critical reading of it, even better. It asks from knowledge questions such as 'who and what? how? why? for whom?' These questions announce and demand the restitution of the context. The city cannot therefore be conceived as *a* signifying system, determined and closed as a system. The taking into consideration the *levels* of reality forbids, here as elsewhere, this sytematization. None the less, the city has this singular capacity of appropriating all significations for saying them, for writing them (to stipulate and to 'signify' them), including those from the countryside, immediate life, religion and political ideology. In the cities, monuments and festivities had this *meaning*.

During each critical period, when the spontaneous growth of the city stagnates and when urban development oriented and characterized by hitherto dominant social relations ends, then appears a planning thought. This is more a symptom of change than of a continuously mounting rationality or of an internal harmony (although illusions on these points regularly reproduce themselves), as this thinking merges the philosophy of the city in search of a with the divisive schemes for urban space. To confuse this anxiety with rationality and organization it is the *ideology* previously denounced. Concepts and theories make a difficult path through this ideology.

At this point the city should be defined. If it is true that the concept emerges little by little from these ideologies which convey it, it must be conceived during this progress. We therefore here propose a first definition of the city as a *projection of society on the ground*, that is, not only on the actual site, but at a specific level, perceived and conceived by thought, which determines the city and the urban. Long-term controversies over this definition have shown its lacunae. Firstly, it requires more accuracy. What is inscribed and projected is not only a *far order*, a social whole, a mode of production, a general code, it is also a time, or rather, times, rhythms. The city is heard as much as music as it is read as a discursive writing. Secondly, the definition calls for supplements. It brings to light certain historical and generic or genetic differences, but leaves aside other real differences: between the types of cities resulting from history, between the effects of the division of labour in the cities, between the persistent 'city–territory' relations. Hence another definition which perhaps does not destroy the first: the city *as the ensemble of differences* between cities. In turn, this definition reveals itself to be insufficient, as it places emphasis on particularities rather than on generalities, neglecting the singularities of urban life, the ways of living of the city, more properly understood as *to inhabit*. Hence another definition, of plurality, coexistence and simultaneity in the urban of *patterns*, ways of living urban life (the small house, the large social housing estates, co-ownership, location, daily life and its changes for intellectuals, craftsmen, shopkeepers, workers, etc.).

These definitions (relative to the levels of social reality), are not in themselves exhaustive and do not exclude other definitions. If a theoretician sees in the city the place of confrontations and of (conflictual) relations between *desire* and *need*, between satisfactions and dissatisfactions, if he goes as far as to describe the city as 'site of desire', these determinations will be examined and taken into consideration. It is not certain that they have a meaning limited to the fragmentary science of psychology. Moreover, there would be the need to emphasize the historical role of the city: the quickening of processes (exchange and the market, the accumulation of knowledge and capitals, the concentration of these capitals) and site of revolutions.

Today, by becoming a centre of decision-making, or rather, by grouping centres of decision-making, the modern city intensifies by organizing the *exploitation* of the whole society (not only the working classes, but also other non-dominant social classes). This is not the passive place of production or the concentration of capitals, but that of the *urban* intervening as such in production (in the *means* of production).

9

Levels of Reality and Analysis

The preceding considerations are sufficient to show that the analysis of urban phenomena (the physical and social morphology of the city, or if one prefers, the *city*, the *urban* and their connexion) requires the use of all the methodological tools: form, function, structure, levels, dimensions, text, context, field and whole, writing and reading, system, signified and signifier, language and metalanguage, institutions, etc. One also knows that none of these terms can attain a rigorous purity, be defined without ambiguity, or escape multiple meaning. Thus the word *form* takes on various meanings for the logician, for the literary critic, for the aesthetician, and for the linguist.

The theoretician of the city and the urban will say that these terms are defined as *form of simultaneity*, as field of encounters and exchanges. This acceptance of the word *form* must be clarified. Let us again consider the term *function*. The analysis distinguishes the functions internal to the city, the functions of the city in relation to territory (countryside, agriculture, villages and hamlets, smaller towns subordinated within a network), and lastly, the functions of the city – each city – in the social whole (the technical and social division of labour between cities, various networks of relations, administrative and political hierarchies). It is the same for *structures*. There is the structure of the city (of each city, morphologically, socially, topologically and topically), then the urban structure of society, and finally the social structure of town–country relations. Hence a muddle of analytical and partial determinations and the difficulties of a global conception. Here as elsewhere *three* terms most often meet, whose conflictual and (dialectical) relations are hidden under *term by term oppositions*. There is the countryside, and the city and society with the State which manages and dominates it (in its relations with the class structure of that society). There is also as we have attempted to show, general (and global) processes, the city as specificity and intermediary level, then relations of immediacy (linked to a way of life, to inhabiting, and to regulating daily life). This requires therefore more precise definitions of each level, which we will not be able to separate or confuse, but of which we shall have to show the articulations and disarticulations, the projections of one upon the other, and the different connections.

The highest level is found *at the same time* above and in the city. This does not simplify the analysis. The social structure exists in the city, makes itself apparent, signifies an order. Inversely, the city is a part of the social whole; it reveals, because contains and incorporates them within sentient matter, institutions and ideologies. Royal, imperial and presidential buildings are a part of the city: the political part (the capital). These buildings do not coincide with institutions, with dominant social relations. And yet, these relations act upon them, by representing social efficacy and 'presence'. At its specific level, the city also contains the projection of these relations. To elucidate this analysis by a particular case, social order in Paris is represented at the highest level in/by the Ministry of the Interior, and at the specific level by the prefecture of police and also by neighbourhood police stations, without forgetting various police agencies acting either at a global level, or in the subterranean shadow. Religious ideology is signified at the highest level by the cathedral, by seats of large religious organizations of the Church, and also by neighbourhood churches and presbyteries, various local investments of institutionalized religious practice.

At this level, the city manifests itself as a group of groups, with its double morphology (practico-sensible or material, on the one hand, social on the other). It has a code of functioning focused around particular institutions, such as the municipality with its services and its problems, with its channels of information, its networks, its powers of decision-making. The social structure is projected on this plane, but this does not exclude phenomena unique to the city, to a particular city, and the most diverse manifestations of urban life. Paradoxically, taken at this level, the city is made up of uninhabited and even uninhabitable spaces: public buildings, monuments, squares, streets, large or small voids. It is so true that 'habitat' does not make up the city and that it cannot be defined by this isolated function.

At the ecological level, *habitation* becomes essential. The city envelops it; it is form, enveloping this space of 'private' life, arrival and departure of networks of information and the communication of orders (imposing the *far order* to the *near order*).

Two approaches are possible. The first goes from the most general to the most specific (from institutions to daily life) and then uncovers the city as specific and (relatively) privileged mediation. The second starts from this plan and constructs the general by identifying the elements and significations of what is observable in the urban. It proceeds in this manner to reach, from the observable, 'private', the concealed daily life: its rhythms, its occupations, its spatio-temporal organization, its clandestine 'culture', its underground life.

Isotopies are defined at each level: political, religious, comercial, etc. space. In relation to these isotopies, other levels are uncovered as *heterotopies*. Meanwhile, at each level spatial oppositions are uncovered which enter in this relationship of isotopy–heterotopy. For example, the opposition between social and owner-occupied housing. Spaces at the specific level can also be classified according to the criterion of isotopy–heterotopy, the city as a whole being the most expanded isotopy, embracing others, or rather, superimposing itself over others (over the spatial sub-wholes which are at one and the same time subordinated and constitutive). Such a classification by opposition should not exclude the analysis of levels, nor that of the movement of the whole with its conflictual aspects (class relations among others). At the ecological level, that of inhabiting, are constituted significant ensembles, partial systems of signs, of which the 'world of the detached house' offers a particularly interesting case. The distinction between levels (each level implying in turn secondary levels) has the greatest use in the analysis of essential relations, for example in understanding how the 'values of detached housing' in France become the reference point of social consciousness and the 'values' of other types of housing. Only the analysis of relations of inclusion–exclusion, of belonging or non-belonging to a particular space of the city enables us to approach these phenomena of great importance for a theory of the city.

On its specific plane the city can appropriate existing political, religious and philosophical meanings. It seizes them to say them, to *expose* them by means – or through the voice – of buildings, monuments, and also by streets and squares, by voids, by the spontaneous theatricalization of encounters which take place in it, not forgetting festivities and ceremonies (with their appropriate and designated places). Beside the writing, there is also the even more important utterance of the urban, these utterances speaking of life and death, joy or sorrow. The city has this capacity which makes of it a significant whole. None the less, to stress a previous remark, the city does not accomplish this task gracefully or freely. One does not ask it. Aestheticism, phenomenon of decline, comes later. Such as planning! In the form of meaning, in the form of simultaneity and encounters, in the form, finally of an 'urban' language and writing, the city dispatches *orders*. The *far order* is projected into the *near order*. This *far order* is never or almost never unitary. There is religious order, political order, moral order, each referring to an ideology with its practical implications. Among these orders the city realizes on its plane a unity, or rather, a syncretism. It dissimulates and veils their rivalries and conflicts by making them imperative. It translates them as *instructions* for action, as time management. It stipulates (signifies) with the management of time a meticulous hierarchy of place, moments, occupations, people. Moreover, it refracts these imperatives in a style, inasmuch as there is a genuine urban life. This style characterizes itself as *architectural* and is associated to art and the study of art objects.

Therefore the semiology of the city is of greatest theoretical and practical interest. The city receives and emits messages. These messages are or are not understood (that is, are or are not coded or decoded). Therefore, it can be apprehended from concepts derived from linguistics: signifier and signified, signification and meaning. Nevertheless, it is not without the greatest reservation or without precautions that one can consider the city as a *system*, as a unique system of significations and meanings and therefore of values. Here as elsewhere, there are several systems (or if one prefers, several sub-systems). Moreover, semiology does not exhaust the practical and ideological reality of the city. The theory of the city as system of significations tends towards an ideology; it separates the *urban* from its morphological basis and from social practice, by reducing it to a 'signifier–signified' relation and by extrapolating from actually perceived significations. This is not without a great naïvety. If it is true that a Bororo village signifies, and that the Greek city is full of meaning, are we to build vast Bororo villages full of signs of Modernity? Or restore the agora with its meaning at the centre of the new town?

The fetishization of the formal 'signifier–signified' relationship entails more serious inconveniences. It passively accepts the ideology of organised consumption. Or rather, it contributes to it. In the ideology of consumption and in 'real' consumption (in quotations), the consumption of *signs* plays an increasing role. It does not repress the consumption of 'pure' spectacles, without activity and participation, without *œuvre* or product. It adds to it and superimposes itself upon it as a determination. It is thus that advertising of consumer goods becomes the principal means of consumption; it tends to incorporate art, literature, poetry and to supplant them by using them as rhetoric. It thus becomes itself the ideology of society; each 'object', each 'good' splits itself into a reality and an image, this being an essential part of consumption. One consumes signs as well as objects: signs of happiness, of satisfaction, of power, of wealth, of science, of technology, etc. The production of these signs is integrated to global production and plays a major integrative role in relation to other productive and organizing social activities. The sign is bought and sold; language becomes exchange value. Under the appearance of signs and significations in general, it is the significations of this society which are handed over to consumption. Consequently, he who conceives the city and urban reality as system of signs implicitly hands them over to consumption as integrally consumable: as exchange value in its pure state. Changing sites into signs and values, the practico- material into formal significations, this theory also changes into pure consumer of signs he who receives them. Would not the Paris *bis* or *ter* conceived by developers be the centres of consumption promoted to a superior level by the intensity of the consumption of signs? Urban semiology is in danger of placing itself at their service if it loses its naïvety.

In truth, semiological analysis must distinguish between multiple levels and dimensions. There is the *utterance* of the city: what happens and takes place in the street, in the squares, in the voids, what is said there. There is the *language* of the city: particularities specific to each city which are expressed in discourses, gestures, clothing, in the words and use of words by the inhabitants. There is *urban language*, which one can consider as language of connotations, a secondary system and derived within the denotative system (to use here Hjemslev and Greimas's terminology). Finally, there is the *writing* of the city: what is inscribed and prescribed on its walls, in the layout of places and their linkages, in brief, the *use of time* in the city by its inhabitants.

Semiological analysis must also distinguish between levels, that of *semantemes* or signifying elements (straight or cured lines, writing, elementary forms of entry, doors and windows, corners, angles, etc.), *morphemes* or signifying objects (buildings, streets, etc.) and lastly, significant ensembles or super-objects, of which the city itself.

One must study how the global is signified (the semiology of *power*), how the city is signified (that is the properly *urban* semiology) and how are signified ways of living and inhabiting (that is the *semiology of daily life*, of to inhabit and habitat). One cannot confuse the city as it apprehends and exposes significations coming from nature, the country and the landscape (the tree for example) and the city as place of consumption of signs. That would be to confuse festivities with ordinary consumption.

Let us not forget *dimensions*. The city has a *symbolic* dimension; monuments but also voids, squares and avenues, symbolizing the cosmos, the world, society, or simply the State. It has a *paradigmatical* dimension; it implies and shows oppositions, the inside and the outside, the centre and the periphery, the integrated and non-integrated to urban society. Finally, it also possesses the *syntagmatic* dimension: the connection of elements, the articulation of isotopies and heterotopies.

At its specific level, the city presents itself as a privileged sub-system because it is able to reflect and expose the other sub-systems and to present itself as a 'world', a unique whole, within the illusion of the immediate and the lived. In this capacity resides precisely the charm, the tonicity, and the tonality specific to urban life. But analysis dissipates this impression and unveils a number of systems hidden in the illusion of oneness. The analyst has no right to share this illusion and to consolidate it by maintaining himself at an *urban* level. He must uncover instead the features of a greater knowledge.

We have not finished making an inventory of sub-systems of significations, and therefore of what semiological analysis can bring to an understanding of the city and the urban. If we consider the sector of owner-occupation and that of new social housing estates, we already know that each of them constitutes a (partial) system of significations, and that another system which overdetermines each of them is established from their opposition. This is how the owner-occupiers of small houses perceive and conceive themselves in the make-believe of habitat, and in turn, the estates establish the logic of habitat and perceive themselves according to this coercive rationality. At the same time and at the same stroke, the sector of owner-occupation becomes the reference by which habitat and daily life are appreciated; that practice is cloaked in make-believe and signs.

Among systems of significations, those of *architects* deserve the greatest critical attention. It often happens that talented men believe themselves to be at the centre of knowledge and experience whereas they remain at the centre of systems of writing, projections on paper, visualizations. Architects tending on their part towards a system of significations which they often call 'planning', it is not impossible for analysts of urban reality, grouping together their piecemeal facts, to constitute a somewhat different system of significations that they can also baptize planning while they leave its programming to machines.

Critical analysis dissipates the privilege of the lived in urban society. It is only a 'plane', or a level. Yet analysis does not make this plane disappear. It exists – as a book. Who reads this open book? Who crosses over its writing? It is not a well-defined subject and yet a succession of acts and encounters constitute on this plane itself urban life, the *urban*. This urban life tends to turn against themselves the messages, orders and constraints coming from above. It attempts to *appropriate* time and space by foiling dominations, by diverting them from their goal, by deceit. It also intervenes more or less at the level of the city and the way of inhabiting. In this way the *urban* is more or less the *oeuvre* of its citizens instead of imposing itself upon them as a system, as an already closed book.

10

Town and Country

A theme which has been used and over-used, hyperinflated and extra-polated, namely, 'nature and culture', originates from the relation be-tween town and country and deflects it. There are three terms in this relation. In the same way, there are three terminologies in existing reality (rurality, urban fabric, centrality) whose dialectical relations are hidden beneath term to term oppositions, but also come to reveal themselves in them. Nature as such escapes the hold of rationally pursued action, as well as from domination and appropriation. More precisely, it remains outside of these influences: it 'is' what flees: it is reached by the imaginary; one pursues it and it flees into the cosmos, or in the underground depths of the world. The countryside is the place of production and *oeuvres*. Agricultural production gives birth to products: the landscape is an *oeuvre*. This *oeuvre* emerges from the earth slowly moulded, linked originally to the groups which occupy it by a reciprocal consecration, later to be desecrated by the city and urban life (which capture this consecration, condense it, then dissolve it over through the ages by absorbing it into rationality). Where does this ancient consecration of the ground to the tribes, peoples and nations come from? From the obscure and menacing presence/absence of nature? From the occupation of the ground which excludes strangers from this possessed ground? From the social pyramid, which has its basis on this ground and which exacts many sacrifices for the maintenance of a threatened edifice? One does not prevent the other. What is important is the complex movement by which the political city uses this sacred–damned character of the ground, so that the economic (commercial) city can desecrate it.

Urban life includes original mediations between town, country and nature. As the village, whose relationship with the city, in history and in actuality, is far from being well known. As are parks, gardens, channelled waters. These mediations cannot be understood as such by city dwellers without symbolisms and *representations* (ideological and imaginary) of nature and the countryside.

The town and country relation has changed deeply during the course of history, according to different periods and to modes of production. It has been sometimes profoundly conflictual, and at other times appeased and close to an association. Moreover, during the same period, very different kinds of relations are manifested. Thus in Western feudalism, the territorial lord threatens the re-emerging city, where the merchants find their meeting place, their homebase, the place of their strategy. The city responds to this action of landed power, and a class struggle ensues, sometimes quiescent, sometimes violent. The city liberates itself, not by integrating itself by becoming an aristocracy of commoners, but by integrating itself with the monarchic State (for which it provided an essential condition). On the other hand, during the same period, in so far as one can speak of an Islamic feudalism, the 'lord' rules over the city of craftsmen and shopkeepers and from it, over a surrounding countryside, often reduced to gardens and to sparse and insignificant cultivations. In such a relationship, there is neither the kernel nor the possibility of a class struggle. From the outset this takes away any historical dynamism and future from this social structure, although not without conferring upon it other charms, those of an exquisite urbanism. The class struggle, creative, productive of *oeuvres* and new relations, takes place with a certain barbarism which characterizes the West (including the most 'beautiful' of its cities).

Today, the town and country relation is changing, an important aspect of a general transformation. In industrial countries, the old exploitation by the city, centre of capital accumulation, of the surrounding countryside, gives way to more subtle forms of domination and exploitation, the city becoming centre of decision-making and apparently also of association. However that may be, the expanding city attacks the countryside, corrodes and dissolves it. This is not without the paradoxical effects already mentioned. Urban life penetrates peasant life, dispossessing it of its traditional features: crafts, small centres which decline to the benefit of urban centres (commercial, industrial, distribution networks, centres of decision-making, etc.). Villages become ruralized by losing their peasant specificity.

They align themselves with the city but by resisting and sometimes by fiercely keeping themselves to themselves.

Will the urban fabric, with its greater or lesser meshes, catch in its nets all the territory of industrialized countries? Is this how the old opposition between town and country is overcome? One can assume it, but not without some critical reservations. If a generalized confusion is thus perceived, the countryside losing itself into the heart of the city, and the city absorbing the countryside and losing itself in it, this confusion can be theoretically challenged. Theory can refute all strategies resting on this conception of the urban fabric. Geographers have coined to name this confusion an ugly but meaningful neologism: the rurban. Within this hypothesis, the expansion of the city and urbanization would cause the urban (the urban life) to disappear. This seems inadmissible. In other words, the overcoming of opposition cannot be conceived as a reciprocal neutralization. There is no theoretical reason to accept the disappearance of centrality in the course of the fusion of urban society with the countryside. The 'urbanity-rurality' opposition is accentuated rather than dissipated, while the town and country opposition is lessened. There is a shifting of opposition and conflict. What is more, we all know that worldwide, the town and country conflict is far from being resolved. If it is true that the town and country separation and contradiction (which envelops without reducing to itself the opposition of the two terms) is part of the social division of labour, it must be acknowledged that this division is neither overcome nor mastered. Far from it. No more than the separation of nature and society, and that of the material and the intellectual (spiritual). Overcoming this today cannot not take place from the opposition between urban fabric and centrality. It presupposes the invention of new urban forms.

As far as industrial countries are concerned, one can conceive polycentric cities, differentiated and renovated centralities, even mobile centralities (cultural ones for example). The critique of planning as ideology can be about such and such a conception of centrality (for example, the distinction between the *urban* and the centres of information and decision-making). Neither traditional city (separated from the countryside to better dominate it), nor the Megalopolis without form or fabric, without woof or warp, would be the guiding idea. The disappearance of centrality is neither called for theoretically nor practically. The only question that can be asked is this one: 'What social and political forms, what theory will one entrust with the realization on the ground of a renovated centrality and fabric, freed from their degradations?'

11

Around the Critical Point

Let us trace hypothetically from left to right an axis going from zero point in urbanization (the non-existence of the city, the complete predominance of agrarian life, agricultural production and the countryside) to full urbanization (the absorption of the countryside by the city and the total predominance of industrial production, including agriculture). This abstract picture momentarily places the discontinuities in parentheses. To a certain extent it will enable us to locate the critical points, that is, the breaks and discontinuities themselves. Quite quickly on the axis, quite near to the beginning, let us mark the political city (in effect achieved and maintained in the Asiatic mode of production) which organizes an agrarian environment by dominating it. A little further, let us mark the appearance of the commercial city, which begins by relegating commerce to its periphery (a heterotopy of outlying areas, fairs and markets, places assigned to foreigners, to strangers specialized in exchanges) and which later integrates the market by integrating itself to a social structure based on exchanges, expanded communications, money and movable wealth. There then comes a decisive critical point, where the importance of agriculture retreats before the importance of craft and industrial production, of the market, exchange value and a rising capitalism. This critical point is located in Western Europe around the sixteenth century. Soon it is the arrival of the industrial city, with its implications (emigration of dispossed and disaggregated peasant populations towards the city – a period of great urban concentration). Urban society is heralded long after society as a whole has tilted towards the urban. Then there is the period when the expanding city proliferates, produces far-flung peripheries (suburbs), and invades the countryside. Paradoxically, in this period when the city expands inordinately, the form (the practico-material morphology, the form of urban life) of the traditional city explodes. This double process (industrialization–urbanization) produces the double movement: explosion–implosion, condensation–dispersion (the explosion already mentioned). It is therefore around this critical point that can be found the present problematic of the city and urban reality.

Political Town Commercial Town   Industrial Town Critical Point

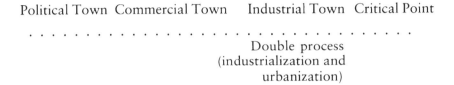

Double process
(industrialization and
urbanization)

The phenomena which unfold around the situation of crisis are not less complex than the physical phenomena which accompany the breaking of the sound barrier (to use a simple metaphor). It is to this end – the analysis in the proximity of the critical point – that we have previously attempted to assemble the essential conceptual tools. Knowledge which would dissociate itself from this situation would fall back into blind speculation or myopic specialization.

Too badly placed, the critical points, breaks and lacunae can have as serious consequences as organicist, evolutionist or continuist negligence. Today, sociological thinking and political strategy, and so-called planning thought, tend to jump from the level of habitat and to inhabit (ecological level, housing, buildings, neighbourhood and thus the domain of the architect), to the general level (scale of land use planning, planned industrial production, global urbanization), passing over the city and the urban. Mediation is placed into parentheses and the specific level is omitted. Why? For significant reasons related firstly to the disregard of the critical point.

The rational planning of production, land use planning, global industrialization and urbanization are essential aspects of the "socialization of society". Let us pause for a moment on these words. A Marxist tradition with reformist inflections uses them to designate the complexification of society and social relations, the rupture of compartimentalization, the growing multiplicity of connexions, communications and information, the fact that an accentuated technical and social division of labour implies a stronger unity in branches of industry, market functions and production itself. This approach insists on *exchanges* and places of exchange: it emphasizes the quantity of economic exchanges and leaves aside quality, the essential difference between use value and exchange value. In this perspective, the exchanges of merchandise and of consumer goods level and align direct exchanges to themselves, that is, communications which do not go through existing networks, and through institutions (namely at the 'inferior' level, the immediate relations, and at the 'superior' level, the political relations resulting from knowledge). The answer given to reformist continuism is the thesis of discontinuism and radical revolutionary voluntarism: a rupture, a break, are essential for the social character of productive labour to abolish relations of production linked to private ownership of these means of production. However, the thesis of the 'socialization of society', an evolutionist, continuist and reformist interpretation, takes on another meaning if one observes that these words refer to, badly and incompletely, the *urbanization of society*. The multiplication and complexification of exchanges in the widest sense of the term cannot take place without the existence of privileged places and moments, without these places and moments of meeting freeing themselves from the constraints of the market, without the law of exchange value being mastered, and without the relations which condition profits be altered. Until then culture dissolves, becoming an object of consumption, an opportunity for profit, production for the market: the 'cultural' dissimulates more than one trap. Until now a revolutionary interpretation has not taken into account these new elements. Would it not be possible that the more rigorous definition of the relations between industrialization and urbanization, in the situation of crisis, and around the critical point, will help to overcome the contradiction of absolute continuism and discontinuism, of reformist evolutionism and total revolution? If one wants to go beyond the market, the law of exchange value, money and profit, is it not necessary to define the place of this possibility: urban society, the city as use value?

The paradox of this critical situation, a crucial element of the problem, is that the crisis of the city is world-wide. It presents itself as a dominant aspect of universality in progress as do technology and the rational organization of industry. Yet, the practical causes and ideological reasons of this crisis vary according to political regimes, the societies, and even the countries concerned. A critical analysis of these phenomena could only be legitimated by comparison, but many elements of this comparison are missing. In underdeveloped countries, highly industrialized capitalist countries, socialist countries unevenly developed, everywhere the city explodes. The traditional form of agrarian society is transforming itself, but differently. In a number of poor countries, shanty towns are a characteristic phenomenon, while in highly industrialized countries, the proliferation of the city into 'urban fabric', suburbs, residential areas, and its relation with urban life is what causes the problem.

How gather together the elements of such a comparison? In the United States, the difficulties of Federal administration, its conflicts with local authorities, the terms of reference of 'urban government', divided among the manager, the political boss and the mayor and his municipality, cannot be explained in the same way as the power conflicts (administrative and juridical) in Europe and in France, where the consequences of industrialization besiege and explode urban cores dating from precapitalist or pre-industrial times. In the United States, the urban core hardly exists except in some privileged cities, yet local authorities have greater legal guarantees and more extensive powers than in France where monarchical centralization attacked these urban 'freedoms' very early on. In Europe, as elsewhere, one cannot attribute only to the growth of cities, or only to problems of traffic, difficulties which are both different and comparable. Here and there, from one part or another, the whole society is questioned one way or another. As it is preoccupied (through ideologues and statesmen) to principally plan industry and organize enterprise, modern society appears little able to give solutions to the urban problematic and to act otherwise than by small technical measures which only protract the current state of affairs. Everywhere the relation between the three levels analysed above becomes confused and conflictual, the dynamic element of the contradiction changing according to the social and political context. In so-called developing countries, the breakdown of agrarian structure pushes dispossessed peasants, ruined and eager for change, towards the cities. The shanty town welcomes them and becomes the (inadequate) mediator between town and country, agricultural and industrial production. It often consolidates itself and offers a substitute of urban life, miserable and yet intense, to those which it shelters. In other countries, particularly in socialist countries, planned urban growth attracts labour to the cities recruited from the countryside resulting in overcrowding, the construction of neighbourhoods or residential sectors whose relation to urban life is not always discernible. To sum up, a world-wide crisis in agriculture and traditional peasant life accompanies, underlies and aggravates a world-wide crisis of the traditional city. This is a change on a planetary scale. The old rural animal and urban animal (Marx), disappear together. Do they leave room to 'man'? That is the basic problem. The major theoretical and practical difficulty comes from the fact that the urbanization of industrial society does not happen without the breakup of what we still call 'the city'. Given that urban society is built on the ruins of the city, how can we grasp the breadth and manifold contradictions of these phenomena? That is the *critical point*. The distinction between the three levels (global process of industrialization and urbanization – urban society, the specific scale of the city – ways of living and conditions of daily life in the urban) tends to become blurred as does the distinction between town and country. And yet, this difference between the three levels is more than ever crucial to avoid confusion and misunderstandings, to combat strategies which find in this conjuncture an opportunity to disintegrate the urban into industrial and or residential planning.

Yes, this city which has gone through so much adversity and so many metamorphoses, since its archaic cores so close to the village, this admirable social form, this exquisite *oeuvre* of praxis and civilization, unmakes and remakes itself under our very eyes. The urgency of the housing question in conditions of industrial growth has concealed and still conceals the problems of the city. Political strategists, more attentive to the immediate, perceived and still perceive only these issues. When these overall problems emerged, under the name of *planning*, they have been subordinated to the general organization of industry. Attacked both from above and below, the city is associated to industrial enterprise: it figures in planning as a cog: it becomes the material device apt to organize production, control the daily life of the producers and the consumption of products. Having been reduced to the status of device, it extends this management to the consumers and consumption; it serves to regulate, to lay one over the other, the production of goods and the destruction of products with that devouring activity, 'consumption'. It did not have, it has no meaning but as an *oeuvre*, as an end, as place of free enjoyment, as domain of use value. Or, it is subjugated to constraints, to the imperatives of an 'equilibrium' within narrowly restrictive conditions; it is no more than the instrument of an organization which moreover is unable to consolidate itself by determining its conditions of stability and equilibrium, an organization according to whose catalogue and teleguide individual needs are satisfied by annihilating catalogued objects whose probability of durability (obsolescence) is itself a scientific field. In the past, reason had its place of birth, its seat, its home in the city. In the face of rurality, and of peasant life gripped by nature and the sacralized earth full of obscure powers, urbanity asserted itself as reasonable. Today, rationality seems to be (or appears to be, or pretends to be) far from the city, above it, on a national or continental scale. It refuses the city as a moment, as an element, as a condition; it acknowledges it only as an instrument and a means. In France and elsewhere, State bureaucratic rationalism and that of industrial organization supported by the demands of large private enterprises, are going the same way. Simultaneously there is enforced a simplifying functionalism and social groups which go beyond the urban. The organism disappears under the guise of organization, so that organicism coming from the philosophers appears as an ideal model. The statutes of urban 'zones' and 'areas' are reduced to a juxtaposition of spaces, of functions, of elements on the ground. Sectors and functions are tightly subordinated to centres of decision-making. Homogeneity overwhelms the differences originating from nature (the site), from peasant surroundings (territory and the soil), from history. The city, or what remains of it, is built or is rearranged, in the likeness of a sum or combination of elements. Now, as soon as the combination is conceived, perceived and anticipated as such, combinations are not easily recognizable; the differences fall into the perception of their whole. So that while one may rationally look for diversity, a feeling of monotony covers these diversities and prevails, whether housing, buildings, alleged urban centres, organized areas are concerned. The urban, not conceived as such but attacked face on and from the side, corroded and gnawed, has lost the features and characteristics of the *œuvre*, of appropriation. Only constraints are projected on the ground, in a state of permanent dislocation. From the point of view of housing, the ordering and arrangement of daily life, the massive use of the car ('private' means of transport), mobility (besides contained and insufficient), and the influence of the mass media, have detached from site and territory individuals and groups (families, organized bodies).

Neighbourhood and district fade and crumble away: the people (the 'inhabitants') move about in a space which tends towards a geometric isotopy, full of instructions and signals, where qualitative differences of places and moments no longer matter. Certainly these are inevitable processes of dissolution of ancient forms, but which produce contempt, mental and social misery. There is a poverty of daily life as soon as nothing has replaced the symbols, the appropriations, the styles, the monuments, the times and rhythms, the different and qualified spaces of the traditional city. Urban society, because of the dissolution of this city submitted to pressures which it cannot withstand, tends on the one hand to blend with the planned land use of the territory into the 'urban fabric' determined by the constraints of traffic, and on the other hand, into dwelling units such as those of the detached house and the housing estates. The extension of the city produced suburbs, then the suburb engulfed the urban core. The problems have been inversed, when they are not misunderstood. Would it not be more coherent, more rational and agreeable to work in the suburbs and live in the city rather than work in the city while living in a hardly habitable suburb? The centralized management of 'things' and of 'culture' tries to avoid this intermediary tier, the city. And more: the State, centres of decision-making, the ideological, economic and political powers, can only consider with a growing suspicion this social form which tends towards autonomy, which can only live specifically, which comes between them and the 'inhabitant', worker or not, productive or unproductive worker, but man and citizen as well as city dweller. Since the last century, what is the essence of the city for power? It ferments, full of suspect activities, of delinquence, a hotbed of agitation. State powers and powerful economic interests can think only of one strategy: to devalorize, degrade, destroy, urban society. In the course of these processes, there are determinisms, there are strategies, spontaneities and concerted acts. Subjective and ideological contradictions, 'humanist' worries impede but do not halt these strategic actions. The city prevents the powers that be from manipulating at will the citizen-city dweller, individuals, groups, bodies. As a result, the crisis of the city is linked not to rationality as such, definable from a philosophical tradition, it relates to explicit forms of rationality: state, bureaucratic, economic, or rather, 'economistic', economism being an ideology endowed with an apparatus. This crisis of the city is accompanied here and there with a crisis of urban institutions (municipal) due to the double pressure from the State and industrial enterprise. Sometimes the State, sometimes private enterprise, sometimes both (rivals in competition, but often associates) tend to commandeer the functions, duties, and prerogatives of urban society. In certain capitalist countries, does 'private' enterprise leave to the State, to institutions, and 'public' bodies any other thing than what it refuses to assume because it is too costly?

And yet, it is on this shaky foundation that urban society and the *urban* persist and even intensify. Social relations continue to become more complex, to multiply and intensify through the most painful contradictions. The form of the urban, its supreme reason, namely simultaneity and encounter, cannot disappear. Urban reality, at the very heart of its dislocation, persists and becomes more dense in the centres of decision-making and information. The inhabitants (which ones? – it's up to research and researchers to find them!) reconstitute centres, using places to restitute even derisory encounters. The use (use value) of places, monuments, differences, escape the demands of exchange, of exchange value. A big game is played before us, with various episodes whose meaning is not always evident. The satisfaction of basic needs is unable to kill the disaffectation of fundamental desires (or of the fundamental desire). As a place of encounters, focus of communication and information, the *urban* becomes what it always was: place of desire, permanent disequilibrium, seat of the dissolution of normalities and constraints, the moment of play and of the unpredictable. This moment includes the implosion–explosion of latent violence under the terrible constraints of a rationality which identifies itself with the absurd. From this situation is born a critical contradiction: a tendency towards destruction of the city, as well as a tendency towards the intensification of the urban and the urban problematic.

This critical analysis calls for a decisive addition. To attribute the crisis of the city to a confining rationality, productivism and economism, and to a planning centralization first and foremost concerned with growth, to the bureaucracy of State and enterprise is not incorrect. Yet, this viewpoint does not go much beyond the horizon of the most classical philosophical rationalism, that of liberal humanism. He who wishes to propose the form of a new urban society by strengthening this kernel, the *urban*, which survives in the fissures of planned and programmed order, must go further. If one wants to conceive an 'urban man' no longer in the image of classical humanism, theoretical elaboration owes it to itself to refine concepts. Until now, in theory as in practice, the double process of industrialization and of urbanization has not been mastered. The incomplete teachings of Marx and Marxist thought have been misunderstood. For Marx himself, industrialization contained its finality and meaning, later giving rise to the dissociation of Marxist thought into economism and philosophism. Marx did not show (and in his time he could not) that urbanization and the *urban* contain the *meaning* of industrialization. He did not see that industrial production implied the urbanization of society, and that the mastery of industrial potentials required specific knowledge concerning urbanization. Industrial production, after a certain *growth*, produces urbanization, providing it with conditions, and possibilities. The problematic is displaced and becomes that of urban *development*. The works of Marx (notably *Capital*) contained precious indications on the city and particularly on the historical relations between town and country. They do not pose the urban problem. In Marx's time, only the housing problem was raised and studied by Engels. Now, the problem of the city is immensely greater than that of housing. The limits of Marxist thought have not been really understood. Supporters as well as adversaries have sowned trouble, by poorly assimilating the methodological and theoretical principles of this thought. Neither criticism from the right, nor criticism from the left have assessed the contributions and the limits. These limits have not yet been overtaken by an approach which does not reject, but deepens acquired knowledge. The implicit sense of industrialization has therefore been badly clarified. In theoretical reflection this process has not acquired its meaning. Moreover, one has looked for meaning elsewhere, or one has abandoned the meaning and the research of meaning.

The 'socialization of society', misunderstood by reformists has prevented urban transformation (in, by, for, the city). It has not been understood that this socialization has urbanization as its essence. What has been 'socialized'? By turning them over to consumption, signs. Signs of the city, of *urban* life, as the signs of nature and the countryside, as those of joy and happiness, delivered to consumption without an effective social practice enabling the *urban* to enter daily life. Urban life faces needs only reluctantly, through the poverty of social needs of 'socialized society', through daily consumption and its own signs in advertising, fashion, aestheticism. At this new moment of analysis, is thus conceived the dialectical movement which carries the forms, the contours, the determinisms and the constraints, the servitudes and the appropriations towards a troubled horizon.

Urban life, urban society and the *urban*, detached by a particular social practice (whose analysis will continue) from their half ruined morphological base, and searching for a new base, these are the contexts of the critical point. The *urban* cannot be defined either as attached to a material morphology (on the ground, in the practico-material), or as being able to detach itself from it. It is not an intemporal essence, nor a system among other systems or above other systems. It is a mental and social form, that of simultaneity, of gathering, of convergence, of encounter (or rather, encounters). It is a *quality* born from quantities (spaces, objects, products). It is a *difference*, or rather, an ensemble of differences. The *urban* contains the meaning of industrial production, as *appropriation* contains the sense of *technical domination over nature*, the latter becoming absurd without the former. It is a *field* of relations including notably the relation of time (or of times; cyclical rhythms and linear durations) with space (or spaces: isotopies and heterotopies). As place of desire and bond of times, the *urban* could present itself as *signifiers* whose *signified* we are presently looking for (that is, practico-material 'realities' which would enable, with an adequate morphological and material base, to realize it in space).

Lacking adequate theoretical elaboration, the double process (industrialization–urbanization) has been severed and its aspects separated, to be therefore consigned to the absurd. Grasped by a higher and dialectical rationality, conceived in its duality and contradictions, this process could not leave the *urban* aside. On the contrary: *it understands it*. Therefore, what should be incriminated is not reason, but a particular rationalism, a constricted rationality, and its limits. The world of merchandise has its immanent logic of money and exchange value generalized without limits. Such a form, that of exchange and equivalence, is indifferent towards urban form; it reduces simultaneity and encounters to those of the exchangers and the meeting place to where the contract or quasi-contract of equivalent exchange is concluded: the market. Urban society, a collection of acts taking place in time, privileging a space (site, place) and privileged by it, in turn signifiers and signified, has a logic different from that of merchandise. It is another world. The *urban* is based on use value. This conflict cannot be avoided. At most, economic and productivist rationality seeks to push beyond all limits the production of products (exchangeable objects of exchange value) by suppressing the *oeuvre*, this productivist rationality makes itself out to be knowledge, while containing an ideological component tied to its very essence. Maybe it is only ideology, valorizing constraints, those which come from existing determinisms, those of industrial production and the market of products, those coming from its fetishism of policy. Ideology presents these real constraints as rational. Such a rationality is not innocuous. The worse danger which it harbours comes from it wanting itself and calling itself *synthetical*. It purports to lead to synthesis and make 'men of synthesis' (either from philosophy, or from science, or lastly, from an 'interdisciplinary' research). Now, this is an ideological illusion. Who has *right of synthesis*? Certainly not a civil servant of synthesis, accomplishing this function in a way guaranteed by institutions. Certainly not he who extrapolates from an analysis or several analyses. Only the practical capacity of realization has the right to collect the theoretical elements of synthesis, by doing it. Is it the role of political power? Maybe, but not any political force: not the political State as an institution or sum of institutions, not statesmen as such. Only the critical examination of strategies enables us to give an answer to this questioning. The *urban* can only be confined to a strategy prioritizing the urban problematic, the intensification of urban life, the effective realization of urban society (that is, its morphological, material and practico-material base).

12

On Urban Form

The ambiguity, or more exactly, the *polysemy* or plurality of meanings, of this term, 'form', has already been remarked upon. It was not really necessary, being obvious. The same goes for the polysemy of the terms 'function', 'structure' etc. None the less we cannot rest there and accept the situation. How many people believe they have said and resolved everything when they use one of these fetish words! The plurality and confusion of the meanings serve an absence of thought and poverty which takes itself for wealth.

The only way to clarify the meaning of the term is to begin from its most abstract acceptance. Only scientific abstraction without contents, distinguished from verbal abstraction and opposed to speculative abstraction, enables transparent definitions. Therefore, to define form, one must begin from formal logic and logico-mathematical structures. Not so as to isolate or fetishize them, but, on the contrary, to catch their relation to the 'real'. This is not without some difficulties and disadvantages. The transparency and clarity of 'pure' abstraction are not accessible to all. Most people are either myopic or blind to it. A 'culture' is necessary not only to understand the abstract, but far more to attain the disturbing frontiers which at one and the same time distinguish and unite the concrete and the abstract, knowledge and art, mathematics and poetry. To elucidate the meaning of the word 'form', one will have to refer to a very general, very abstract theory, the *theory of forms*. It is close to a philosophical theory of knowledge, extending it and yet very different, since on the one hand it designates its own historical and 'cultural' conditions and on the other it rests upon difficult logico-mathematical considerations.

Proceeding by stages a socially recognized 'form' will be examined; for example, the *contract*. There are many kinds of contracts: the marriage contract, the work contract, the sales contract, etc. The contents of social acts defined as contractual are therefore very different. Sometimes they relate to the regulation of relations between two individuals of different sexes (the sexual relationship taking second place in the social regulation of assets and their transmission as they relate to children and inheritance). Sometimes they relate to the regulation of relations between two individuals of different social and even class status: employer and employee, boss and worker. Sometimes what is involved is the submission to a social regularity of the relationship between seller and buyer, etc. These particular situations have none the less a common feature: *reciprocity* in a socially constituted and instituted engagement. Each engages himself *vis-à-vis* the other to accomplish a certain sort of action explicitly or implicitly stipulated. Moreover, one knows that this reciprocity entails some fiction, or rather, that as soon as it is concluded, it reveals itself to be fictional, inasmuch as it does not fall into contractual stipulation and under the rule of law. Sexual reciprocity between spouses becomes social and moral fiction (the 'conjugal duty'). The reciprocity of engagement between boss and worker establishes them on the same level only fictionally. And so on and so forth. Nevertheless, these fictions have a social existence and influence. They are the various contents of a general juridical *form* with which jurists operate and which become the *codification* of social relations: the civil code.

It is the same for reflective thought which has extremely diverse contents: objects, situations, activities. From this diversity emerge more or less fictional or real domains: science, philosophy, art, etc. These many objects, these domains somewhat small in number, relate to a logical formulation. Reflection is codified by a form common to all contents, which is born out of their differences.

Form detaches itself from content, or rather, contents. Thus freed, it emerges pure and transparent: intelligible. That much more intelligible as decanted from content, 'purer'. But here is the paradox. As such, in its purity, it has no existence. It is not real, it is not. By detaching itself from its content, form detaches itself from the concrete. The summit, the crest of the real, the key to the real (of its penetration by knowledge and the action which changes it), it places itself outside the real. Philosophers have tried to understand for two thousand years.

None the less, philosophy brings the theoretical elements to this knowledge. The approach is in several stages and has a strategic objective. That is to grasp through the movement of reflection which purifies forms and its own form, and which codifies and formalizes the inherent and hidden movement of the relation between form and content. There is no form without content. No content without form. What offers itself to analysis is always a *unity* of form and content. Analysis breaks this unity. It allows the purity of form to appear, and form refers back to content. Yet, this indissoluble unity, broken by analysis, is conflictual (dialectical). By turns thought goes from transparent form to the opacity of contents, of the substantiality of these contents to the inexistence of 'pure' form, in a ceaseless if not momentary movement. Nevertheless, on the one hand, reflection tends to dissociate forms (and its own logical form) from contents, by constituting absolute 'essences', by establishing the reign of essences. And on the other hand, practice and empiricism tend to ascertain contents, to be satisfied with such certitude, to sojourn in the opacity of various contents, accepted in their differences. For dialectical reason, contents overflow form and form gives access to contents. Thus form has a double 'existence'. It is and is not. It has reality only in contents, and yet detaches itself from them. It has a mental and a social existence. Mentally the contract is defined by a form quite close to logic: reciprocity. Socially, this form regulates countless situations and activities; it confers upon them a structure, it maintains them and even valorizes them, including as form an evaluation and involving a 'consensus'. As for the logico-mathematical form, its mental existence is obvious. What is less obvious is that it involves a fiction: the purely reflective disembodied theoretical man. As for its social existence, it should be shown at length. Indeed, to this form are attached multitudinous social activities: to count, define, classify (objects, situations, activities), rationally organized, predicted, planned and even programmed.

Reflection which (in new terms) extends the long meditation and the problematic of philosophers, can elaborate a *scheme of forms*. It is a sort of analytical grid to decipher the relations between the real and thought. This (provisional and modifiable) grid moves from the most abstract to the most concrete, and therefore from the least to the most immediate. Each form presents itself in its double existence as mental and social.

I. Logical form

Mentally: it is the principle of identity: A=A. It is void essence without content. In its absolute purity it is supreme transparency (difficult to grasp, for reflection can neither hold it or keep itself within it and yet it has *tautology* as its point of departure and return). Indeed, this tautology is what all propositions have in common which otherwise have nothing in common with each other by content, or the designated (*designatum*, denoted). As Wittgenstein has shown, this tautology A=A is the centre, emptied of substance of all enunciated, of all propositions.

Socially: understanding and the conventions of understanding over and above misunderstandings. The impossible possibility to make effective stopping, to define everything, to say everything and to agree on the rules of understanding. But also, verbalism, verbiage, repetitions, pure talk. But again pleonasms, vicious circles (including the great social pleonasms, for bureaucracy which engenders bureacracy to maintain the bureaucratic form – social logics which tend towards their pure maintenance to the extent of destroying their content and thus themselves, showing their emptiness).

II. Mathematical form

Mentally: identity and difference, equality in difference. Enumeration (of the elements of a whole, etc). Order and measure.

Socially: distributions and classifications (in space, generally privileged as such, but also in time). Scheduling. Quantification and quantitative rationality. Order and measure subordinating to themselves desires and desire, quality and qualities.

III. Form of language

Mentally: coherence, the capacity to articulate distinct elements, to confer to them significations and meanings, to emit and decipher messages according to their coded conventions.

Socially: the cohesion of relations, their subordination to the demands and constraints of cohesion, the ritualization of relations, their formalization and codification.

IV. Form of exchange

Mentally: confrontation and discussion, comparison and adjustments of activities, needs, products of labour, etc., that is, *equivalence*.
Socially: exchange value, the commodity form (as identified, formulated and formalized by Marx in chapter I of *Capital*, with an implicit reference to formal logic and to logico-mathematical formalism).

V. Contractual form

Mentally: reciprocity.
Socially: the codification of social relations based on mutual engagement.

IV. Form of the practico-material object

Mentally: internal equilibrium perceived and conceived as 'objective' (or 'objectal') property. *Symmetry*.
Socially: the anticipation of this equilibrium and this symmetry, demanded by objects or denied (including among living and thinking 'beings'), as well as social objects such as houses, buildings, utensils and instruments, etc.

VII. Written form

Mentally: recurrence, synchronic fixation of what has occurred over time, going backwards and returning along a fixed becoming.
Socially: the accumulation in time on the basis of fixation and the conversation of what is acquired, the constraint of writing and writings, terror before the written and the struggle of the spirit against the letter, the power of speech against the inscribed and the prescribed, the becoming against the immutable and the reified.

VIII. Urban form

Mentally: simultaneity (of events, perceptions, and elements of a whole in the 'real').

Socially: the encounter and the concentration of what exists around, in the environment (assets and products, acts and activities, wealth) and consequently, urban society as privileged social site, as meaning of productive and consuming activities, as meeting between the *oeuvre* and the product.

We will leave aside *repetition* which some (among them Nietzsche), have considered to be the supreme form, existential form, or form of existence.

It is almost evident that in so-called modern society, simultaneity is intensified and becomes more dense, that the capacities for encounter and assembly become strengthened. Communications speed up to quasi-instantaneity. Ascendent or descendent circuits of information flow and are diffused from this *centrality*. This aspect of the 'socialization of society' has already been emphasized (reservations having been made about the 'reformist' nature of this well-known formulation).

It is just as evident that under the same conditions dispersion increases: the division of labour is pushed to the extreme segregation of social groups and material and spiritual separations. These dispersions can only be conceived or appreciated by reference to the form of simultaneity. Without this form, dispersion and separation are purely and simply glimpsed, accepted, confirmed as facts. Thus form enables us to designate the content, or rather, contents. Movement in its emergence reveals a hidden movement, the dialectical (conflictual) movement of content and urban form: the problematic. The form in which is inscribed this problematic asks questions which are a part of it. Before whom and for whom is simultaneity established, the contents of urban life assembled?

13

Spectral Analysis

In fact, the rationality we see used in practice (including applied planning), this limited rationality is exercised especially according to the modalities of a very advanced and prepared analytical intelligence, endowed with great means of pressure. This analytical intellect endows itself with the privileges and prestige of synthesis. In this way it hides what it conceals: strategies. One could impute it with the peremptory concern of the functional, or rather, the *unifunctional*, as well as the subordination of details minutely inventoried for the representation of a social globality. Thus disappear *mediations* between an ideological ensemble assumed to be rational (technologically or economically) and detailed measures, objects of tactics and prediction. This placing in parenthesis of theoretical, practical, social and mental mediations does not lack black humour in a society where intermediaries (shopkeepers, financiers, publicists, etc.) have immense privileges. One covers the other! Thus a gulf is dug between the global (which hovers over the void) and the manipulated and repressed partial, upon which institutions weigh.

What is questioned here is not an uncertain 'globality', it is an *ideology* and the class *strategy* which uses and supports this ideology. After a sort of 'spectral' analysis of social elements, the already mentioned use of analytical intelligence is related as much to extreme fragmentation of work and specialization pushed to the limits (including specialized planning studies), as projection on the ground. *Segregation* must be highlighted, with its three aspects, sometimes simultaneous, sometimes successive: *spontaneous* (coming from revenues and ideologies) – *voluntary* (establishing separate spaces) – programmed: under the guise of planning and the plan).

There are unquestionably strong tendencies in all countries opposing segregationist tendencies. One cannot state that the segregation of groups, ethnic groups, social strata and classes comes from a constant and uniform strategy of the powers, nor that one should see in it the efficient projection of institutions or the will of political leaders. Moreover, there exist the will and organized actions to combat it. And yet, even where separation of social groups does not seem to be patently evident on the ground, such a pressure and traces of segregation appear under examination. The extreme case, the last instance, the ghetto. We can observe that there are several types of ghetto: those of Jews and the blacks, and also those of intellectuals or workers. In their own way residential areas are also ghettos; high status people because of wealth or power isolate themselves in ghettos of wealth. Leisure has its ghettos. Wherever an organized action has attempted to mix social strata and classes, a spontaneous decantation soon follows. The phenomenon of segregation must be analysed according to various indices and criteria: *ecological* (shanty towns, slums, the rot in the heart of the city), *formal* (the deterioration of signs and meanings of the city, the degradation of the *urban* by the dislocation of its architectural elements), and *sociological* (standards of living and life styles, ethnic groups, cultures and sub-cultures, etc.)

Anti-segregationist tendencies would be rather more ideological. They sometimes relate to liberal humanism, sometimes to a philosophy of the city considered as 'subject' (as a community or social organism). Despite good humanist intentions and philosophical goodwill, *practice* tends towards segregation. Why? For theoretical reasons and by virtue of social and political causes. At the theoretical level, analytical thought separates and delineates. It fails when it wants to reach a synthesis. Socially and politically (conscious or unconscious) class strategies aim for segregation.

In democratic countries public powers cannot overtly decree segregation as such. Therefore they often adopt a humanist ideology which in the most old-fashioned sense becomes a utopia, when it does not become a demagogy. Segregation always wins over, even in those parts of social life more or less easily and more or less thoroughly controlled by public powers. Let us say that the State and private enterprise strive to absorb and suppress the city as such. The State proceeds rather from above and private enterprise from below (by ensuring housing and the function of inhabiting in workers' towns and housing estates, which depending on a 'society' and also assuring leisure, even culture and social promotion). Despite their differences and sometimes their conflicts, the State and private enterprise both converge towards segregation.

Let us leave open the issue of knowing whether the political forms of the State (capitalist, socialist or in transition, etc.), engender different strategies towards the city. Let us not attempt for the time being to know where or how, at whom and with whom these strategies are developed. We substantiate strategies by observing them as significant orientations. Segregations which morphologically destroyed the city and threaten urban life cannot be passed off as the effect of hazards or local conjunctures. Let us be contented with the notion that the *democratic* character of a regime is identifiable by its attitude towards the city, urban 'liberties' and urban reality, and therefore towards *segregation*. Among the criteria to retain would not this one be one of the most important? It is fundamental in what concerns the city and its problematic. Nevertheless one must distinguish between political power and social pressures which can annihilate the effects of (good or bad) will of politicians. With regards to private enterprise, let us also leave this an open question. What are the relations between (ideological and practical) rationality in general, between (general and urban) planning on the one hand, and on the other the rational management of large firms? We can nevertheless put forward a hypothesis and research direction. Rationality in the firm always implies an analysis pushed to the extreme of tasks, operations and sequences. In addition, the reasons and causes of class strategy are fully played out in the capitalist firm. It is therefore highly probable that the firm as such favours the extreme segregation, acts accordingly and applies social pressure when this is not a decision.

The State and the firm seek to appropriate urban functions and to assume and ensure them by destroying the form of the *urban*. Can they? Do not these strategic objectives exceed their strengths, combined or not? It would be most interesting to investigate this point. The conditions and modalities of the crisis of the city are gradually uncovered and accompanied by a city-wide institutional crisis of urban jurisdiction and administration. What was specific to the city (the municipality, local expenditures and investments, schools and educational programmes, universities, etc.) fall increasingly under the control of the State, and by institutionalizing itself in a global context, the city tends to disappear as a specific institution. This abolishes it as an *oeuvre* of original groups which were themselves specific. However, can the powers and institutions at the top dispense with this relay, this mediation, the city? This, of course, would need to be shown by researches into juridical, economic, cultural and administrative sociology. Can they abolish the *urban*? It is at this level that daily life, governed by institutions which regulate it from above, consolidated and set up according to multiple constraints, constitutes itself. Productivist rationality which tends to suppress the city at the level of general planning rediscovers it in the controlled and organized consumption of a supervised market. After having been kept away from the global level of decision-making, the city is reconstituted at the level of executions and application, by institutions of power. The outcome – inasmuch as such a situation in France and elsewhere can make sense – is an incredible entanglement of measures (all reasonable), regulations (all very complicated), and constraints (all motivated). The functioning of bureacratic rationality becomes confused with its own presuppositions and consequences which overcome and elude it. Conflicts and contradictions resurface, giving rise to 'structuring' activities and 'concerted' actions aimed at their revocation. It is here on the ground that the absurdity of a limited rationality of bureaucracy and technocracy becomes evident. Here is grasped the falsehood of an illusory identification between the rational and the real in the State, and the true identity between the absurd and a certain authoritarian rationalism.

On our horizon, the city and the *urban* are outlined as virtual objects, as projects of a synthetic reconstitution. Critical analysis confirms the failure of an analytical but uncritical thought. What does this analytical practice retain of the city and the urban whose results one can detect on the ground? Aspects, elements and fragments. It places before our eyes the spectre, the spectral analysis of the city. When we speak of *spectral analysis*, its meaning is almost literal and not metaphorical. Before our eyes, under our gaze, we have the 'spectre' of the city, that of urban society and perhaps simply of society. If the spectre of Communism no longer haunts Europe, the shadow of the city, the regret of what has died because it was killed, perhaps guilt, have replaced the old dread. The image of urban hell in the making is not less fascinating, and people rush towards the ruins of ancient cities to consume them touristically, in the belief that they will heal their nostalgia. Before us, as a spectacle (for spectators 'unconscious' of what is before their 'conscience') are the dissociated and inert elements of social life and the *urban*. Here are 'social housing estates' without teenagers or old people. Here are women dozing while the men work far away and come home exhausted. Here are private housing developments which form a microcosm and yet remain urban because they depend on centres of decision-making and each house has a television. Here is a daily life well divided into fragments: work, transport, private life, leisure. Analytical separation has isolated them as ingredients and chemical elements, as raw materials (whereas they are the outcome of a long history and imply an appropriation of materiality). It is not finished. Here is the dismembered and dissociated human being. Here are the senses of smell, taste, sight, touch, hearing – some atrophied, some hypertrophied. Here is functioning separately perception, intelligence and reason. Here is speech, discourse and writing. Here is daily life and celebration, the latter moribund. It is obvious, urgently. *Synthesis* then becomes an item on the order of the day, the order of the century. But this synthesis, with its analytical intellect, appears only as a *combination* of separate elements. But combination is not and can never be synthesis. The city and the *urban* cannot be recomposed from the signs of the city, the *semanthemes* of the *urban*, although the city is a signifying whole. The city is not only a language, but also a practice. Nobody therefore, and we have no fear to repeat it, is entitled to pronouce or announce this synthesis. No more is the sociologist or community worker than the architect, the economist, the demographer, the linguist or semiologist. Nobody has the power or the right. Only the philosopher might perhaps have the right, if philosophy in the course of the centuries had not demonstrated its incapacity to attain concentrate totalities (although it has always aimed at totality and has posed global and general questions). Only a *praxis*, under conditions to be determined, can take charge of the possibility and demand of a synthesis this objective: the gathering together of what gives itself as dispersed, dissociated, separated, and this in the form of simultaneity and encounters.

We have here therefore before us, projected separately on the ground, groups, ethnic groups, ages and sexes, activities, tasks and functions, knowledge. Here is all that is necessary to create a world, an urban society, or the developed *urban*. But this world is absent, this society is before us only in a state of virtuality. It may perish in the bud. Under existing conditions, it dies before being born. The conditions which give rise to possibilities can also sustain them in a virtual state, in presence–absence. Would this not be the root of this drama, the point of emergence of nostalgia? The urban obsesses those who live in need, in poverty, in the frustration of possibilities which remain only possibilities. Thus the integration and participation obsess the non-participants, the non-integrated, those who survive among the fragments of a possible society and the ruins of the past: excluded from the city, at the gates of the *urban*. The road travelled is staked out with contradictions between the total (global) and the partial, between analysis and synthesis. Here is a new one which reveals itself, high and deep. It does not interest theory but practice. The same *social practice*, that of society today (in France, in the second half of the twentieth century) offers to critical analysis a double character which cannot be reduced to a significant opposition, although it signifies.

On the one hand, this social practice is *integrative*. It attempts to integrate its elements and aspects into a coherent whole. Integration is accomplished at different levels and according to various modalities. The market, the 'world of commodities', that is, by consumption and ideology of consumption, by 'culture', put forward as unitary and global; by 'values', including art; by the actions of the State, including national consciousness and the political options and strategies at national level. This integration is firstly aimed at the working class, but also the intelligentsia and intellectuals, and critical thought (not excluding Marxism). Planning could well become essential to this integrative practice.

At the same time this society practices *segregation*. This same rationality which sees itself as global (organizing, planning, unitary and unifying) concretizes itself at the analytical level. On the ground it projects separation. It tends (as in the United States), to form ghettos or parking lots, those of workers, intellectuals, students (the campus), foreigners, and so forth, not forgetting the ghetto of leisure or 'creativity', reduced to miniaturization or hobbies. Ghetto in space and ghetto in time. In planning, the term 'zoning' already implies separation, segregation, isolation in planned ghettos. The fact becomes rationality in the project.

This society wants itself and sees itself as *coherent*. It seeks coherence, linked to rationality both as feature of efficient organizational action, and as value and criterion. Under examination the ideology of coherence reveals a hidden but none the less blatant incoherence. Would coherence not be the obsession of an incoherent society, which searches the way towards coherence by wishing to stop in a conflictual situation denied as such?

This is not the only obsession. *Integration* also becomes an obsessional theme, an aimless aspiration. The term 'integration' used in all its meanings, appears in texts (newspapers, books, and speeches) with such frequency that it must reveal something. On the one hand, this term designates a *concept* concerning and enclosing social practice divulging a strategy. On the other, it is a *social connotator*, without concept, objective or objectivity, revealing an obsession with integrating (to this or that, to a group, an ensemble or a whole). How could it be otherwise in a society which superimposes the whole to the parts, synthesis to analysis, coherence to incoherence, organization to dislocation? It is from the city that the urban problematic reveals this constitutive duality with its conflictual content. What results from this? Without a doubt paradoxical phenomena of disintegrating integration which refer particularly to urban reality.

This does not mean that this society is disintegrating and falling apart. No. It is functionning. How? Why? That creates a problem. It must also mean that this functionning is not without an enormous *malaise* – its obsession.

Another obsessional theme is *participation*, linked to integration. This is not a simple obsession. In practice, the ideology of participation enables us to have the acquiescence of interested and concerned people at a small price. After a more or less elaborate pretence at information and social activity, they return to their tranquil passivity and retirement. Is it not clear that real and active participation already has a name? It is called *self-management*. Which poses other problems.

Very powerful forces tend to destroy the city. A particular kind of planning projects on the ideological terrain a practice whose aim is the death of the city. These social and political forces ravage the *urban* in the making. This kernel, so powerful, in its own way, can it grow in the cracks which still subsist between these masses? Does science, or rather, scientificity, which puts itself at the service of existing rationality, legitimize these masses of the State, private enterprise, culture which allow the city to perish while offering its images and "*oeuvres*" for consumption sentence. 'Does science . . . legitimize these masses . . .

for consumption?' Construction is? Could urban life recover and strengthen its capacities of *integration* and *participation* of the city, which are almost entirely lost, and which cannot be stimulated either by authoritarian means or by administrative prescription, or by the intervention of specialists? The foremost theoretical problem can be formulated thus. The political meaning of class segregation is clear, whether it is a 'subject' for analysis, whether it is the end result of a series of unplanned actions, or whether it is the effect of a will. For the *working class*, victim of segregation and expelled from the traditional city, deprived of a present or possible urban life, there is a practical and therefore *political* problem even if it is not posed politically and even if until now the housing question has for it and its representatives concealed the problematic of the city and the *urban*.

14

The Right to the City

Theoretical thought sees itself compelled to redefine the forms, functions and structures of the city (economic, political, cultural, etc.) as well as the social needs inherent to urban society. Until now, only those individual needs, motivated by the so-called society of consumption (a bureaucratic society of managed consumption) have been prospected, and moreover manipulated rather than effectively known and recognized. Social needs have an anthropological foundation. Opposed and complimentary, they include the need for security and opening, the need for certainty and adventure, that of organization of work and of play, the needs for the predictable and the unpredictable, of similarity and difference, of isolation and encounter, exchange and investments, of independence (even solitude) and communication, of immediate and long-term prospects. The human being has the need to accumulate energies and to spend them, even waste them in play. He has a need to see, to hear, to touch, to taste and the need to gather these perceptions in a 'world'. To these anthropological needs which are socially elaborated (that is, sometimes separated, sometimes joined together, here compressed and there hypertrophied), can be added specific needs which are not satisfied by those commercial and cultural infrastructures which are somewhat parsimoniously taken into account by planners. This refers to the need for creative activity, for the *oeuvre* (not only of products and consumable material goods), of the need for information, symbolism, the imaginary and play. Through these specified needs lives and survives a fundamental desire of which play, sexuality, physical activities such as sport, creative activity, art and knowledge are particular expressions and *moments*, which can more or less overcome the fragmentary division of tasks. Finally, the need of the city and urban life can only be freely expressed within a perspective which here attempts to become clearer and to open up the horizon. Would not specific urban needs be those of qualified places, places of simultaneity and encounters, places where exchange would not go through exchange value, commerce and profit? Would there not also be the need for a time for these encounters, these exchanges?

At present, an analytical science of the city, which is necessary, is only at the outline stage. At the beginning of their elaboration, concepts and theories can only move forward with urban reality in the making, with the *praxis* (social practice) of urban society. Now, not without effort, the ideologies and practices which blocked the horizon and which were only bottlenecks of knowledge and action, are being overcome.

The *science of the city* has the city as object. This science borrows its methods, approaches and concepts from the fragmentary sciences, but synthesis escapes it in two ways. Firstly, because this synthesis which would wish itself as total, starting from the analytic, can only be strategic systematization and programming. Secondly, because the object, the city, as consummate reality is falling apart. Knowledge holds in front of itself the historic city already modified, to cut it up and put it together again from fragments. As social text, this historic city no longer has a coherent set of prescriptions, of use of time linked to symbols and to a style. This text is moving away. It takes the form of a document, or an exhibition, or a museum. The city historically constructed is no longer lived and is no longer understood practically. It is only an object of cultural consumption for tourists, for a estheticism, avid for spectacles and the picturesque. Even for those who seek to understand it with warmth, it is gone. Yet, the *urban* remains in a state of dispersed and alienated actuality, as kernel and virtuality. What the eyes and analysis perceive on the ground can at best pass for the shadow of a future object in the light of a rising sun. It is impossible to envisage the reconstitution of the old city, only the construction of a new one on new foundations, on another scale and in other conditions, in another society. The prescription is: there cannot be a going back (towards the traditional city), nor a headlong flight, towards a colossal and shapeless agglomeration. In other words, for what concerns the city the object of science is not given. The past, the present, the possible cannot be separated. What is being studied is a *virtual object*, which thought studies, which calls for new approaches.

The career of the old classical humanism ended long ago and badly. It is dead. Its mummified and embalmed corpse weighs heavily and does not smell good. It occupies many spaces, public or otherwise, thus transforms into cultural cemeteries under the guise of the human: museums, universities, various publications, not to mention new towns and planning procedures. Trivialities and platitudes are wrapped up in this 'human scale', as they say, whereas what we should take charge of are the excesses and create 'something' to the scale of the universe.

This old humanism died during the World Wars, during the demographic growth which accompanied great massacres, and before the brutal demands of economic growth and competition and the pressure of poorly controlled techniques. It is not even an ideology, barely a theme for official speeches.

Recently there have been great cries of 'God is dead, man too' as if the death of classical humanism was that of man. These formulae spread in best-sellers, and taken in by a publicity not really responsible, are nothing new. Nietzschean meditation, a dark presage for Europe's culture and civilization, began a hundred years ago during the 1870–1 Franco-Prussian war. When Nietzsche announced the death of God and man, he did not leave a gaping hole, or fill this void with makeshift material, language or linguistics. He was also announcing the Superhuman which he thought was to come. He was overcoming the nihilism he was identifying. Authors transacting these theoretical and poetic treasures, but with a delay of a century, plunge us back into nihilism. Since Nietzsche, the dangers of the Superhuman have been cruelly evident. Moreover, this 'new man' emerging from industrial production and planning rationality has been more than disappointing. There is still another way, that of urban society and the human as *oeuvre* in this society which would be an *oeuvre* and not a product. There is also the simultaneous overcoming of the old 'social animal' and man of the ancient city, the urban animal, towards a polyvalent, polysensorial, urban man capable of complex and transparent relations with the world (the environment and himself). Or there is nihilism. If man is dead, for whom will we build? How will we build? It does not matter that the city has or has not disappeared, that it must be thought anew, reconstructed on new foundations or overcome. It does not matter whether terror reigns, that the atomic bomb is dropped or that Planet Earth explodes. What is important? Who thinks? Who acts? Who still speaks and for whom? If meaning and finality disappear and we cannot even declare them in a praxis, nothing matters. And if the capacities of the 'human being', technology, science, imagination and art, or their absence, are erected as autonomous powers, and that reflective thought is satisfied with this assessment, the absence of a 'subject', what to reply? What to do?

Old humanism moves away and disappears. Nostalgia lessens and we turn back less and less often to see its shape lying across the road. It was the ideology of the liberal bourgeoisie, with its Greek and Latin quotes sprinkled with Judeo-Christianity, which bent over the people and human sufferings and which covered and supported the rhetoric of the clear consciences of noble feelings and of the sensitive souls. A dreadful cocktail, a mixture to make you sick. Only a few intellectuals (from the 'Left' – but are there still any intellectuals on the 'Right'?) who are neither revolutionary nor openly reactionary, nor Dionysiacs or Apollonians, still have a taste for this sad potion.

We thus must make the effort to reach out towards a new humanism, a new praxis, another man, that of urban society. We must avoid those myths which threaten this will, destroy those ideologies which hinder this project and those strategies which divert this trajectory. Urban life has yet to begin. What we are doing now is to complete an inventory of the remains of a millenarian society where the countryside dominated the city, and whose ideas, values, taboos and prescriptions were largely agrarian, with rural and 'natural' dominant features. A few sporadic cities hardly emerged from a rustic ocean. Rural society was (still is), a society of scarcity and penury, of want accepted or rejected, of prohibitions managing and regulating privations. It was also the society of the *Fête*, of festivities. But that aspect, the best, has been lost and instead of myths and limitations, this is what must be revitalized! A decisive remark: for the crisis of the traditional city accompanies the world crisis of agrarian civilization, which is also traditional. It is up to us to resolve this double crisis, especially by creating with the new city, a new life in the city. Revolutionary societies (among which the USSR ten or fifteen years after the October Revolution), intimated the development of society based on industry. But they only intimated.

The use of 'we' in the sentences above has only the impact of a metaphor to mean those concerned. The architect, the planner, the sociologist, the economist, the philosopher or the politician cannot out of nothingness create new forms and relations. More precisely, the architect is no more a miracle-worker than the sociologist. Neither can create social relations, although under certain favourable conditions they help trends to be formulated (to take shape). Only social life (praxis) in its global capacity possesses such powers – or does not possess them. The people mentioned above can individually or in teams clear the way; they can also propose, try out and prepare forms. And also (and especially), through a maieutic nurtured by science, assess acquired experience, provide a lesson from failure and give birth to the possible.

At the point we have arrived there is an urgent need to change intellectual approaches and tools. It would be indispensable to take up ideas and approaches from elsewhere and which are still not very familiar.

Transduction. This is an intellectual operation which can be methodically carried out and which differs from classical induction, deduction, the construction of 'models', simulation as well as the simple statement of hypothesis. Transduction elaborates and constructs a theoretical object, a *possible* object from information related to reality and a problematic posed by this reality. Transduction assumes an incessant feed back between the conceptual framework used and empirical observations. Its theory (methodology), gives shape to certain spontaneous mental operations of the planner, the architect, the sociologist, the politician and the philosopher. It introduces rigour in invention and knowledge in utopia.

Experimental utopia. Who is not a *utopian* today? Only narrowly specialized practioners working to order without the slightest critical examination of stipulated norms and constraints, only these not very interesting people escape utopianism. All are utopians, including those futurists and planners who project Paris in the year 2,000 and those engineers who have made Brasilia! But there are several utopianisms. Would not the worst be that utopianism which does not utter its name, covers itself with positivism and on this basis imposes the harshest constraints and the most derisory absence of technicity?

Utopia is to be considered experimentally by studying its implications and consequences on the ground. These can surprise. What are and what would be the most successful places? How can they be discovered? According to which criteria? What are the times and rhythms of daily life which are inscribed and prescribed in these 'successful' spaces favourable to happiness? That is interesting.

There are other indispensable intellectual approaches to identify without dissociating them the three fundamental theoretical concepts of structure, function and form, and to know their import, the spheres of their validity, their limits and their reciprocal relations. To know that they make a whole but that the elements of this whole have a certain independence and relative autonomy. To not privilege one over the other, otherwise this gives an ideology, that is, a closed and dogmatic system of significations: structuralism, formalism, functionalism. To be used equally and in turn for the analysis of the real (an analysis which is never exhaustive or without residue), as well as for that operation known as 'transduction'. It is important to understand that a function can be accomplished by means of different structures, and that there is no unequivocal link between the terms. That is, that functions and structures clothe themselves with forms which reveal and veil them – that the triplicity of these aspects make a whole which is more than these aspects, elements and parts.

We have among our intellectual tools one which deserves neither disdain nor privilege of the absolute: that of *system* (or rather *sub-system* of significations.

Policies have their systems of significations – ideologies – which enable them to subordinate to their strategies social acts and events influenced by them. At the ecological level, the humble inhabitant has his system (or rather, his sub-system) of significations. The fact of living here or there involves the reception, adoption and transmission of such a system, for example that of owner-occupied housing. The system of significations of the inhabitant tells of his passivities and activities: he is received but changed by practice. He is perceived.

Architects seem to have established and dogmatized an ensemble of significations, as such poorly developed and variously labelled as 'function', 'form', 'structure', or rather, functionalism, formalism, and structuralism. They elaborate them not from the significations perceived and lived by those who inhabit, but from their interpretation of inhabiting. It is graphic and visual, tending towards metalanguage. It is graphism and visualization. Given that these architects form a social body, they attach themselves to institutions, their system tends to close itself off, impose itself and elude all criticism. There is cause to formulate this system, often put forward without any other procedure or precaution, as *planning* by extrapolation.

This theory which one could legitimately call planning, close to the meanings of that old practice of *to inhabit* (that is, the human) which would add to these partial facts a general theory of urban *time-spaces*, which would reveal a new practice emerging from this elaboration can be envisaged only as the practical application of a comprehensive theory of the city and the urban which could go beyond current scissions and separations, particularly those existing between philosophy and the sciences of the city, the global and the partial. Current planning projects could figure in this development – but only within an unwavering critique of their ideological and strategic implications. Inasmuch as we can define it, our object – the urban – will never today be entirely present in our reflections. More than any another object, it possesses a very complex quality of totality in act and potential the object of research gradually uncovered, and which will be either slowly or never exhausted. To take this object as a given truth is operate a mythifying ideology. Knowledge must envisage a considerable number of methods to grasp this object, and cannot fasten itself onto a particular approach. Analytical configurations will follow as closely as possible the internal articulations of this 'thing' which is not a thing; they will be accompanied by reconstructions which will never be realized. Descriptions, analyses and attempts at synthesis can never be passed off as being exhaustive or definitive. All these notions, all these batteries of concepts will come into play: form, structure, function, level, dimension, dependent and independent variables, correlations, totality, ensemble, system, etc. Here as elsewhere, but more than elsewhere, the residue reveals itself to be most precious. Each 'object' constructed will in turn be submitted to critical examination. Within the possible, this will be accomplished and submitted to experimental verification. The science of the city requires a historical period to make itself and to orient social practice.

This science is necessary but not sufficient. We can perceive its limits at the same time as its necessity. Planning thought proposes the establishment or reconstitution of highly localized, highly particularized and centralized social units whose linkages and tensions would re-establish an urban unity endowed with a complex interior order, with its hierarchy and a supple structure. More specifically, sociological thought seeks an understanding and reconstitution of the integrative capacities of the urban as well as the conditions of practical participation. Why not? But only under one condition: never to protect these fragmented and therefore partial attempts from criticism, practical assessment and global preoccupation.

Knowledge can therefore construct and propose models. In this sense each object is but a model of urban reality. Nevertheless, such a reality will never become manageable as a thing and will never become instrumental even for the most operational knowledge. Who would not hope that the city becomes again what it was – the act and *oeuvre* of a complex thought? But it cannot remain at the level of wishes and aspirations and an *urban strategy* is not defined. An urban strategy cannot take into account existing strategies and acquired knowledge: science of the city, with its disposition towards the planning of growth and the control of development. Whoever says 'strategies' says the hierarchy of 'variables' to be considered, some having a strategic capacity and others remaining at the tactical level – and says also the power to realize these strategies on the ground. Only groups, social classes and class fractions capable of revolutionary initiative can take over and realize to fruition solutions to urban problems. It is from these social and political forces that the renewed city will become the *oeuvre*. The first thing to do is to defeat currently dominant strategies and ideologies. In the present society that there exist many divergent groups and strategies (for example between the State and the private) does not alter the situation. From questions of landed property to problems of segregation, each project of *urban reform* questions the structures, the immediate (individual) and daily relations of existing society, but also those that one purports to impose by the coercive and institutional means of what remains of urban reality. In itself *reformist*, the strategy of urban renewal becomes 'inevitably' revolutionary, not by force of circumstance, but against the established order. Urban strategy resting on the science of the city needs a social support and political forces to be effective. It cannot act on its own. It cannot but depend on the presence and action of the working class, the only one able to put an end to a segregation directed essentially against it. Only this class, as a class, can decisively contribute to the reconstruction of centrality destroyed by a strategy of segregation and found again in the menacing form of *centres of decision-making*. This does not mean that the working class will make urban society all on its own, but that without it nothing is possible. Without it integration has no meaning and disintegration will continue under the guise of nostalgia and integration. There is there not only an option but an horizon which opens or closes. When the working class is silent, when it is quiescent and cannot accomplish what theory has defined as its 'historical mission', then both the 'subject' and 'object' are lacking. Reflection confirms this absence, which means that it is appropriate to consider two series of propositions:

1   *A political programme of urban reform* not defined by the framework and the possibilities of prevailing society or subjugated to a 'realism', although based on the study of realities. In other words, reform thus understood is not limited to reformism. This programme will therefore have a singular and even paradoxical character. It will be established to be proposed to political forces, parties. One could even add that preferentially it would be presented to 'left' parties, political formations representing or wishing to represent the working class. But it would not be established as a function of these forces and formations. It will have in relation to them a specific character which comes from knowledge, a scientific part. It will be *proposed* (free to be altered) by those who take control of it. Let political forces take their responsibilities. In this domain which engages the future of modern society and that of producers, ignorance and misunderstanding entail responsibilities before history.

2   Mature *planning projects* which consist of models and spatial forms and urban times without concern for their current feasibility or their utopian aspect. It does not seem possible that these models result either from a simple study of existing cities and urban typologies, or from a combination of elements. Other than contrary to experience, the forms of space and time will be invented and proposed to praxis. That imagination be deployed, not the imaginary of escape and evasion which conveys ideologies, but the imaginary which invests itself in *appropriation* (of time, space, physiolocal life and desire). Why not oppose ephemeral cities to the eternal city, and movable centrality to stable centres? All audacities can be premissed. Why limit these propositions only to the morphology of time and space? They could also include the way of living in the city and the development of the urban on this basis.

In these two series there will also be long, medium and short-term propositions constituting urban strategy understood as such.

The society in which we live appears to tend towards plenitude – or at least towards fullness (durable goods and objects, quantity, satisfaction and rationality). In fact it allows a colossal gulf to be dug into which ideologies agitate themselves and the fog of rhetoric spreads. Having left speculation and contemplation, incomplete knowledge and fragmentary divisions, one of the greatest projects active thought can propose for itself is to fill this lacuna – and not only with language.

In a period during which ideologists pronounce abundantly on structures, the destructuration of the city manifests the depth of phenomena, of social and cultural disintegration. Considered as a whole, this society finds itself *incomplete*. Between the sub-systems and the structures consolidated by various means (compulsion, terror, and ideological persuasion), there are holes and chasms. These voids are not there due to chance. They are the places of the possible. They contain the floating and dispersed elements of the possible, but not the power which could assemble them. Moreover, structuring actions and the power of the social void tend to prohibit action and the very presence of such a power. The conditions of the possible can only be realized in the course of a radical metamorphosis.

In this conjuncture, ideology claims to provide an absolute quality to 'scientificity', science appertaining to the real, dissecting it, reconstituting it, and by this fact isolating it from the possible and closing the way. Now, in such a conjuncture science which is fragmentary science can only have a *programmatic* impact. It brings elements to a programme. If one concedes that these elements already constitute a totality, and one wishes to execute this programme literally, one treats the virtual object as a pre-existent technical object. A project is accomplished without criticism and this project fulfills an ideology by projecting it on the ground – that of the technocrats. Although necessary, policy is not enough. It changes during the course of its implementation. Only social force, capable of investing itself in the urban through a long political experience, can take charge of the realization of a programme concerning urban society. Conversely, the science of the city brings to this perspective a theoretical and critical foundation, a positive base. Utopia controlled by dialectical reason serves as a safeguard against supposedly scientific fictions and visions gone astray. Besides, this foundation and base prevent reflection from losing itself in pure policy. Here the dialectical movement presents itself as a relation between science and political power, as a dialogue which actualizes relations of 'theory–practice' and 'critical positive–negative'.

As necessary as science, but not sufficient, *art* brings to the realization of urban society its long meditation on life as drama and pleasure. In addition and especially, art restitutes the meaning of the *oeuvre*, giving it multiple facets of *appropriated* time and space; neither endured nor accepted by a passive resignation, metamorphosed as *oeuvre*. Music shows the appropriation of time, painting and sculpture that of space. If the sciences discover partial determinisms, art and philosophy show how a totality grows out of partial determinisms. It is incumbent on the social force capable of creating urban society to make efficient and effective the unity of art, technique and knowledge. As much the science of the city, art and the history of art are part of a meditation on the urban which wants to make efficient the images which proclaim it. By overcoming this opposition, this meditation striving for action would thus be both utopian and realistic. One could even assert that the maximum of utopianism could unite with the optimum of realism.

Among the contradictions characteristic of our time there are those (particularly difficult ones) between the realities of society and the facts of civilization. On the one hand, genocide, and on the other, medical and other interventions which enable a child to be saved or an agony prolonged. One of the latest but not least contradictions has been shown in this essay: between the *socialization of society* and *generalized segregation*. There are many others, for example, the contradiction between the label of *revolutionary* and the attachment to an obsolete productivist rationalism. The individual, at the centre of social forces due to the pressure of the masses, asserts himself and does not die. *Rights* appear and become customs or prescriptions, usually followed by enactments. And we know how, through gigantic destructions, World Wars, and the terror of nuclear threats, that these concrete rights come to complete the abstract rights of man and the citizen inscribed on the front of buildings by democracy during its revolutionary beginnings: the rights of ages and sexes (the woman, the child and the elderly), rights of conditions (the proletarian, the peasant), rights to training and education, to work, to culture, to rest, to health, to housing. The pressure of the working class has been and remains necessary (but not sufficient) for the recognition of these rights, for their entry into customs, for their inscription into codes which are still incomplete.

Over the last few years and rather strangely, the *right to nature* entered into social practice thanks to *leisure*, having made its way through protestations becoming commonplace against noise, fatigue, the concentrationary universe of cities (as cities are rotting or exploding). A strange journey indeed! Nature enters into exchange value and commodities, to be bought and sold. This 'naturality' which is counterfeited and traded in, is destroyed by commercialized, industrialized and institutionally organized leisure pursuits. 'Nature', or what passes for it, and survives of it, becomes the ghetto of leisure pursuits, the separate place of pleasure and the retreat of 'creativity'. Urban dwellers carry the urban with them, even if they do not bring planning with them! Colonized by them, the countryside has lost the qualities, features and charms of peasant life. The urban ravages the countryside: this urbanized countryside opposes itself to a dispossessed rurality, the extreme case of the deep misery of the inhabitant, the habitat, of to inhabit. Are the rights to nature and to the countryside not destroying themselves?

In the face of this pseudo-right, the *right to the city* is like a cry and a demand. This right slowly meanders through the surprising detours of nostalgia and tourism, the return to the heart of the traditional city, and the call of existent or recently developed centralities. The claim to nature, and the desire to enjoy it displace the right to the city. This latest claim expresses itself indirectly as a tendency to flee the deteriorated and unrenovated city, alienated urban life before at last, 'really' living. The need and the 'right' to nature contradict the right to the city without being able to evade it. (This does not mean that it is not necessary to preserve vast 'natural' spaces).

The *right to the city* cannot be conceived of as a simple visiting right or as a return to traditional cities. It can only be formulated as a transformed and renewed *right to urban life*. It does not matter whether the urban fabric encloses the countryside and what survives of peasant life, as long as the 'urban', place of encounter, priority of use value, inscription in space of a time promoted to the rank of a supreme resource among all resources, finds its morphological base and its practico-material realization. Which presumes an integrated theory of the city and urban society, using the resources of science and art. Only the working class can become the agent, the social carrier or support of this realization. Here again, as a century ago, it denies and contests, by its very existence, the class strategy directed against it. As a hundred years ago, although under new conditions, it gathers the interests (overcoming the immediate and the superficial) of the whole society and firstly of all those who *inhabit*. Who can ignore that the

Olympians of the new bourgeois aristocracy no longer inhabit. They go from grand hotel to grand hotel, or from castle to castle, commanding a fleet or a country from a yacht. They are everywhere and nowhere. That is how they fascinate people immersed into everyday life. They transcend everyday life, possess nature and leave it up to the cops to contrive culture. Is it essential to describe at length, besides the condition of youth, students and intellectuals, armies of workers with or without white collars, people from the provinces, the colonized and semi-colonized of all sorts, all those who endure a well-organized daily life, is it here necessary to exhibit the derisory and untragic misery of the inhabitant, of the suburban dweller and of the people who stay in residential ghettos, in the mouldering centres of old cities and in the proliferations lost beyond them? One only has to open one's eyes to understand the daily life of the one who runs from his dwelling to the station, near or far away, to the packed underground train, the office or the factory, to return the same way in the evening and come home to recuperate enough to start again the next day. The picture of this generalized misery would not go without a picture of 'satisfactions' which hides it and becomes the means to elude it and break free from it.

15

Perspective or Prospective?

Since its beginnings, classical philosophy, which has had as social base and theoretical foundation the city, thought the city, and endeavours to determine the image of the ideal city. The *Critias* of Plato sees in the city an image of the world, or rather of the cosmos, a microcosm. Urban time and space reproduce on earth the configuration of the universe as the philosopher discovers it.

If today one wants a representation of the 'ideal' city and of its relations to the universe, one will not find this image with the philosophers and even less in an analytical vision which divides urban reality into fractions, sectors, relations and correlations. One has to find it among the writers of science fiction. In science fiction novels, every possible and impossible variation of future urban society has been foreseen. Sometimes the old urban cores agonize, covered with an urban fabric more or less thick, more or less sclerosed or cancerous, which proliferates and spreads over the planet. In these cores destined to disappearance after a long decline, live or vegetate failures, artists, intellectuals and gangsters. Sometimes colossal cities reconstitute themselves and carry onto a higher level former struggles for power. In Azimov's magistral work, *The Foundation*, an entire planet is covered by a giant city, Trentor, which has all the means of knowledge and power with which it dominates, as a centre of decision-making, a whole galaxy. After many gigantic episodes, Trentor saves the universe and brings it to its end, that is, to the 'reign of endings', joy and happiness, for excesses are finally overcome and the time of the world finally appropriated in a cosmic space. Between these two extremes, the visionaries of science fiction have also their intermediary versions: the city ruled by a powerful computer, the city of a highly specialized and vital production which moves among planetary systems and galaxies, etc.

Is it necessary to explore so far ahead the horizon of horizons? The ideal city, the New Athens, is already there to be seen in the image which Paris and New York and some other cities project. The centre of decision-making and the centre of consumption meet. Their alliance on the ground based on a strategic convergence creates an inordinate centrality. We already know that this decision-making centre includes all the channels of information and means of cultural and scientific development. Coercion and persuasion converge with the power of decision-making and the capacity to consume. Strongly occupied and inhabited by these new Masters, this centre is held by them. Without necessarily owning it all, they possess this privileged space, axis of a strict spatial policy. Especially, they have the privilege to possess time. Around them, distributed in space according to formalized principles, there are human groups which can no longer bear the name of slaves, serfs, vassals or even proletarians. What could they be called? Subjugated, they provide a multiplicity of services for the Masters of this State solidly established on the city. These Masters have around for them every cultural and other pleasure, from nightclubs to the splendours of the opera – not excluding remote controlled amusements. Could this not be the true New Athens, with its minority of free citizens, possessing and enjoying social spaces, dominating an enormous mass of subjugated people, in principle free, genuinely and perhaps voluntarily servants, treated and manipulated according to rational methods? Are not the scholars, sociologists leading, in this very different from ancient philosophers, not themselves the servants of State and Order, under the pretence of empiricism and rigour, of scientificity? The possibilities can even be assessed. Directors, heads, presidents of this and that, elites, leading writers and artists, well-known entertainers and media people, make up one per cent, or just under half a million of the new notables in France in the twenty-first century, each with their family and their following, and their own 'firm'. The domination of and by centrality in no way denies the possession of secondary domains – the enjoyment of nature, the sea, the mountains, ancient cities (available through trips, hotels, etc.). Next are about four per cent of executives, administrators, engineers and scholars. After selection, the most eminent of these are admitted into the heart of the city. For this selection, incomes and society rituals might be sufficient. State capitalism has carefully organized for other privileged subordinates domains distributed according to a rational plan. Before reaching this goal State capitalism has carefully prepared it. Without omitting the realization of several urban ghettos, it has organized for scholars and for science a severely competitive sector: in the universities and laboratories, scholars and intellectuals have confronted each other on a purely competitive basis, with a zeal worthy of a better job, for the best interest of the Masters, the economic and political, for the glory and joy of the Olympians. Indeed, these secondary elites are assigned to residence in science parks, university campuses – ghettos for intellectuals. The mass, under pressure from many constraints, spontaneously houses itself in satellite cities, planned suburbs, and other more or less residential ghettos. There is for it only carefully measured space. Time eludes it. It leads it daily life bound (perhaps unwittingly), to the requirement of the concentration of powers. But this is not a concentrationary universe. All this can quite do without the ideology of freedom under the pretence of rationality, organization, and programming. These masses who do not deserve the name of people, or popular classes, or working class live relatively well. Apart from the fact that their daily life is remote-controlled and the permanent threat of unemployment weighs heavily on them, contributing to a latent and generalized terror.

If someone smiles at this utopia, he is wrong. But how to prove it? When his eyes will open, it will be too late. He demands proof. How do you show light to a blind person, or the horizon to a myopic one – even if he knows the theory of wholes, or of 'clusters', the finesses of variance analysis, or the precise charms of linguistics?

Since the Middle Ages, each epoch of European civilization has had its image of the possible, its dream, its fantasies of hell and paradise. Each period, and perhaps each generation has had its representation of the best of all possible worlds, or of a new life, an important, if not essential part of all ideologies. In order to accomplish this function, the eighteenth century, seemingly so rich, had only the rather feeble image of the noble savage and exotic islands. To this exoticism, some men of that century added a closer but somewhat prettified representation of England. In relation to them, *we* are richly endowed. By *we* is meant a poorly defined crowd, generally intellectuals, living and thinking in France at the beginning of the second half of the twentieth-century. We have many models, horizons, and avenues which do not converge to imagine the future: the

USSR and the United States, China, Yugoslavia, Cuba, Israel, even Sweden or Switzerland – and without forgetting the Bororos.

While French society is becoming urbanized and Paris is being transformed, and certain powers, if not State power, are modelling France of the year 2,000, nobody is thinking about the ideal city or what is happening to the real city. Utopia attaches itself to numerous more or less distant and unknown or misunderstood realities, but no longer to real and daily life. It is no longer begotten in the absences and lacunae which cruelly puncture surrounding reality. The gaze turns away, leaves the horizon, loses itself in the clouds, elsewhere. Such is the power of diversion of ideologies, at the exact moment when we no longer believe in ideology, but in realism and rationalism!

Previously, by refuting partial disciplines and their interdisciplinary attempts, one was also asserting that *synthesis belongs to the political* (that is, that all synthesis of analytical facts about urban reality conceals under philosophy or an ideology a *strategy*). Statesmen, experts and specialists should certainly not be given control of decision-making. The term *political* is not here used so narrowly. Such a proposition must be understood in the opposite way to what has been expressed here. The capacity of synthesis belongs to political forces which are in fact social forces (classes and fractions of classes, groupings or class alliances). They exist or not, they manifest and express themselves or not. They speak or do not speak. It is up to them to indicate social needs, to influence existing institutions, to open the horizon and lay claims to a future which will be their *oeuvre*. If the inhabitants of various categories and strata allow themselves to be manoeuvred and manipulated, displaced anywhere under the pretext of social mobility, if they accept the conditions of an exploitation more refined and extensive than before, too bad for them. If the working class is silent, if it does not act, either spontaneously or by the mediation of its institutional representatives and mandatories, segregation will continue resulting again in a vicious circle. Segregation is inclined to prohibit protest, contest, action, by dispersing those who protest, contest, and act. In this perspective political life will either challenge or reaffirm the centre of political decision-making. For parties and men, this option is the *criterion of democracy*.

The politician needs a *theory* to help him determine its course but this presents some great difficulties. How can there be a theory of urban society, the city and *the urban*, of realities and possibilities, without synthesis?

Two dogmatic disciplines, philosophical systematization and systematization from partial analyses under the pretence of such disciplines or of so-called interdisciplinary research have already been rejected. There can be no possibility of an analysis accomplished in the context of knowledge. The unity outlined is defined by a convergence which only practice can actualize between:

1 the goals, spread over time of political action, from the possible to the impossible, that is, what is possible here and now, to what is impossible today, but will become possible tomorrow in the course of this very action
2 the theoretical elements brought to the analysis of urban reality, that is, the ensemble of knowledge brought into play during the course of political action, ordered, used and dominated by this action
3 the theoretical elements contributed by philosophy, which appear in a new light, as its history inscribes itself in another perspective – philosophical meditation transforming itself according to reality or rather, the realization to accomplish.
4 the theoretical elements brought by art, conceived as a capacity to transform reality, to *appropriate* at the highest level the facts of the 'lived', of time, space, the body and desire.

From this convergence, one can define the preceding conditions. It is essential to consider no longer industrialization and urbanization separately, but to perceive in urbanization the meaning, the goal and the finality of industrialization. In other words, it is essential to aim no longer for economic growth for its own sake, and economistic ideology which entails strategic objectives, namely, superprofit and capitalist overexploitation, the control of the economic (which fails precisely because of this) to the advantage of the State. Concepts of economic equilibrium, harmonious growth, structural maintenance (structured–structuring relations being existing relations of production and property) must be subordinated to more powerful concepts potentially of development, and of concrete rationality emerging from conflicts.

In other words, *growth must be guided*. Very common formulations which pass for democratic (growth, well-being for all, the general

interest) lose their meaning and this applies to liberalism as economistic ideology as much as to centralized State planning. Such an ideology, whether or not prospective, reduces the outlook on such issues
as the increase of wages and the better distribution of national
revenue, or even on the review and ajustment of the capital–labour
relation.

To direct growth towards development, therefore towards *urban
society*, means firstly to prospect *new needs*, knowing that such needs
are discovered in the course of their emergence and are revealed in the
course of their prospection. They do not pre-exist as objects. They do
not feature in the 'real' described by market studies and studies of
'individual' motivation. Consequently, this means substituting social
planning whose theory is hardly elaborated. Social needs lead to the
production of new 'goods' which are not this or that *object*, but social
objects in space and time. Man of urban society is *already* a man rich
in needs: the man of rich needs awaiting their objectification and
realization. Urban society overtakes the old and the new poverty, as
much the destitution of isolated subjectivity as that humdrum old need
for money with its worn symbols of the 'pure' gaze, the 'pure' sign, the
'pure' spectacle.

Thus, direction is not defined by an effective synthesis, but by a
convergence, a virtuality which is outlined but realized only at the
limit. This limit is not somewhere in the infinite, and yet it be can
reached by successive leaps and bounds. It is impossible to settle in it
and to establish it as an accomplished reality. Hence this is the
essential feature of the method already considered and named 'transduction', the construction of a virtual object approached from experimental facts. The horizon opens up and calls for actualization.

The orientation reacts upon researched facts. In this way research
ceases to be either indeterminate, that is, empiricist, or a simple
confirmation of a thesis, that is, *dogmatist*. In this light, philosophy
and its history, art and its metamorphoses appear transformed.

As for the analytical aspect of urban research, it modifies itself by
the fact that research has already found 'something' at the outset and
that the direction or orientation influences the hypothesis. There is no
more question of isolating the points of space and time, of considering
separately activities and functions, or of studying apart from each
other behaviours or images, distributions and relations. These various
aspects of social production, that of the city and urban society, are

situated in relation to a framework of explanation and forecasting. Since method consists as much in overcoming ecological description as structural and functional analysis, in order to reach out to the concrete of urban drama, formal evidence could be provided by the general theory of forms. According to this theory, there is a form of the city: assembly, simultaneity, encounter. Transduction is the intellectual approach linked to these operations which codifies them or supports them methodologically.

Scientifically speaking, the distinction between *strategic variables* and *tactical variables* seems fundamental. The first ones, as soon as they are identified, subordinate the second. Increase of wages? Better distribution of national revenue? Nationalization of this or that? Very well. But these are tactical variables. In the same way the suppression of urban related constraints would affect the municipalization, nationalization or socialization of building plots. Fine and well. But for what purpose? The increase of rates and rhythms of growth between strategic variables, given that quantitative growth already poses qualitative problems of finality and development. The issue is not only rates of growth, production and revenues, but distribution. Which part of increased production and global revenue will be attributed to social needs, to 'culture', to urban reality? Is not the transformation of daily life part of strategic variables? One could think it so. To take an example, flexible working hours are of interest. This is only a minuscule tactical action. The creation of new networks concerning the life of children and adolescents (crèches, playing fields and sports, etc.), the constitution of a very simple apparatus of social pedagogy, which would inform as much social life itself as sexual life, the art of living and art *tout court*. Such an institution would have much more impact: it would mark the passage from the tactical to the strategic in this field.

The variables of projects elaborated by economists also depend on generally poorly defined strategies. Against class strategies which often use very powerful scientific instruments and which tend to abuse science (no: scientificity – a rigid and coercive ideological apparatus) as means to persuade and impose, what is needed is to turn knowledge around by putting it back on its feet.

Socialism? Of course, that is what it is about. But what socialism? According to which concept and theory of socialist society? Is the definition of this society by the planned organization of production enough? No. Socialism today can only be conceived as production oriented towards social needs, and consequently, towards the needs of urban society. The goals borrowed from simple industrialization are being overtaken and transformed. Such is the thesis or hypothesis formulated here. Conditions and preconditions? We know them: a high level of production and productivity (by breaking with an exploitation reinforced by a relatively decreasing minority of highly productive manual and intellectual workers), and a high technical and cultural level. In addition, the institution of new social relations, especially between governing and governed, between 'subjects' and 'objects' of decision-making. These conditions have virtually been realized in advanced industrial countries. Their formulation does not arise from the *possible*, even if this possible seems far from real and is really far away.

Possibilities relate to a double examination: the *scientific* (project and projection, variations of projects, predictions) and the *imaginary* (at the limit, science fiction). Why should the imaginary enter only outside the real instead of nurturing reality? When there is a loss of thought in and by the imaginary, it is being manipulated. The imaginary is also a social fact. Do not specialists claim for themselves the intervention of imagination and the imaginary when they acclaim the 'man of synthesis', or when they are disposed to welcome the 'nexialist' or the 'generalist'?

For two centuries, industrialization has been promoting commodities – which although they pre-existed, were limited by agrarian and urban structures. It has enabled the virtually unlimited extension of exchange value. It has shown how merchandise is not only a way of putting people in relation to each other, but also a logic, a language, and a world. Commodities have swept away barriers. And this process is not over: the car, the current pilot-object in the world of commodities, is overcoming this last barrier – the city. It was therefore the time of political economy and the two variations of its rule: liberal and state economis. Today the overtaking of economism is being outlined. Towards what? Towards an ethic or an aesthetic, a moralism or an aestheticism? Towards new 'values'? No. What is at stake is an overtaking by and in practice of a change in social practice. Use value, subordinated for centuries to exchange value, can now come first again. How? By and in urban society, from this reality which still resists and preserves for us use value, the city. A weakened but true vision of this truth is an urban reality for 'users' and not for capitalist speculators, builders and technicians.

Here we can envisage a strategic variable: to limit the importance of the car industry in the economy of a country and the place of the 'car-object' in daily life. To substitute the car for other techniques, other objects, other means of transport such as public ones. This is a rather simple and trivial example but demonstrates the subordination of the 'real' to a strategy.

The problem of *leisure* forces one to think even more clearly of a strategy. To define it in its full scope, it is important to firstly destroy a few fantasies mixed up with ideology. The social imaginary furnished by ideology and advertising, as well as the sad reality of 'hobbies' and miniaturized 'creativity' blocks the horizon. Neither holidays, nor industrialized cultural production, nor leisure in or outside daily life resolve this problem. Their images prevent it from being posed. The problem is to put an end to the separations of 'daily life – leisure' or 'daily life – festivity'. It is to restitute the *fête* by changing daily life. The city was a space occupied at one and the same time by productive labour, by *oeuvres*, and by festivities. It should find again this function beyond functions, in a metamorphosed urban society. One of the strategic aims can be formulated in this way, although it is only a formulation of what is happening today without grace or splendour in cities which attempt to recreate the *fête* with festivities and festivals.

Each type of society and each mode of production has had its type of city. The relative discontinuity of modes of production defines the history of urban reality, although this is not exclusive and other periodization are possible. Another periodization resting on a specific centrality would show more closely the succession of urban types but would not coincide completely with the primary periodization.

The oriental city, reason and result of the Asiatic mode of production, offers its triumphal way for gatherings and meetings. Armies which protect and oppress the agricultural territories administered by the city leave and return through this way on which are deployed military parades and religious processions. The palace of the prince, the *umbilical*, the *omphalos*, is the centre of the world, the point of departure and arrival. The sacred enclosure captures and condenses sacredness diffused over the whole of the territory. It manifests the eminent right of the sovereign, inseparable possession and sacredness.

The triumphal way penetrates into the enclosure through a door, monument among monuments. It is the door of the true urban centre, the centre of the world not open to gatherings. Around the door are gathered guards, caravaneers, vagrants and robbers. The tribunal sits here and gathers the inhabitants for spontaneous assemblies. It is the place of urban order and disorder, of revolts and repressions.

In the Greek and Roman antique city, centrality is attached to an empty space, the agora and the forum. It is a place for assembly. There is an important difference between the agora and the forum. Prohibitions characterize the latter and buildings will quickly cover it up, taking away from it its character of open space. It is not disjointed from the centre of the world: the hole, the sacred–damned *mundus*, the place from which souls leave, where the condemned and unwanted children are thrown. The Greeks did not put emphasis on horror, on the links between urban centrality and the underworld of the dead and the souls. Their thought of their city is related to the Cosmos, a luminous distribution of places in space, rather than to the world, passage to darkness and of underworld wanderings. This shadow, more Roman than Hellenic, weighs over the West.

For its part, the medieval city soon integrated merchants and commodities and established them in its centre; the market-place. A commercial centre characterized by the proximity of the church and the exclusion of the enclosure – a heterotopy of territory. The symbolism and the functions of this enclosure are different from that of the oriental or antique city. The territory belongs to the lords, peasants, vagrants and plunderers. Urban centrality welcomes produce and people. It forbids its access to those who threaten its essential and economic function, thus heralding and preparing capitalism. Nevertheless, centrality thus functionalized and structured remains the object of all attentions. It is embellished. The smallest hamlet, the smallest barbican have their arcades, the possibly sumptuous monumental hall and municipal buildings which are places of pleasure. The church blesses commerce and gives a good conscience to the busy citizens. Within the limits of commercial rationality, gatherings which are part of this double feature of the religious and the rational take place in the square, between the church and the market. How these two features associate by colliding together in combination or in conflict, is another story.

The capitalist city has created the centre of consumption. Industrial production did not constitute centrality as such, except in the special cases – if one can say that – of big enterprise around which a workers' city was erected. We already know the double character of the capitalist city: place of consumption and consumption of place. Businesses densify in the centre, and attract expensive shops, luxury foodstuffs and products. The establishment of this centrality is partial to the old cores, the spaces appropriated during the course of a previous history. It cannot go without it. In these privileged sites, the consumer also comes to consume space; the collection of objects in the windows of boutiques becomes the reason and the pretext for the gathering of people. They look, they see, they talk and talk with each other. And it is the place of encounters amongst the collection of things. What is said and written, comes before everything else: it is the world of commodities, of the language of commodities, of the glory and the extension of exchange value. It tends to absorb use value in exchange and exchange value. Yet, use and use value resist irreducibly. This irreducibility of the urban centre plays an essential role in this argument.

It is neo-capitalism which superimposes, without denying or destroying it, the centre of consumption upon the centre of decision-making. It no longer gathers together people and things, but data and knowledge. It inscribes in an eminently elaborated form of simultaneity the conception of the whole incorporated into an electronic brain, using the quasi-instantaneity of communications, thus overcoming obstacles such as the loss of information, the meaningless accumulations of elements, redundancies, etc. With a disinterested aim? Certainly not. Since the problem is political, those who constitute specific centrality aim for power or are its instruments. The issue is not simply to 'master technique' in general, but to master clearly defined techniques with socio-political implications. What is at stake is to control the potential masters: those whose power appropriates all possibilities.

The controversy has been taken up again and pushed towards new conclusions to propose and defend another centrality. The possibility of an urban society here outlined cannot be satisfied with centralities of the past, although it does not destroy them and appropriates them by altering them. What to project? There is something barren about cultural centrality. It easily allows itself to be organized, institutionalized, and later, bureaucratized. There is nothing more derisive than the bureaucrat of culture. The educational is attractive, but neither seduces nor enchants. Pedagogy implies localized practices, not so-cialized centrality. Moreover, there is nothing to prove that there is 'one' or 'a' culture. Subordinated to this entity, 'culture' and its ideology, 'culturalism', theatre, the greatest of games, is threatened with boredom. The elements of a superior unit, the fragments and aspects of 'culture', the educational, the formative and the informa-tional, can be collected together. But from where can the contents of the principle of assembly be derived? From play, *ludo*, a term which must be understood here in its broadest and deepest meaning. Sport is play and so is the theatre, in a way more involving than the cinema. Fairs, collective games of all sorts, survive at the interfaces of an organized consumer society, in the holes of a serious society which perceives itself as structured and systematical and which claims to be technical. As for the old places of assembly, they are largely devoid of meaning: the *fête* dies or leaves it. That they should find a meaning again does not preclude the creation of places appropriate to a renewed *fête* fundamentally linked to play.

No doubt that so-called consumer society suggests this direction. Leisure centres, leisure societies, cities of luxury and pleasures, holiday places, show this eloquently with the particular rhetoric of advertis-ing. Therefore, all that is needed is to give form to this tendency which is still subordinated to the industrial and commercial production of culture in this society. The proposition of this project is to gather together by subordinating to play rather than to subordinate play to the 'seriousness' of culturalism and scientificism, although this does not exclude 'cultural' elements. On the contrary. It collects them together by restoring them in their truth. Only relatively recently and through institutions has the theatre become 'cultural', while play has lost its place and value in society. Would culture not be the accom-modation of the *oeuvre* and style to exchange value, thus allowing for its commercialization, its production and consumption as specific product?

There are implications to the *centrality of play* which is the restora-tion of the meaning of the *oeuvre* that philosophy and art can bring so as to prioritize time over space, not forgetting that time comes to inscribe itself and to be written in a space – and thus replace domina-tion by appropriation.

The space of play has coexisted and still coexists with spaces of exchange and circulation, political space and cultural space. Projects within quantified and accounted 'social space' which lose their qualitative and differentiated spaces relate to a schizophrenia which is concealed under the veils of precision, scientificity and rationality. We have shown above the inevitable outcome of an analytical thought which without safeguards perceives itself as global. This globality is the formalized space of social pathology. There is a continuous path from the concept of *habitat* to schizophrenic space projected as social model. The orientation envisaged here does not consist in suppressing qualified spaces as existing historical differences. On the contrary. These already complex spaces can be further articulated, by emphasizing differences and contrasts, and by stressing quality which implies and overdetermines quantities. To these spaces, one can apply formalized principles of differences and articulation, of superimpositions of contrasts. Thus conceived, social spaces are related to social times and rhythms which are prioritized. One understands more clearly how and up to what point in urban reality elements distribute themselves over a period of time. It is the truth of urban time which lucidly reclaims this role. To *inhabit* finds again its place over habitat. The quality which is promoted presents and represents as *playful*. By *playing* with words, one can say that there will be *play* between the parts of the social whole (plasticity) – to the extent that *play* is proclaimed as supreme value, eminently solemn, if not serious, overtaking use and exchange by gathering them together. And if someone cries out that this utopia has nothing in common with socialism, the answer is that today only the working class still knows how to really play, feels like playing, over and above the claims and programmes, of economism, and political philosophy. How is this shown? Sport and the interest shown in sport and games, including, in television and elsewhere, the degraded forms of ludic life. Already, to city people the urban centre is movement, the unpredictable, the possible and encounters. For them, it is either 'spontaneous theatre' or nothing.

To the extent that the contours of the future city can be outlined, it could be defined by imagining the reversal of the current situation, by pushing to its limits this inverted image of the world upside down. There are currently attempts to establish fixed structures, 'equilibrium structures', stabilities submitted to systematization, and therefore to existing power. At the same time there is a tactical wager on the accelerated obsolescence of consumer goods, ironically known as 'durables'. The ideal city would involve the obsolescence of space: an accelerated change of abode, emplacements and prepared spaces. It would be the *ephemeral city*, the perpetual *oeuvre* of the inhabitants, themselves mobile and mobilized for and by this *oeuvre*. Time comes first. There is no doubt that technology makes possible the ephemeral city, the apogee of play and supreme *oeuvre* and luxury. One can cite the world exhibition in Montreal among other examples! In Montreal.

To put art at the service of the urban does not mean to prettify urban space with works of art. This parody of the possible is a caricature. Rather, this means that time-spaces become works of art and that former art reconsiders itself as source and model of *appropriation* of space and time. Art brings cases and examples of appropriate 'topics': of temporal qualities inscribed in spaces. Music shows how expression and lyricism uses numbering, order and measure. It shows that time, tragic or serious, can absorb and reabsorb calculation. With less force but more precision than music, this is the same for sculpture and painting. Let us not forget that gardens, parks, and landscapes were part of urban life as much as the fine arts, or that the landscape around cities were the works of art of these cities. For example, the Tuscan landscape around Florence, inseparable from its architecture, plays an immense role in Renaissance arts. Leaving aside representation, ornamentation and decoration, art can become *praxis* and *poiesis* on a social scale: the art of living in the city as work of art. Coming back to style and to the *oeuvre*, that is, to the meaning of the monument and the space appropriated in the *fête*, art can create 'structures of enchantment'. Architecture taken separately and on its own, could neither restrict nor create possibilities. Something more, something better, something else, is needed. Architecture as art and technique also needs an orientation. Although necessary, it could not suffice. Nor could architecture set and define its own aims and strategy. In other words, the future of art is not artistic, but urban, because the future of 'man' is not discovered in the cosmos, or in the people, or in production, but in urban society. In the same way art and philosophy must reconsider itself in relation to this perspective. The problematic of the *urban* renews the problematic of philosophy, its categories and methods. Without a need to break or reject them, these categories *accept* something else new: a meaning.

The right to the city manifests itself as a superior form of rights: right to freedom, to individualization in socialization, to habitat and to inhabit.

The right to the *oeuvre*, to participation and *appropriation* (clearly distinct from the right to property), are implied in the right to the city.

With regards to philosophy, three periods are identifiable. This is a periodization which is particular among those which mark the continuum of becoming. In the first stage, philosophy meditates on the city as partial whole at the heart of totality, world and cosmos. In the second, philosophy reflects on a transcending totality of the city: history, 'man', society, State. It accepts and even confirms several separations in the name of totality. It sanctions the analytical hold by believing it is refuting or overcoming it. In the third period philosophy competes for the promotion of a rationality and a practice which transform themselves into urban rationality and planning practice.

16

The Realization of Philosophy

Let us take up again the thread of the argument and show its continuity to its conclusions. Knowledge is in an untenable situation. Philosophy wanted to reach the total but passed by it, unable to grasp it and even less to realize it. By giving it a representation which was systematized, speculative and contemplative, in its own way it mutilated totality. And yet, only philosophy had and still has the sense of the total. Partial and fragmentary knowledge claimed to have achieved certainties and realities, but have only delivered fragments. They cannot go without synthesis, yet cannot legitimize their right to it.

From its beginnings Greek philosophy linked itself to greatness, and also the miseries and limitations of the Greek city – slavery and the subordination of the individual to the *Polis*. Two thousand years later, Hegel declared the realization of philosophical rationality released by centuries of reflection and meditation, but in and by the State. How to get out of these quandaries? How to resolve contradictions?

Industrial production has upset notions concerning the social capacity to act, to create anew, and to master material nature. Philosophy could no longer sustain its traditional mission, nor the philosopher his vocation, to define man, the human, society and the world while taking charge of the creation of man by his effort, his will, his struggle against determinisms and hazards. Science and the sciences, technology, the organization and rationalization of industry were coming onto the scene. Were 2,000 years of philosophy to go to the grave? No. Industry contributes new means but has no purpose or meaning in itself. It throws *products* into the world. Philosophy (with art and works of art), a supreme *oeuvre*, says what is *appropriation*, not the technical mastery of material nature which produces products and exchange values. Therefore, the philosopher must speak, *say the meaning* of industrial production, as long as he does not speculate on it and use it as a theme to prolong the old manner of philosophizing. Instead he must take it as *means of realizing philosophy*, that is, the *philosophical project* of man in the world: desire and reason, spontaneity and reflection, vitality and containment, domination and appropriation, determinisms and liberties. Philosophy cannot realize itself without art (as model of appropriation of time and space), accomplishing itself fully in social practice and without science and technology, as means, not being fully used, without the proletarian condition being overcome.

This theoretical revolution begun by Marx was later obscured, industrial production, economic growth, organizational rationality, the consumption of products, becoming ends rather than means, subordinated to a superior end. Today, the *realization of philosophy* can take up again its meaning, that is, give a meaning as much to history as to actuality. The thread interrupted for a century is renewed. The theoretical situation is released and the gulf is filled between the total and the partial or fragmentary, between the uncertain whole and the all too certain fragments. From the moment that urban society reveals the meaning of industrialization, these concepts play a new role. Theoretical revolution continues and urban revolution (the revolutionary side of urban reform and urban strategy), comes to the fore. Theoretical revolution and political change go together.

Theoretical thought aims at the realization of humanity other than that of a society of low productivity (that of the epochs of non-abundance, or rather, of the non-possibility of abundance), and that of a productivist society. In a society and an urban life delivered from its ancient limitations, those of rarity and economism, technologies, art and knowledge come to the service of daily life so as to metamorphose it. Thus can be defined the realization of philosophy. It is no longer a question of a philosophy of the city and of an historico-social philosophy alongside a science of the city. The realization of philosophy gives a meaning to the sciences of social reality. At the outset, it refutes the accusation of 'sociologism' which will no doubt be made against the hypotheses and theses expressed here. Neither philosophism, nor scientism, nor pragmatism nor sociologism, nor psychologism, nor economism. Something else is proclaimed.

17

Theses on the City, the Urban and Planning

(1) Two groups of questions and two orders of urgency have disguised the problems of the city and urban society: questions of housing and the 'habitat' (related to a housing policy and architectural technologies) and those of industrial organization and global planning. The first from below, the second from above, have produced, hidden from attention, a rupture of the traditional morphology of cities, while the urbanization of society was taking place. Hence, a new contradiction adding to other unresolved contradictions of existing society, aggravating them and giving them another meaning.

(2) These two groups of problems have been and are posed by economic growth and industrial production. Practical experience shows that there can be growth without social development (that is, quantitative growth without qualitative development). In these conditions, changes in society are more apparent than real. Fetishism and ideology of change (in other words, the ideology of modernity) conceal the stagnation of essential social relations. The development of society can only be conceived in urban life, by the realization of urban society.

(3) The double process of industrialization and urbanization loses all meaning if one does not conceive urban society as aim and finality of industrialization, and if urban life is subordinated to industrial growth. The latter provides the conditions and the means of urban society. To proclaim industrial rationality as necessary and sufficient is to destroy the sense (the orientation, the goal) of the process. At first industrialization produces urbanization negatively (the breakup of the

traditional city, of its morphology, of its practico-material reality) and then is ready to get down to work. Urban society begins on the ruins of the ancient city and its agrarian environment. During these changes, the relation between industrialization and urbanization is transformed. The city ceases to be the container the passive receptacle of products and of production. What subsists and is strengthened of urban reality in its dislocation, the *centre of decision-making*, henceforth enters into the *means of production and the systems of exploitation of social labour* by those who control information, culture and the powers of decision-making themselves. Only one theory enables the use of these practical facts and the effective realization of urban society.

(4) For this realization, neither the organization of private enterprise, nor global planning, although necessary, suffice. A leap forward of rationality is accomplished. Neither the State, nor private enterprise can provide indispensable models of rationality and reality.

(5) The realization of urban society calls for a planning oriented towards social needs, those of urban society. It necessitates a science of the city (of relations and correlations in urban life). Although necessary, these conditions are not sufficient. A social and political force capable of putting these means into *oeuvres* is equally indispensable.

(6) The working class suffers the consequences of the rupture of ancient morphologies. It is victim of a segregation, a class strategy licensed by this rupture. Such is the present form of the negative situation of the proletariat. In the major industrial countries the old proletarian immiseration declines and tends to disappear. But a new misery spreads, which mainly affects the proletariat without sparing other social strata and classes: the poverty of the habitat that of the inhabitant submitted to a daily life organized (in and by a bureaucratized society of organized consumption). To those who would still doubt its existence as class, what identifies the working class on the ground is segregation and the misery of its 'to inhabit'.

(7) In these difficult conditions, at the heart of a society which cannot completely oppose them and yet obstructs them, rights which define

civilization (in, but often *against* society – *by*, but often *against* culture) find their way. These rights which are not well recognized, progressively become customary before being inscribed into formalized codes. They would change reality if they entered into social practice: right to work, to training and education, to health, housing, leisure, to life. Among these rights in the making features the *right to the city* (not to the ancient city, but to urban life, to renewed centrality, to places of encounter and exchange, to life rhythms and time uses, enabling the full and complete *usage* of these moments and places, etc.). The proclamation and realization of urban life as the rule of use (of exchange and encounter disengaged from exchange value) insist on the mastery of the economic (of exchange value, the market, and commodities) and consequently is inscribed within the perspectives of the revolution under the hegemony of the working class.

(8) For the working class, rejected from the centres towards the peripheries, dispossessed of the city, expropriated thus from the best outcomes of its activity, this right has a particular bearing and significance. It represents for it at one and the same time a means and an end, a way and a horizon: but this virtual action of the working class also represents the general interests of civilization and the particular interests of all social groups of 'inhabitants', for whom integration and participation become obsessional without making their obsession effective.

(9) The revolutionary transformation of society has industrial production as ground and lever. This is why it had to be shown that the urban centre of decision-making can no longer consider itself in the present society (of neo-capitalism or of monopoly capitalism associated to the State), outside the means of production, their property and their management. Only the taking in charge by the working class of planning and its political agenda can profoundly modify social life and open another era: that of socialism in neo-capitalist countries. Until then transformations remain superficial, at the level of signs and the consumption of signs, language and metalanguage, a secondary discourse, a discourse on previous discourses. Therefore, it is not without reservations that one can speak of urban revolution. Nevertheless, the orientation of industrial production on social needs is not a secondary fact. The finality thus brought to plans transforms them. In this way

urban reform has a revolutionary bearing. As in the twentieth century agrarian reform gradually disappears from the horizon, urban reform becomes a revolutionary reform. It gives rise to a strategy which opposes itself to class strategy dominant today.

(10) Only the proletariat can invest its social and political activity in the realization of urban society. Equally, only it can renew the meaning of productive and creative activity by destroying the ideology of consumption. It therefore has the capacity to produce a new humanism, different from the old liberal humanism which is ending its course – of *urban man* for whom and by whom the city and his own daily life in it become *oeuvre, appropriation*, use value (and not exchange value), by using all the means of science, art, technology and the domination over material nature.

(11) Nevertheless, difference persists between *product* and *oeuvre*. To the meaning of the production of products (of the scientific and technical mastery of material nature) must be added, to later predominate, the meaning of the *oeuvre*, of *appropriation* (of time, space, the body and desire). And this in and by urban society which is beginning. Now, the working class does not spontaneously have the sense of the *oeuvre*. It is dimmed, having almost disappeared along with crafts and skills and 'quality'. Where can be found this precious deposit, this sense of the *oeuvre*? From where can the working class receive it to carry it to a superior degree by uniting it with productive intelligence and dialectic practical reason? Philosophy and the whole of philosophical tradition on the one hand, and on the other all of art (not without a radical critique of their gifts and presents) contain the sense of the *oeuvre*.

(12) This calls for, apart from the economic and political revolution (planning oriented towards social needs and democratic control of the State and self-management), a permanent cultural revolution.

There is no incompatibility between these levels of total revolution, no more than between urban strategy (revolutionary reform aiming at the realization of urban society on the basis of an advanced and planned industrialization) and strategy aiming at the transformation of traditional peasant life by industrialization. Moreover in most countries today the realization of urban society goes through the agrarian form and industrialization. There is no doubt that a world front is possible, and equally that it is impossible today. This utopia projects as it often does on the horizon a 'possible–impossible'. Happily, or otherwise, time, that of history and social practice, differs from the time of philosophies. Even if it does not produce the irreversible, it can produce the difficult to repair. Marx wrote that humanity does not only ask itself problems that it can resolve. Some today believe that men now only ask themselves insoluble problems. They deny reason. None the less, there are perhaps problems which are easy to resolve, whose solutions are near, very near, and that people do not ask themselves.

Paris 1967 – centenary of *Capital*

PART III

Space and Politics

18

Introduction

When a text wants to have a theoretical reach and claims to be self-sufficient, it is because the author has firstly proceeded to delineate and attribute to himself part of a field which he is attempting to close. A fairly crude, always suspect, yet habitual operation of private appropriation which passes off as legitimate given that private property includes ideas and knowledge! More than one scholar should apologize for putting up fences around his garden in order to cultivate it at leisure. Here, the author apologizes because none of the articles in this volume can be read without referring to works published elsewhere on everyday life, space, various rights (the right to the city, the right to difference) and on the reproduction of social relations of production, etc.

Research on the city and the urban refer to that concerning space which will be the object of a work to be published under the title *Production of Space*. This theory of social space encompasses on the one hand the critical analysis of urban reality and on the other that of everyday life. Indeed, everyday life and the urban, indissolubly linked, at one and the same time products and production, occupy a social space generated through them and inversely. The analysis is concerned with the whole of practico-social activities, as they are entangled in a complex space, urban and everyday, ensuring up to a point the reproduction of relations of production (that is, social relations). The global synthesis is realized through this actual space, its critique and its knowledge.

In this way is constructed an ensemble in which each item has a specificity, relating to a certain level on a certain aspect or element. Despite the connection between its elements and aspects, this ensemble has nothing to do with a system or a 'synthesis' in the usual sense. Its meaning? Its aim? It is not to show a coherence or cohesion, but to seek by trial and error where can be located in time and space the *point of no return* and of *no recourse* – not on an individual or group scale, but on a global scale. This moment has nothing to do with historicism or a classical theory of crises: it would be nevertheless crucial. It is a question of metamorphosis or self-destruction (one not excluding the other). It would be the moment when the reproduction of existing relations of production would cease either because degradation and dissolution sweep it away, or because new relations are produced displacing and replacing old ones. The possibility of such a moment (a perspective which does not coincide exactly with the usual theory of revolution) defines a strategic hypothesis. It is not an indisputable and positively established certainty. It does not exclude other possibilities (for example, the destruction of the planet).

Haunted by this moment, many exert themselves to put it off, cast it aside, and exorcize through ideological magic the images which have been conjured up. Councils meet to discourse gravely and to maintain the representations (ideologies) which disguise the actual due date. Indeed, pollution, the environment, ecology and ecosystems, growth and its finality, all fragment and conceal the problems of space. Meanwhile, others invoke a fateful moment, wishing to hasten destiny by worsening it. They are nihilists driven by what they call the 'death wish'. Perhaps the best choice for a reflection which wishes itself knowledge and act, consists in not giving in to catastrophism, in determining a limited but quite precise point of attack, involving a tactic and strategy of thought.

Here we are trying neither to dramatize the situation nor neutralize it. It is possible that the moment of no return is nigh, that one should prepare oneself for it. The forces of destruction can no longer be described; they no longer have, as Jean-Clarence Lambert writes in *Opus* (June 1972) name or face. They are System, the only one, that of negation and death, which under a positive appearance attacks in its innermost depth existence itself. Sometimes, in the current prosperity of capitalist France, one wants to cry out: 'Beware! Revolution or death . . .' This does not mean, 'Let us die for the revolution', but rather 'If you do not want us to die, make the revolution, swiftly, totally'. This total world revolution should put an end to power, to this power which dominates human beings and the being of 'man' without dominating any of the forces which come from them and turn against them: neither technique, demography, or space! Over whom is it exercised? On those who could appropriate for themselves these forces which have become foreign, these deadly realities. There is no abuse of power, for always and everywhere power abuses. Total revolution should put an end to this *abstract power* which claims to use means for an unknown end, while it has become an end in itself. This revolution would put an end to it by substituting *powers* of appropriation and re-appropriation. The idea of complete *subversion*, that of *revolution* aims at the destruction of politics, because all State power is destructive. Upon close examination, the first objective must be the *limitation* of power. For this the threat of its complete destruction is essential. Accordingly, the Church allowed its ambitions to be curtailed only when faced with atheism which threatened it. Scientism and technicism do not back down from philosophical criticism but from occultism and magic. 'Necessary rights' of habeas corpus and right to the city, are no longer sufficient. The urban must also make itself threatening.

This total and planetary revolution – economic, demographic, psychic, cultural, etc., is today *par excellence* the impossible – possible (that is, possibility, necessity and impossibility)! There is nothing closer and more urgent, nothing more fleeting and more remote. The idea of revolution refers to the global and to the conjunctural, to total and immediate practice; that is, to the existence of an enormous majority of people, silent or not, who subscribe to the present and go as far as to accept millenarism because it postpones until later the eventuality of a catastrophe. After us nothingness! Thus, so-called 'concerned' people waver between the jovial tone of optimism and radical nihilism, postponing deadlines.

At the centre, recognized here and elsewhere, is the process of *reproduction of relations of production*, which unfolds before one, which is accomplished with each social activity, including the most ostensibly anodyne (leisure activities, everyday life, dwelling and habitat, the use of space) and which has yet to be the subject of a global study. It was inherent in social practice and as such went unnoticed. It overcomes (until when?) reasons and causes of dissolution. The lots divided up from this vast field by specialities – political economy, sociology, demography, etc. – implied the global and left it in the shade, a blind field. Approached in this way, the analysis of globality (which cannot be labelled 'system' in the usual sense of the word) cannot be found here. However, the articles included in this collection do not refer to unworthy although partial aspects of the global process. They offer stages of discovery. At a certain level they insert themselves into an aforementioned specificity, within a theoretical framework and reality approached critically.

To *dwell* is only reduced to a designated function which can be isolated and localized, that of *habitat*, reasons for which have been put forward in *Right to the City*. Here the reader will find these reasons again, considered anew and perhaps more detailed: the action of State bureaucracy, the planning of space according to the requirements of the (capitalist) mode of production, that is, the reproduction of relations of production. An important, perhaps essential, aspect of this practice will come to light: the fragmentation of space for sale and purchase (exchange), in contradiction with the technical and scientific capacity of the production of social space on a planetary scale, the consequence of which is a critical analysis of a current and disastrous procedure. In a binary correspondence needs, functions, places, social objects are placed directly (point by point) in a supposedly neutral, innocuous and innocently objective space; after which linkages are set up. This procedure which bears an obvious relationship although never made explicit as such, with the fragmentation of social space, the theory of direct correspondence between terms (functions, needs, objects, places) leads to *projects* which as visual projections appear clear and correct on paper and the *plan* of a space distorted from the start. Fragmentation results in a false and uncritical analysis which believes itself precise because *visual*, of places and sitings. A more advanced and especially more concrete analysis modifies terms which seemed more positive, 'operational'. Indeed they are within a certain 'framework'. This analysis gives rise to a truly specific operation. It is not a question of *localizing* in pre-existing space a need or a function, but on the contrary, of *spatializing* a social activity, linked to the whole of a practice by *producing* an appropriate space.

So what is *architecture*? It has been talked about a great deal and for a long time, since architecture has existed and therefore architecture as a craft, in the division of labour. Could it be an art? This definition only still tempts those who love to draw façades, persist in turning out mouldings, skilfully distribute materials and pleasantly sculpt volumes. There are some. Could it be a technique? If so the engineer supplants the architect, whether he specializes in concrete or road-works. Could it be a science? In which case it would be necessary to construct a methodology, an epistemology or a doctrinal corpus. Now the fruitlessness of this hypothesis is obvious. Supposing it could be established, this corpus would be self-sufficient and without any other effectiveness than its transmission. Architecture cannot be conceived other than as a social practice among others (for example, medicine) in the practical ensemble which sustains and which society at present supports (the mode of production): a relationship to be ascertained. The doctor calls upon a number of sciences, perhaps all of them, and uses many techniques. Therefore medicine cannot be a specific science given that it must borrow knowledge from physics, biology, physio-logy, mathematics as well as from semiology and sociology. It includes many specialities. On the one hand it stretches from dietetics, hygiene, the control of the most 'normal' activities such sport and preventive medecine; and on the other to so-called mental medicine – which does not simplify matters. Consciously or otherwise, the doctor uses very general concepts related to philosophy: the normal and the abnormal, health and illness, equilibrium and disequilibrium, system (nervous, glandular, etc). These concepts justify a theoretical refletion and yet a medical epistemology seems difficult and of little use. Doctors vacillate between the use of computers to process data, and the intuition of the general practitioner who knows his patients personally. Whatever his choice, the doctor cannot easily reduce knowledge to a narrow spe-ciality; nevertheless he almost always specializes and increasingly so. If he divides up his field of experiences and applications, he must restitute the global, the body, the organism, the relation to the envi-ronment, the living unity of the human being in society. And conver-sely. Finally, who will say that medicine and doctors are not affected by the influence of capitalism? There is no doubt that there exists a capitalist medical practice and another, non-capitalist, 'social' or 'so-cialist' one. None the less, as a practice, medicine came before capital-ism: it will continue after it, whatever its end will be. Whether capitalist relations of production stimulate medical research and effi-ciency by giving them adequate motivations and directions or whether they hinder them is uncertain. Biology and biochemistry it seems are making giant strides, but not without adding to a list of already impressive threats of other risks, other anxieties, other deadlines. How can medicine break away from this hold and find better forms of

research and action? The question is posed with only some seriousness. The answer is not certain, the solutions are not obvious.

It is the same for architecture and the architect. Of course, architectural practice predates capitalism. As with urbanism, from which it
was not separate, it was submitted to the orders of more or less
enlightened despots. The architect, artist as well as learned man,
accepted the major fact of the priority of monumentality, the importance of religious or political buildings, over *dwelling*. With the industrial period, architecture disengages itself, but badly, from religious
and political constraints. It falls into ideology – that of functions
which are impoverished, structures which are homogeneous, forms
which are frozen. Today, after the revolutions of the industrial era,
architecture approaches the urban era with difficulty. The architect
too calls upon all the sciences: mathematics, informatics, physics,
chemistry, politics, economics, even semiology, psychology, sociology.
As the doctor, he puts into action an encyclopedic knowledge. Yet, his
practice remains fixed, limited on all sides. He is awkwardly placed
between the engineer and the draughtsman; he does not know where
he fits between developers, users, financial backers and public authorities. If he does have a specific role in the (social) division of labour,
the product of this labour does not appear to be clearly specified. He
too avails himself of a number of stock concepts (carefully catalogued:
scale, proportions, 'options', etc.) which justify a reflection close to
that of philosophy but which are not self-sufficient and are not enough
to construct a doctrinal corpus. Finally, architecture differs from
painting, sculpture and the arts, in that they are related to social
practice only indirectly and by mediations; while the architect and
architecture have an immediate relationship with dwelling as social
act, with construction as a practice.

The architect, producer of space (but never alone) operates over a
specific space. Firstly he has before him, before his eyes, his drawing
board, his blank drawing paper. Of course, the blackboard is not very
different. This drawing paper, who does not consider it for a simple
and a faithful mirror? Whereas all mirrors are deceptive and besides,
this blank sheet is more and something else than a mirror. The
architect uses it for his *plans* in every sense of the term: a flat surface
upon which a more or less nimble and skilful pencil leaves traces
which the author takes for the reproduction of things, of the tangible
world, while in fact this surface forces a decoding and recoding of the

'real'. The architect cannot, as he easily tends to believe, *localize* his thought and his perceptions on the drawing board, *visualize* things (needs, functions, objects) by *projecting* them. He confuses *projection* and *project* in a confused ideality which he believes to be 'real', even rigorously conceived, and so escapes him because the procedures of coding and decoding through drawing are routine and traditional. The sheet at hand, before the eyes of the draughtsman, is as blank as it is flat. He believes it to be neutral. He believes that this neutral space which passively receives the marks of his pencil corresponds to the neutral space outside, which receives things, point by point, place by place. As for the 'plan', it does not remain innocently on paper. On the ground, the bulldozer realises 'plans'.

And this is why and how drawing (and by this one must also understand design) is not only a skill and a technique. It is a mode of representation, a stipulated and codified know-how. *Therefore it is a filter* selective towards contents, eliminating this or that part of the 'real', in its own way filling the lacuna of the text. In aggravating circumstances this filtering goes further than being an ideological specialization. It may even conceal social demand.

What is a code? What is a coding–decoding? Let's quickly say that apart from a number of blatant examples (the highway code), a code does not consist of a system of prefabricated rules. All codes define a focused space by opening up a horizon around a text (message), by deploying it and consequently encircling and closing it. This text can be practico-material and social, and therefore not always necessarily written. Images also can be coded and decoded! The complexity of operations executed escapes as much the readers, as language and its production escape the speakers. The agent (here the draughtsman) believes himself to be in the only practice. He thinks he is reproducing while in fact he produces! He skips over intermediaries, going from one result to another result. Every coding brings a placing into context and 'production' of a certain meaning which substitutes itself to the given text and can either impoverish it or valorize it by enriching it. Hence ambiguity. Coding–decoding implies an effect or mirage effects, for the formal structure of a code appears only at the moment when production declines, or the appearance of meaning fades. The code that is formulated is no more than its shadow! Nowadays the most subtle of semiologists are saying that a code is a voice and a way: from the 'text' – the message – arise several possibilities, choices, various utterances, a plurality, a fabric rather than a line. Hence, a certain 'work' on the text (message) which produces meaning starting from attempts and fragments which provoke a complex movement: valorizations and devalorizations, advances coming up against obstacles, with 'fading'. Each coding would be a proposed outline, taken up again, abandoned, always at the outline stage, engendering a meaning among many others. The hand searches, the pencil hesitates. The hand believes it reproduces and substitutes. It obeys a voice which speaks, which says and interprets the thing, believing that it is seizing it. The voice, the hand, the instrument, believe that they are 'expressing' (reproducing) whereas they are acting, 'producing'; but the product of this work does not have the qualities and properties with which the author credits it. He is doing other than what he says and believes.

More than one good draughtsman will have trouble recognizing himself in this ironic picture of his professional lived experience. Yet, drawing obviously entails a risk, that of a substitution to objects, especially people, bodies, their gestures and acts, of graphic arts. He is *reducer* even if it does not seem so for the draughtsman during the course of his action. With 'design', form signifies function, and structure only has to incorporate in a matter treated in a profitable way this 'signifier–signified' relation. The distance between these three terms, function, form, structure, which formerly made it possible to bring them together into an organic unity, not visible as such, has been reduced. The signs of objects give rise to signs of signs, to an increasingly sophisticated *visualization*, where the limit is reached when inevitable figurines come on the stage, in charge of 'animating' space. These fixed signifiers of mobility and activity speak of symbolic murder. They make the procedure of coding–decoding by concealing it. They must be used to condemn it by putting an end to two myths: the expression of reproduction and fabulous creation.

Legibility passes for a great quality, which is true, but one forgets that that all quality has its counterpart and its faults. Whatever the coding, legibility is bought at a very high price: the loss of part of the message, of information or content. This loss is inherent in the movement which rescues from the chaos of tangible facts, a meaning, a single one. The emergence of this meaning breaks the network, often very fine and richly disorderly from which the elaboration began. It completes its erasure by *making another thing*. The snare of legibility is therefore everywhere, especially when the *auteur*, here the architect, believes to be holding up to and have well in hand the 'thing' from which he started, namely, to dwell. In fact what he has done is to substitute it for habitat! Visual legibility is even more treacherous and better ensnared (more precisely, ensnaring) than graphic legibility, that is, writing. Every legibility stems from a paucity: from redundance. The fullness of text and space never go together with legibility. No poetry or art obeys this simple criteria. At best legibility is blank, the poorest of texts!

Ensnared and ensnaring, legibility hides what it omits and which a more attentive, analytical and critical reader detects. Is not the homology (homogeneity) of all the spaces represented and recorded on the surfaces the most efficient of reductive ideologies? An ideology very useful to the reproduction of existing social relations, transported into space and the *reproductibility* of spaces!

It goes without saying that such a code does not stay within the narrow confines of individual know-how. It becomes a question of skill. To this effect, it enters into social labour and the social division of labour. Thus, it is transmitted and taught by self-enhancement to become tradition and pedagogy. The visual code, as such insufficiently or poorly formulated, has been the basis of the teaching of drawing, of fine arts and architecture over a long period. Challenged, but still influential, it perpetuates itself as the only solid pedagogic skill (not only in France, but in Italy, and probably elsewhere).

The architect cannot confine himself to drawing and cannot avoid oral consultation with other agents of this production, space. Foremost the user, but also the bureaucrat, the politician, the financier, and so on and so forth. To such an extent that there is a tendency to present the architect no longer traditionally as a man of drawing, but as a 'man of words'. An interesting but questionable assumption, for it forgets the general problematic of space (and its production), to retain from the particular problematic of architecture the desire to legitimize the profession. Moreover, we all know that for the user and the architect, neither the 'signifiers' nor the 'signified', nor their sequences coincide.

The general problematic of space requires particular questions to be approached in another way, for example, that of the profession. It subordinates the profession to general questions. It rejects the separation between the architect and the planner. Sharing space and sharing it with other agents, including proprietors, they divide and fragment it each in their own way; and thus fragmentation appears theoretically justified. To each his level and scale of intervention and thus the global escapes and flees. Each operates over an abstract space, at his level, at his scale, the architect at the micro, the planner at the macro. Now, given their pathetic results, the problem today is to overcome these fragmentations and therefore determine the junction, the articulation of these two levels, of the micro and the macro, the *near* and *far order*, neighbouring and communication.

Would it not be precisely at this scale, that nowadays thought can intervene and intervention be situated? At the lower level, that of the building, all has been stated, restated, fiddled with. For the time being the higher level belongs to road and highway engineers. Exploration begins from an all too complex urban space: it is too early to make concepts operative. Many studies lose themselves in gigantism by making the building higher or larger (see Soleri, Aldo Rossi, etc). Most famous architects today have not broken with monumentality. They attempt a compromise between the monument and the building whereas others disperse social space into ephemeral units, atoms and flows of housing. What can be thought and projected is situated at the intermediary level, as can be witnessed in the studies and projects of Constant, Ricardo Bofill, the studies of Mario Gaviras in Spain, etc. The lower level is that of the village and the neighbourhood, and the macro level is that of the urban. Between the two and at the sharp end is the population, for which one could now attempt the production of an *appropriated* space, for between ten and twenty thousand inhabitants. For now – as a stage! It is at this scale that the 'right to the city' can intervene operationally and stimulate research.

Who can be surprised that urbanism has not been able to constitute itself as either science or practice, but instead has only been able to institute itself (that is, become an institution) by pouring forth heavy ideological clouds? Only an especially sharp critical thought could free urbanism from a prevailing and fettering ideology. But this critical thought, after a few moments of hope soon dashed (about fifteen years ago), could only but turn against urbanism.

If it is true that the words and concepts 'city', 'urban', 'space', correspond to a global reality (not to be confused with any of the levels defined above), and do not refer to a minor aspect of social reality, the *right to the city* refers to the globality thus aimed at. Certainly, it is not a natural right, nor a contractual one. In the most 'positive' of terms it signifies the right of citizens and city dwellers, and of groups they (on the basis of social relations) constitute, to appear on all the networks and circuits of communication, information and exchange. This depends neither upon an urbanistic ideology, nor upon an architectural intervention, but upon an essential quality or property of urban space: centrality. Here and elsewhere we assert that there is no urban reality without a centre, without a gathering together of all that can be born in space and can be produced in it, without an encounter, actual or possible, of all 'objects' and 'subjects'.

To exclude the *urban* from groups, classes, individuals, is also to exclude them from civilization, if from not society itself. The *right to the city* legitimates the refusal to allow oneself to be removed from urban reality by a discriminatory and segregative organization. This right of the citizen (if one wants, of 'man') proclaims the inevitable crisis of city centres based upon segregation and establishing it: centres of decision-making, wealth, power, of information and knowledge, which reject towards peripheral spaces all those who do not participate in political privileges. Equally, it stipulates the right to meetings and gathering; places and objects must answer to certain 'needs' generally misunderstood, to certain despised and moreover transfunctional 'functions': the 'need' for social life and a centre, the need and the function of play, the symbolic function of space (close to what exists over and above classified functions and needs, which cannot be objectified as such because of its figure of time, which gives rise to rhetoric and which only poets can call by its name: desire).

The right to the city therefore signifies the constitution or reconstitution of a spatial-temporal unit, of a gathering together instead of a fragmentation. It does not abolish confrontations and struggles. On the contrary! This unity could be, according to ideologies, called the subject (individual and collective) in an external morphology which enables it to affirm its interiority the accomplishment (of oneself, of the 'being'); life the 'security – happiness' pair already defined by Aristotle as finality and meaning of the *polis*. In all these cases, under all these names, philosophers have foretold and perceived from afar the reconstitution of what has been fragmented, dissociated and disseminated, during the course of social history. Having defined the goal, they have badly determined its conditions, of which some are political (involving in this term the criticism of all politics) and others are morphological, spatial-temporal.

Thus conceived, the right to the city implies and applies a knowledge which cannot be defined as a 'science of space' (ecology, geopolitics, ekistics, development planning etc.), but as a knowledge of a *production*, that of space.

In Marx's time, economic science was getting lost in the enumeration, description and accounting of objects produced. Marx replaced the study of things by the critical analysis of the productive activity. Resuming the initiative of the great economists (Smith and Ricard) and connecting to it the critical analysis of the mode of (capitalist) production, he extended knowledge to a higher level. Today a similar approach is necessary with regard to space.

For many years the science of space has been trying to find itself in vain. It cannot find itself. It disperses itself and loses itself in various considerations about what there is in space (objects and things), or over an abstract space (devoid of objects and geometrical). At best, this research describes fragments of space more or less filled up. These decriptions of fragments are themselves fragmentary, according to the compartimentalization of the specialized sciences (geography, history, demography, sociology, anthropology, etc.). Such that 'science' therefore disperses itself in divisions and representations of space, without ever discovering a thought which, as Hegel (see *Philosophy of Right*, sect. 189) says about political economy, recognizes in the infinite mass of details, the principles of understanding which prevail in a field.

This difference between 'science of space' and knowledge of the production of space, its portent and meaning will be indicated elsewhere. Hence the previous referral and further apologies to the reader.

Today, the right to the city, fully understood, appears as *utopian* (not to say pejoratively, utopist). None the less, should it not be included in the imperatives as one says, of plans, projects and programmes? The cost of it can appear to be exorbitant, especially if one accounts for these costs in terms of current administrative and bureaucratic frameworks, for example, those of local authorities. It is obvious that only a great increase of social wealth at the same time as profound alterations in social relations themselves (the mode of production), can allow the entry into practice of the right to the city and some other rights of man and of the citizen. Such a development supposes an orientation of economic growth which would no longer carry within it its 'finality', and no longer aim at (exponential) accumulation for itself, but would instead serve superior 'ends'.

While waiting for something better, one can suppose that the social costs of negation of the right to the city (and of a few others), accepting that we could price them, would be much higher than those of their realization. To estimate the proclamation of the right to the city as more 'realistic' than its abandonment is not a paradox.

It is (implicitly) understood that this little book, and those which accompany or follow it, if only in a dialectical manner, does not cancel out the previous ones: it takes them up again by trying to carry them to a higher level. Discourses of a certain (analytical) type here change themselves into other presumably superior discourses. Concepts, formerly situated in *abstract* spaces because *mental*, are now situated in *social* spaces and in relation to *strategies* which deploy themselves and confront each other on a planetary scale. The mental cannot separate itself from the social and never has been except for (ideological) representations. In classical philosophy, the 'subject' and the 'object' remained one outside the other. They meet in the chasms of the Absolute, of original or terminal Identity. Today, the mental and the social find themselves in practice in *conceived and lived space*.

19

Institutions in a 'Post-technological' Society

In 1971 the Museum of Modern Art (New York) initiated a reflection upon the future. As one knows, the most lucid Americans have abandoned the idea of indefinitely continued economic growth, an idea that remains with the political leaders. For these analysts of American society, growth must cross a threshold (with or without a revolution in the conventional European sense), and pass onto a higher stage. In this new society productivism will be transcended and growth controlled and directed as will be the use of techniques (information, cybernetics, missiles and warheads etc). It is not conceivable that each well-to-do American family own three, then, four, and eventually ten cars, ten then twenty television sets, etc. The future society will not be an industrial society but an *urban society*. It will begin by resolving the problems of the American city presently underestimated, and formulated in terms of the environment.

Why the Museum of Modern Art? Because the group of intellectuals supported by the Rockefeller Foundation or those associated with it believe that the University does not respond to this task. Their project includes the creation of a new University, focused on architectural and urbanistic problems to be surrounded by an experimental city.

In 1971 the instigators of this project sent to the future participants a voluminous black book that presented an initial theoretical outline. The interest of this document was that it used, not without some confusion, Marxist concepts (superstructure, ideology, etc.), together with non-Marxist terminology and concepts (value systems, etc). The term 'design' in the American sense is full of meaning and hopes. The designer, a real demi-god (*demiurge*), would be capable of modifying the environment and creating a new space so long as he is supplied with new values. A design of liberty would have a mission: to embody values and re-establish a correspondence between superstructures and spatial morphology of society.

In January 1972 a symposium examining this project took place at the Museum of Modern Art. Fifty guests, the majority of international reputation, including linguists (Jakobson), writers and poets (Octavio Paz, H. N. Ensensberger), philosophers (Foucault), semiologists (Umberto Eco, Roland Barthes), sociologists, etc. had been approached. In the end only thirty participated in the symposium, among whom were four lecturers and ex-lecturers from The Sociology Department at the University of Nanterre (Jean Baudrillard, Manuel Castells, Alain Touraine, Henri Lefebvre).

The first session was opened with a presentation of the project by its director Emilio Ambasz. It was enhanced by the reading and commentary of a magnificent poem on his city, Mexico by its author Octavio Paz. Then followed the first panel on Law and Value led by a jurist Ronald Dworkin, Professor of Jurisprudence at the University of Oxford. He discussed how the problem of social transformation was thought about in Anglo-Saxon countries. One cannot do anything without changing the Law, the supreme Value, but once the Law is undermined, one doesn't know where one is going and the worst is feared. In other words, it's impossible to change anything without changing everything; but how to change everything without beginning with a beginning, without calling into question the structural keystone of a society, thus without throwing oneself not without risks into a revolutionary enterprise? The imperturbable logic of Anatole Rappaport increased the dilemma and widened the alternative instead of reducing it.

The second panel gave rise to a lively discussion between scientists destined to become part of the new University and to be involved in the creation of the experimental city. The semiologists (especially Umberto Eco and Gillo Dorfles, both from Milan) were subjected to a virulent criticism which virtually led to a kind of autocritique. 'Make nature significant and signs natural', declared Dorfles as watchword. This semiology was caught in a cross-fire: on the one hand, the realists, including M. Schapiro and the economists, referred to the practical aspects of the construction and constitution of the city; on the other, the leftists and the ultra-leftists who showed that signs and significants inevitably emanated today from the failed and condemned society. This is what Jean Baudrillard brilliantly demonstrated, not without adding some very dark remarks indeed about the 'dealth impulse' inherent in any contemporary project. As for Castells, he declared that the massive, and therefore revolutionary, intervention of the people is indispensable for any social transformation, including those of the way we live, of the city and its space.

The third panel was dominated by Christopher Alexander's discourse. He explained why he had abandoned his ambitions and earlier objectives of parametric architecture and the application of cybernetics to construction. The crucial event for him seems to have been the conflict between the students and Senate of a major American university when he as the architect chosen for his audacity, had to redesign the campus. The management wanted to impose upon the students and the architect the division of the campus into specialized spaces, whilst the students wanted multifunctional spaces and rejected single purpose spaces, especially one exclusively devoted to rest and leisure. Incensed, the young and brilliant theoretician of architecture came to the conclusion that one could only devise a space for a concrete community (a concept that was developed at the last session by Susanne Keller). As a result Alexander turned to Buddhism and the doctrine of Zen and left the United States to construct elsewhere the spatial morphology appropriate to life in a community of this type. There followed a discussion, as lively and lengthy as it was obscure, that Hannah Arendt's address was unable to clarify.

The last session was supposed to draw some conclusions from all the debates. Alain Touraine persuasively expounded his thesis that the University must produce knowledge and not ideology, a role that the University does not consciously Ensure. Martin Pawley, going even further, incriminated the techniques of manipulation and the militarization of universities as an authoritarian response to the students' protest in a large number of countries.

Out of these discussions, of which this short résumé fails to convey their richness and confusion, J. Tabibian (California Institute of the Arts) drew optimistic conclusions about the future of the project, the new University and the experimental city.

What of the meaning of this meeting? Well there are several. Certainly the slogan 'save the city' is going to dominate the political, scientific and cultural life of the United States for some time to come from now. The project (University and the City) supported by an economic and financial power can have multiple consequences. But what came out of these debates was the firstly the confusion, the admission of impotence, coming from the specialist sciences and scholars (economists, sociologists, semiologists) as well as from the supposedly relevant authorities. In the United States one does not know exactly how to deal with the city and they are ready to listen to suggestions coming from Europeans, even a Marxist one.

Here then is the complete text of my paper on 'space, the production of space, and the political economy of space' of which only a shortened version was delivered at New York due to lack of time.

The crisis of political economy is today obvious and public despite being carefully covered up and masked by the interested parties, namely economists. It is part of the general crisis of the so-called social sciences. Political economy has failed practically and theoretically, but from this failure we add a few characteristics in describing the crisis.

This crisis differs from that of linguistics or history. Linguistics has counted on an opposition, made into a dogma and authoritative core of knowledge, the opposition being 'signifier–signified' (Saussure and his school). But one becomes aware that the notion of value plays a decisive and specific role even in linguistics: value attaches itself to the polysemy of all words: the relationship signifier–signified, real or reality is not univocal and depends on 'values' which are not simply connotations or elements of a second degree but specific ensembles. As for history, it falls under a reactive critique which denies historicity, and under an active critique which defines it, by showing that the modern world is entering a world 'time' that cannot be thought of any longer according to a traditional historicity but in terms of the concept of 'strategy'.

The totality of these sciences are located without knowing it (and it was the 'unthought' of epistemological reflection itself) in the *reproduction of the relations of production* of existing society. Each scholar accepted this or that partial factor of this reproduction, involved themselves in it and contributed to it. This was primarily the case of economists, though not forgetting sociologists such as Max Weber and Durkheim. Political economy had an ideology and even the principal ideology of this period: productivism, the theory of indefinite growth in the socio-political context of capitalism, models of

growth adapted to State capitalism and the politics of national organizations (recently international). In this context, the crisis means that
the reproduction of relations of production comes to light and is
understood as such. That means that knowledge is being reconstituted
on new grounds and already through the radical criticism of existing
sciences, of their blind contribution to the reproduction of relations of
production . . .

Seen from close, these failures of economists reveal even better their
meaning. In fact, they have confused political economy as science and
political economy as praxis, techniques, acts of power. Their 'modelling' has been directed more and more consciously.

PART IV

Interviews

20

No Salvation away from the Centre?

What one calls a paradox is a series of poorly explained contradictions. The situation of what one still calls today the city is eminently paradoxical. Theoretically there are two opposing points of view.

The first is an anti-city tradition which has a lengthy past. The city is the site of corruption, of Hell, Babylon. In the texts of the prophets (the Apocalypse of John), it is designated as an infamous place. The Chicago School which launched the scientific study of the city was permeated by it. For these authors the city is a place of constraints, where natural groups such as the family and the corporate association are beset by tensions pulling them apart. It is the place not of social life, but of breakup of society. The influence of the Chicago School has been and continues to be considerable; this long anti-urban tradition having repercussions even on Marxism, Marxist practice and in socialist countries. Firstly Marx himself never sought to reflect on the city. There are texts on the rural – urban relationship, but there is nothing on the city. He was far from thinking that the following century, our century would be that of the globalization of the city and of massive urbanization. Engels speaks of housing but very little of the city. The thinking of Marx and Engels seems to revolve around an urban utopia, a medium-sized city of 10,000–20,000 inhabitants itself existing around a firm run by a workers' association. This has had serious consequences: at the outset the Soviet revolution has been anti-urban. There have been architects (very famous ones) rather than urbanists. The Chinese revolution has been a profoundly peasant one. Later it concentrated in medium-sized towns rather than large cities. The Cuban revolution was anti-urbanistic. Havana of course was a place of corruption and oppression. The climax, if one can call it that, of this anti-urban tendency within Marxism was the frenetic action of Pol Pot against Phnom Penh. And this anti-urban tendency goes very far back in thought; in my opinion it runs through Judaism, Protestantism and Marxism and ends up by not thinking about the city and urban growth.

There is another tradition of Greek origin which is that of the City. It is the place where civilization, culture and art develop. It is in the City that art appears and is produced. This tradition is maintained through Roman influence and even the enormous influence of Spain. It is odd that in the United States the conurbations that one would count as cities are of European and Hispanic influence: Boston, San Francisco, New York. The others are sorts of huge villages bereft of any centrality or monumentality.

The modern city is not thought out because we haven't resolved the contradiction between these two traditions. Besides, our modern city is a divided city. The medieval historic city in Europe still has a reality, for example, Paris. Yet at the same time it is split by the phenomenon of explosion and implosion. On the one hand, it is broken up into peripheries, into suburbs, some inner, some further out, in rings where workers and the excluded are relegated. And on the other hand, its centrality is becoming more pronounced. It has become the centre of decision- making, of information, of authority and knowledge. The modern city, with its problematic, its breaking-up, has yet to be considered. To do this it is necessary to think about space, policy, strategy. In France neither government nor policy-makers have urban strategies. This has been done according to the interests of various agents of urbanization: developers, banks, and local authorities acting according to their electoral interests without an overall conception. I have tried to warn of the dangers inherent to these hasty, precipitate and crudely economic solutions. I have uttered all sorts of warnings without getting any results, and so it is a problem I open to public opinion. Now we are beginning to realize that the suburbs are monstrous, that the high rises are unlivable, and that they produce new generations of rebels and delinquents. Symbolically we are demolishing the Minguettes[1] but there are a thousand Minguettes in France.

Of course there have been numerous studies but these are isolated and local without any overall conception. They assume that one must study what one is capable of mastering, that is the local and the micro,

---

[1] Minguettes, a suburb in the Lyon agglomeration, was the site of urban disturbances in 1981.

and this is the paradox that you are witnessing. The concept of the urban itself is unclear. Sometimes one emphasizes historic centrality, the hard core, at other times, the almost endless extension of the suburbs which are in effect urbanized but very badly so.

The Socialist government has paid attention to building. It has adopted interesting measures in relation to housing and favoured large firms such as Bouygues, but it hasn't thought about the city. It is true that they have noticed that the suburbs are unlivable and got Roland Castro[2] to rethink them. But this consists of repairing the disastrous work of dozens of years. The shapeless suburbs, neither town or country, are a collection of ghettos. And the problem is world-wide.

The so much vaunted neo-liberalism in this case simply means submitting everything to circulation. One thinks of this plan by Le Corbusier which gets rid of the city and replaces it by gigantic houses where everything is given over to circulation. Le Corbusier was a good architect but a catastrophic urbanist, who prevented us from thinking about the city as a place where different groups can meet, where they may be in conflict but also form alliances, and where they participate in a collective *œuvre*. I fear that liberalism will be a 'free for all', a space abandoned to speculation and the car.

There are apparently different levels of intervention in the city. I have friends who promote the architectural approach, saying that we must either invent new forms or improve existing cultural models. Others favour the urban viewpoint, the city as a whole. Still others say that it is territorial planning and its networks which are decisive. I wonder if it is a real problem. A real consideration of the city in space must bring together the three levels as well as a strategy and politics of space. There have been some attempts in this direction.

Technology is important. The City is the relatively small Greek city where everyone knew each other. The town is the medieval town, the historic town. It is this which has fragmented into peripheries and suburbs. The urban encompasses the city and the town as historical monuments and expresses the fragmented modern reality. When the

---

[2] Roland Castro and J. M. Cantal-Dupart were responsible for the Banlieues 89 central government programme of urban renewal of working-class suburbs which involved the redesign of public spaces and the commissioning of new social building projects. Urbanism, like decentralization, was supposed to be one of the big issues of Mitterrand's first presidency. See Roland Castro *Civilisation urbaine ou barbarie?*, Plon, Paris, 1994.

young and the unemployed are pushed towards the periphery, they return to the city. They come back. I live, not entirely by chance, in the centre of Paris, and I see the young of the suburbs who come by RER to the Forum and Beaubourg. They come from far away to see the centre, this Palm Beach of the poor, and that sometimes makes for frightening crowds. This shows that we have not succeeded in recreating a town where every space is interesting and moving and has its religious, political and aesthetic pulsations.

It is extremely difficult to give an answer to the question of which city one likes and dislikes, for detestable cities are also fascinating, for example, Los Angeles. For a European it is appalling and unlivable. You can't get around without a car and you pay exorbitant sums to park it. And yet at the same time, it is unbelievably fascinating. What fascinates and disgusts me are the streets of luxury shops with superb windows but which you can't enter into. They are shut and you have to give them advance warning by phone if you want to visit them. They enquire after your bank account, offer you champagne and you make your purchase. These streets are empty. And not far from there, you have a street, a neighbourhood where 200,000 Salvadorean immigrants are exploited to death in cellars or lofts. A parallel and underground illegal economy. But there, there is singing and dancing. There is something stupendous and fascinating. You are and yet are not in the city. You cross a series of mountains and you are still in the city, but you don't know when you are entering it or leaving it. It stretches for 150 km, twelve million inhabitants. Such wealth! Such poverty! Chicanos, Salvadoreans. And at the same time you feel that the Hispanics have a counter culture, and they make the society, the music, painting (the murals which are beautiful and which they have created).

My favourite city is Florence which has ceased recently to be a mummified city, a museum city, and which has found again an activity, thanks to the small modern industries of the periphery. But of course I love Paris with its enormous problems and its centre. I came to live in this city thirty years ago. So what I like is Los Angeles for the fascination, Florence for the pleasure and Paris to live in.

The globalization of the city is a fundamental phenomenon. In the future, the city will inevitably be polycentric, a multiplicity of centres, diversified but conserving a Centre. There is no urbanity without a centre. I believe in a general urbanization. There will remain vast spaces but deserted, little inhabited.

21

The Urban in Question

Société Française: In your book *La révolution urbaine*, written twenty years ago, you announced the coming of an urban society. This remains today a virtuality and you said recently that the concept of the urban itself remains uncertain. What changes have taken place over the last few years?

Henri Lefebvre: I have the impression that architectural and urbanistic interventions have not matched the transformations of the city. I have lived in the centre of Paris for the past thirty years and have seen it transformed. Only a few years ago the centre was virtually abandoned, then reoccupied in an elitist fashion. Why? This phenomenon is also observable in other large cities. The extension of cities occurred for peripheries and centres, originally centres of decision-making, and which have been somewhat left behind for peripheries which have been places of production, business and residence. Then after a time it was as if there was a return to the centre. This is a movement fairly characteristic of Paris where the centre is now hyperfrequented by French and foreign tourists, students and businessmen. People come to see the museums, the monuments, but also the recently constructed buildings. It is this that gives it a lively appearance. But is it lively in urbanistic terms? I wouldn't know what to say! This liveliness is due mostly to passers-by who are in transit. The permanent population, its inhabitants, have changed a lot. In my building behind the Pompidou Centre, the old people have for the most part died and apartments are occupied by offices. They also want to push me out to have my apartment. I have the feeling that the centre is becoming 'museumfied' and managerial. Not politically, but financially managerial. The metamorphoses of the city and the urban continue.

S.F.: You have often stressed the increasing rupture between the conceived and the lived. One could say in some ways that this is due to an accentuation of the social division of labour leading to more and more specialization. And yet today the desired efficiency is reaching its limits. That is to say that there is the need for the rigorous constitution of general and specifically urban knowledge and *savoir faire* to be grasped at different scales. At the same time, there is a demand for greater and greater intervention by people themselves.

H.L.: Despite urban struggles which on the whole developed only slightly in the 1970s, the passivity of people has often intrigued me: the city is changing around them and they accept it, internalize it and bear the consequences. In some ten years many people have been thrown out of the centre of cities towards the suburbs to make way for the financial sector. But recently, this passivity seems to have lessened and reactions have been more frequently forthcoming and better informed. In my neighbourhood for example, it seems that people are saying that they can do something. But the essential movement is after all the purchase of property. This attraction to property as a specific security signifies a certain alteration in the relationship of the population to space. On the one hand, there is a greater attention and watchfulness, but on the other, there is only simply the place one owns to which one is almost irrevocably atached, but that doesn't resolve the problems of the appropriation of space. It evolves in a very contradictory fashion. One notices in discussions between friends, in meetings of associations and even during elections, that one speaks more often than before of the neighbourhood. It seems that there is a renewed interest in the urban. But I don't know to what extent this state of affairs is generalized nor whether it will last. I don't know either whether it will be really effective, for it is the private ownership of land and property which remains by far the dominant power and which will continue to grow more powerful.

S.F.: Often when one tries to get people to participate in the planning process, one comes up against a dichotomy between a fragmented, one could almost say divided, daily reality, on the one hand, and on the other, more global scales, totalities, that are not consciously lived, but which nevertheless exert an effect. How in concrete terms can we give inhabitants the means to intervene effectively?

H.L.: This question of people's capacity to participate is crucial. People have been exhorted to participate. They mobilized themselves a little, but the means and the results are not enormous. The property system has not changed, and neither has the relation with the hierarchy of powers. There is a contradiction between the need to organize space according to the demands of society and private property which is increasingly in conflict with collective interests. It is around the resolution of this crucial problem that we should mobilize, whilst urbanization continues to extend world-wide. For even if it is necessary to keep land for agricultural production, and in spite of futuristic solutions (dwellings at the bottom of the seas), when the population of the planet will have reached ten billion, we shall require urban solutions.

Work on the urban cannot limit itself merely to recording what has been produced. We must also look ahead and propose things. However today the city is above all considered according to a historicist model and there are masses of studies on the origins of the evolution of cities. But studies looking into the future are rather few and tentative. This is a serious error. It is how we are surprised about the things which are happening. I have tried to steer urban studies towards possibilities, eventualities, the future, but there is a resistance to it. Even architects are more interested in what has been built than in the future of the city, the form of the city itself and the relations between buildings and monuments. It is difficult to determine exactly the question of urban form which depends on a multitude of factors, from the local configuration of the site, to social relations, and today the global.

S.F.: These urban historical studies, beyond the evolution, the idea and the practice of the city have had the the merit to show the reality of the city as a place of interaction of different historical times. In revealing the existence of permanences, these studies have enabled us at the same time better to grasp changes so as to avoid applying any old abstract model to the city.

H.L.: These studies have had the merit of clearly showing the lines of evolution of such and such a city, their axes and types of development, etc. But these studies do not look to the future. What will happen in the next century? As far as the urban is concerned, we are always in a phase of transition. This affects not only the work of architects and urbanists, but all those concerned with the city: sociologists, economists and geographers . . . One must be predictive. It is true that predictive work, because it includes an element of speculation and uncertainty, does not pay, whilst there is more budget for studies of what has been accomplished. It also shows that urban thinking is at its beginning. It is still a thinking attached to the land, to the logic of agricultural production which leaves traces, outlines. One continues to think in forms shaped by this social base: the land and not the city. One may still need decades to change the way, the method and style of thinking.

S.F.: Does not this refusal to project into the future fit in the general context of a societal crisis, whereby confronted by the uncertainty of the future, one tries to bring the past into a present endlessly extended and lived in its immediacy? Isn't this a bit what the so-called postmodernist discourse is about?

H.L.: This is also a crisis of practice, thought and social philosophy. But we cannot just state this, we have to explore the possibilities. This seems to me both a necessity dictated by the crisis and a way out of this very crisis, which though disastrous, at the same time pushes out, engenders and gives rise to new research and developments. I believe that through all sorts of convulsions and contradictions, we shall see the emergence of new ideas, especially in urbanistic thinking, which seems to me to be a field of creation and exploration. Besides, the urban as a concept designates a reality in crisis. Because if there is a crisis of representation, we should not forget that it is also that which is represented which is in crisis, in transformation, changing. What will be the city of tomorrow? That is a huge question. Let us take the question of centrality. Will we witness the maintenance of a very hierarchical system, or on the contrary, are we moving towards a dispersal of centres, towards their multiplication? And who decides what? If one takes the case of France, conflicts between mayors, general councils, the regions and the State remain strong.

What will be the room for manoeuvre of these centres? Our society is changing more rapidly and profoundly than we generally think, and urban problems, with those of financial production or globalization, are part of the most basic problems.

S.F.: The crisis of the city has forced us to question the simplistic association of the city with certain concepts borrowed from the modern movement and subsequently generalized: the mass production of housing, circulatory logic or zoning. We have rediscovered the complexity of the city as a key place of interactions through a certain hierarchy of urban space, of monumentality, and especially of public space.

H.L.: Of course! It's extraordinary. It was expecially the ideological domination of the bourgeoisie. When it dominated, property was its major preoccupation. It was the owner of land and spaces and this was expressed in its ideology. Now we have noticed that society exists and cannot be reduced to aspects of property. The city has an autonomous reality. It has a life, an existence which cannot be reduced to the distribution of land or space, the street, the square, meeting places, *fêtes*; all this urban life which we could call traditional, has been rediscovered in the past few years. It is coming back but with difficulty, for these traditions have been broken. But we must not hold on to tradition, we must invent. And of course this does not happen in a day. It took centuries and centuries to build ancient Rome! One cannot deny, or push aside urban life. All the more so because we generally only follow the flow, we take account of facts once they have made their mark on space through the built environment. This still shows the necessity to have a thinking that projects into the future.

S.F.: Today architects and urbanists are increasingly in their projects only the conveyors of an iconic message. They render an image which depending on the situation tries to be of historical, technological or conceptual inspiration. And unfortunately, demand, including the public sector's, follows this fashion. This 'illusionism', this 'derealization' of spatial practices, does not contribute much to the invention of a kind of urban life of which you spoke.

H.L.: It is fairly recently that there have been practicians of space. It is a knowledge, a practice which isn't so developed, especially if one considers it from a world-wide point of view. Consider the European, Chinese or American city, they have different features. Los Angeles is not developing in the same way as Rome. The science of the city is in the process of consolidation and its action is still slight. I fervently hope that it becomes more and more important and that political, administrative and financial authorities learn from this knowledge of the city rather than doing whatever, however and wherever. I am caricaturing, but it is a little like that. Look at the mess in the suburbs: it is our society which has gone overboard. On the one hand centrality, on the other, disorder. It is a contradiction which has not yet been sufficiently highlighted. One is beginning to speak of contradictions of society, but not sufficiently of urban contradictions.

S.F.: Nevertheless contradiction is an integral part of the urban, its constitutive elements are contradictory. Take for example suburban roads; they are often at the same time departmental and national routes and streets. In not taking into account the contradiction street/route, current planning in attempting to get rid of or elude part of the problem and not respond to the richness of urban life, rigidifies it.

H.L.: I have tried to shed light on the complexities and richness of urban life. One knew them, but vaguely and especially through his-toric events which unfolded in them (the ancient city: Paris under the Ancien Régime or the Revolution). I especially wanted to show the breadth of the everyday richness of the city. I don't know whether I managed to do so, it's a considerable task. That is part of a decenter-ing–recentering of thought which must conquer new domains, new methods of deduction and construction.

S.F.: Including working on old problematics like time?

H.L.: Yes. There one finds again the problems of the ancient or Greek city which didn't have the same conception of time as we have. Our conception is that of industry, which is especially located around cities. If our cities simply become refuges for the retired, for tourists and intellectuals occupied with abstractions, that would be a disaster. What threatens the city today is the departure of production. What then remains is the central question of the use of free time in cities. That is for each person to invent. One cannot draw up a range of possible uses of time. They are ceaselessly multiplied in a social practice. It is an essential domain of liberty. There is much talk of liberty, but that remains abstract. Liberty is also the maximum of possibilities for each citizen in the city and not in an isolated place. We must find the link between the mode of production and what is called free time. Besides, free time can be fully productive in the widest sense, of art, of knowledge, of the lived. It is a delicate question which supposes the mastery by each person of their time, with a multiplicity of possibilities. This disjunction which we make between 'productive time' and 'free time' is very symptomatic.

S.F.: What are the problems which you see particularly in the constitution of knowledge and *savoir faire* of the city?

H.L.: On the whole I am constantly surprised by the little importance given to urban questions in the university. The number of chairs of urbanism are rather limited, a few in Paris and even fewer in the provinces. In contrast to traditional teaching, it's nothing. Yet its about a more important question. It isn't just a question of culture, of activity, of productivity, of adaptation and of understanding of the modern world. I tried when I was in the university to introduce urban questions into teaching. I was usually told that it was a matter for schools of architecture. On the other hand, courses in sociology and history which leave aside urban questions seem ludicrous, it's like taking away their very substance.

Unfortunately it hasn't changed very much and the resources for urban research are really minimal in relation to the task. It is as if in traditional circles knowledge is little open to the future. It is a question which relates to the very orientation of society, of civilization, conscience and knowledge; it's either traditional or else an exploration of the future.

PART V

Elements of Rhythmanalysis

22

Seen from the Window

(That won't do! This title belongs to the writer Colette. I must write: 'Seen from my windows overlooking a big intersection in Paris, therefore onto the street'.)

Noise. Noises. Rumours. When rhythms are lived and blend into another, they are difficult to make out. Noise, when chaotic, has no rhythm. Yet, the alert ear begins to separate, to identify sources, bringing them together, perceiving interactions. If we don't listen to sounds and noises and instead listen to our body (whose importance cannot be overvalued) usually we do not understand (hear) the rhythms and associations which none the less comprise us. It is only in suffering that a particular rhythm separates itself out, altered by illness. Analysis is closer to pathology than to the usual arhythm.

To understand and analyse rhythms, one has to let go, through illness or technique, but not completely. There is a certain externality which allows the analytical intellect to function. Yet, to capture a rhythm one needs to have been *captured* by it. One has to *let go*, give and abandon oneself to its duration. Just as in music or when learning a language, one only really understands meanings and sequences by *producing* them, that is, by producing spoken rhythms.

Therefore, in order to *hold* this fleeting object, which is not exactly an *object*, one must be at the same time both inside and out. A balcony is perfect for the street and it is to this placing in perspective (of the street) that we owe this marvellous invention of balconies and terraces from which we also dominate the street and passers-by. For want of these you can always be content with a window, as long as it does not look onto a dark corner or a dank interior courtyard – or onto a forever deserted lawn.

From a window open onto R. street facing the famous P. Centre, one does not have to lean over much to see into the distance. To the right, the palace-centre P., the Forum, right up to the Bank of France. To the left, up to the National Archives. Perpendicular to this direction, the Hôtel de Ville and on the other side, the Arts et Métiers. All of Paris ancient and modern, traditional and creative, active and idle.

Over there, the one walking in the street is immersed into the multiplicity of noises, rumours, rhythms (including those of the body, but is the person aware of these, except at the point of crossing the street, because a calculation must be made of the number of steps to be taken). But from the window noises are distinguishable, fluxes separate themselves, rhythms answer each other. Below, towards the right, a traffic light: on red, the cars stop, pedestrians cross, soft murmurings, a babble of voices. One does not converse while crossing a dangerous intersection, threatened by wild animals and elephants about to leap, taxis, buses, trucks and various cars. So there is a relative silence in this crowd. A kind of soft murmur and sometimes a cry, a call.

Therefore, when the cars stop, people produce a completely different sound: feet and words. From left to right and vice versa and on the pavements along the perpendicular street. At the green light, steps and voices stop. A second of silence and its the surge, the burst of speed of tens of cars accelerating as fast as possible. There are risks: pedestrians to the left, buses across, other vehicles. Whence slow down and restart (take off, slow down for turn, brutal restart, foot right down, top speed – unless there is a hold-up . . .). It's incredible what one sees and hears (from the window). Strict harmony. Maybe it is because the other side of the street is filled with this immense boutique nicknamed Beaubourg after the immortalized president. On that side are those who walk to and fro, silent and numerous; tourists and suburbanites, young and old together, alone or in couples. But there are no cars alongside of culture. After the red light, it's instantly the bellowing rush of the large and small beasts: monstrous trucks turn towards Bastille, most of the smaller vehicles dash towards Hôtel de Ville. The noise rises, rises in intensity and power, peaks, becomes unbearable, although rather well borne by the stink of fumes. Then stop. More pedestrians. Intervals: two minutes. During the fury of cars the pedestrians cluster, a clot, a lump here and there; grey predominates with a few multicoloured spots and these heaps break up for the race ahead.

Sometimes cars stagnate in the middle of the road and pedestrians go round them, as waves around a rock, giving withering looks to the drivers of the stranded vehicles. Hard rhythms: silence and uproar alternate, time broken and accented, striking the one who from his window takes to listening. This astonishes him more than the incongruous look of the crowds.

Incongruous crowds, yes. Tourists from far away places – Finland, Sweden, Portugal, whose cars have trouble finding parking places, buyers from afar, wholesalers, lovers of art or of novelties, young suburbanites who pour in between the so-called rush hours, so that there are always people around the enormous metallic knick-knacks: boys and girls lurch forward, often hand in hand as if to support each other in this test of modernity, in this exploration of these aeolites fallen in the middle of old Paris, from a planet several centuries ahead of ours – and on top of that, a complete failure! Many among these young people walk and walk, without respite, around the buildings of Beaubourg, of the Forum. Several times one sees them again, in groups or alone. They walk without cease, chewing gum or a sandwich. They only stop to stretch out, probably exhausted, on the square itself, in the galleries of the Chiraqian Forum, or on the steps of the Fountain of the Innocents, now its only use. The noise that pierces the ears doesn't come from the passers-by, but from the engines revving up. No ear, no apparatus could apprehend this ensemble of flows of metallic or carnal bodies. There must be a little time to capture the rhythms, a sort of mediation over time, the city, people.

To this inexorable rhythm which at night hardly abates, are superimposed other, less intense, slower rythms: children going off to school, a few very noisy even piercing calls, cries of morning recognition. Then, around 9.30, according to a schedule which hardly ever varies except for a few exceptions (such as a downpour or an advertising promotion) the arrival of shoppers, closely followed by tourists. Flows and conglomerates succeed each other; they increase or decrease but always accumulate at the corners then make their way, entangled and disentangled among the cars.

These last rhythms, (those of schoolchildren, shoppers and tourists) would be more *cyclical*, with big and simple intervals, within more intense, *alternating* rhythms with short intervals – cars, regulars, employees, bistro clients. The interactions of various repetitive and different rhythms, as one says, animate the street and the neighbourhood. The linear, that is, succession, consists in comings and goings and combines with the cyclical and spells of longer duration. The cyclical is social organization manifesting itself. The linear is routine, thus the perpetual, made up of chance and encounters.

Night does not interrupt diurnal rhythms, but modifies them and especially slows them down. None the less, even at three or four in the morning there are always a few cars in front of the red lights. Sometimes one of the drivers, coming back from a late evening, goes through them. Sometimes there is no one at the lights and their alternating red, white and green go on flashing. In the emptiness the signal still functions endlessly, a despairing social mechanism marching inexorably through the desert, in front of façades which dramatically proclaim their destiny as ruins.

Should a window suddenly light up or darken it is vain that the solitary dreamer asks himself whether what is going on is a scene of sickness or love, if it is a child or an insomniac waking up too early. Never a head or a face appears in these dozens of windows. Unless something is happening in the street – an explosion, a fire engine speeding non-stop towards a call for help. In short, arhythm rules, except in rare occasions and circumstances.

From my window overlooking courtyard and gardens, the view and the offer of space is very different. Over the gardens, the differences of habitual rythms (daily and therefore linked to day and night) fade; they seems to disappear into a sculptural immobility. Except, of course, the sun or the shadows, the corners that are lit up and those that are dark, quite cursory constrasts. But look at those trees, those lawns, those plantations. they position themselves to your eyes in a permanence, in a spatial simultaneity, in a coexistence. But look more closely and longer. Up to a point, this simultaneity is only apparent; surface and spectacle. Go deeper, dig below the surface, listen closely instead of simply looking, reflecting the effects of a mirror. You then discern that each plant, each tree, has its rhythms, made of several: leaves and flowers, seeds or fruit, each has its own time. The plum tree? The flowers appeared in the spring, before the leaves. The tree was white before it was green. As for this cherry tree, the flowers opened before the leaves which will survive the fruit until they fall, not all at the same time, late in the autumn. Continue and you will see this garden and the *objects* (which have nothing to do with *things*) *polyrhythmically*, or if you prefer, *symphonically*. Instead of a collection of congealed things, you will follow each *being*, each *body*, as having above all, its time. Each therefore having its place, its rhythms, with its immediate past, a near future and hereafter.

Are simultaneity and immobility deceptive? Are synchronicity, the tableau and the spectacle abusive? Yes and no. No: they are the *present*, they constitute. Modernity curiously enlarged, deepened and dilapidated the present. The quasi-suppression of distances and delays (by the media) amplifies the present, but these media only provide reflections and shadows. You attend the incessant festivities or massacres, you look at the cadavers, you contemplate the explosions; the missiles take off under your eyes. You are there! But no, you are not; your present consists of simulacra. The image before you simulates the real, chases it away, is not there and the simulation of drama, the moment has nothing dramatic, except in the verbal.

What this window which opens onto one of the most lively streets of Paris shows, what appears *spectacular*, would it be this *feeling* of spectacle? To attribute this rather derogatory character to this *vision* (as dominant feature) would be unjust and would bypass the *real*, that is, of meaning. The characteristic features are really temporal and rhythmical, not visual. To extricate and to listen to the rhythms requires attentiveness and a certain amount of time. Otherwise it only serves as a *glance* to enter into the *murmurs*, noises and cries. The classical term in philosophy, the 'object', is not appropriate to rhythm. 'Objective'? Yes, but spilling over the narrow framework of objectivity by bringing to it the multiplicity of the *senses* (sensorial and meaningful).

The succession of alternations, of differential repetitions, suggests that somewhere in this present is an order which comes from elsewhere and reveals itself. Where? In the monuments, in the places, in the Archives of the Bank of France, meteorites fallen from another planet into the popular centre so long abandoned, the Cour des Miracles, the place of scoundrels. Therefore, beside the present, a sort of presence–absence, badly localized and powerful: the State does not see itself from the window, but is intimated in this present, the omnipresent State.

In the same way that beyond the horizon, other horizons present themselves without being present, other horizons, beyond material and visible order, which reveals political power, other orders are intimated. Logic, division of labour, *leisure* pursuits are also *products* (and productive) although they are proclaimed as '*free*' and even as '*free time*'. But is this freedom not also a *product*?

In their own way secret objects also speak, issuing out a message. The Palace shouts, screams louder than the cars. It shouts: 'Down with the past! Up with the modern! Down with history, I have swallowed it, digested it, thrown it up . . .' Law and Order – the cop at the junction is perpetual witness and proof, and if someone goes too far, he knows that he will be arrested, hissed at, trapped in such a way that this solitary cop induces the discourse of Order, more and better than the façades of the Square and the junction. Unless he also induces an anarchistic discourse, for he is always there and of little use. The fear of an accident maintains the order at the junctions more efficiently than the police, whose presence gives rise to no protestation, each knowing beforehand the uselessness of it.

Could it be that the lessons of the streets and the teachings of the window are exhausted and dated? Certainly not. They perpetuate themselves by renewing themselves. The window on the street is not a mental place from which the interior gaze would be following abstract perspectives. A practical site, private and concrete, the window offers views that are more than spectacles. Perspectives which are mentally prolonged so that the implication of this spectacle carries its explanation. Familiarity preserves it as it disappears and is reborn, with the everyday life of inside and out. Opacity and horizons, obstacles and perspectives are implicated, for they become complicated, imbricate themselves to the point of allowing the Unknown, the giant city, to be perceived or guessed at. With its diverse spaces affected by diverse temporalities – rhythms.

Once interactions are determined, analysis continues. In this confusion, this scaffolding, is there a hierarchy? A determinant rhythm? A primordial and co-ordinating aspect?

The window suggests a number of hypotheses which restless wandering and the street confirm or invalidate. The bodies (alive and human, besides a few dogs) who move down below, the whole swarming whole wrecked by the cars, would they not be imposing a law? Which one? An order of grandeur. The windows, the doors, the streets, the façades, are measured according to a human scale. Those waving hands, those appendages, although they throw off many messages, cannot be taken for signs. But is there a relationship between these physical flows of gestures and the culture which shows itself (and howls) in the enormous noise of the junction? After all, little *bistrots* and shops of R. Street, are, like the passers-by, on a human scale. The constructions across the street wanted to *transcend* this scale, go beyond familiar dimensions and also all other past and possible models. Hence, this exhibition of metal and solidified piping with the harshest reflections. And this is a meteorite fallen from a planet where rules an absolute technocracy.

Absurd or super-rational? What are these strange contrasts saying? What does the proximity whisper between a certain archaism linked to history and the exhibited supra-modernity? Does it have a secret – or secrets? Will the State-political order be written on this hoarding with the signature of the author? No doubt, but the epoch and time which are also inscribed in this theatre set and give it a meaning should not be forgotten. And why have the *rue de la Truanderie* and the *passage des Menestriers* been preserved through all these upheavals?

The essential and determinant factor is money. But money does not make itself obvious as such, even on the façade of the Banque de France. This centre of Paris carries the imprint of what it hides, but hides it. Money goes through circuits. Not so long ago, this *capital* centre had kept something provincial about it, something medieval, historical and dilapidated. So many discussions and projects for these doomed or abandoned places! Although profitable too – and for a long time! Such an amiable and charming project, very eighteenth-century, signed by Ricardo Boffil, was set aside after its adoption. Another project which converted the centre of Paris into the administrative centre (for the ministries) of the country apparently seduced the Chief. But the project disappeared with him. So a compromise between the different powers, State, money, culture, was attempted. There would be shop windows for all products, including the intellectual ones, the blandness being corrected by Belle Époque images.

How is it that *people* (as it is said now given that certain words such as 'the people' or 'the workers' have lost their prestige) so accept this display that they come in perpetual flows of crowds? So much so that the rhythms of their passing diminish or increase but link up and never disappear (even at night)!

What attracts them that much? Are they coming simply *to look*? But at what? This great building which was conceived not to be seen, but to *offer itself to the gaze*. Yet, one comes to see it, and one casts upon it an absent-minded look upon what it *exposes*. One goes around this void, which fills itself with things and people to empty itself again and so forth. Would it be that these people come especially to see and meet each other? Would not this crowd unconsciously give itself the consciousness of a crowd?

The window answers. Firstly, there is the spectacle of the junction and the perpendicular streets which, not long ago, formed a neighbourhood of the City, peopled by a kind of native, with many craftsmen and small shopkeepers. In short, people from the neighbourhood. Those that remain live in the garrets of attics, with their Chinese or Arab neighbours. Production has left this site and even that part of businesses which involve depots, warehouses, stocks and vast offices. There is nothing to say about these really well-known facts, other than their consequences. For example: the crowds, the masses on the square of Beaubourg, around medieval Saint-Merri or on the Place des Innocents of which it would be too easy to say that it has lost all innocence. The squares have found again their old functions, in peril for long, of meeting places, scene setting and spontaneous popular theatre.

So here on the square explodes a medieval-like festivity, between Saint-Merri and Modernism: fire-eaters, jugglers, snake-men, but also preachers and sit-in discussions. Opening and adventure beside dogmatic armour. Every possible material and spiritual games. Impossible to classify and number. Without doubt, many are deviant and bizarre who seek they do not know what. Perhaps themselves! But many also seek to forget their own place, neither town nor country. And they walk for hours and hours, find again the junctions, go around the squares, closed and enclosed. They hardly ever stop, eating some hot-dog while walking (such quick Americanization). Sometimes, on the square, they stop walking, looking straight ahead of them fixedly, no longer knowing what to do. They look, listen a little to the clap-trappers and then resume their untiring walk.

Here, on the square, there is something maritime about the rhythms. Currents flows across the masses. Streams detach themselves which bring new assistants or take them away; some drifting towards the jaws of the monster who engulfs them to quickly vomit them back. The tide invades the immense square then withdraws: flux and reflux. Agitation and noise are such that the residents have complained. The fatal hour: ten o'clock at night, forbidden sounds. The crowd then becomes silent, calm but more melancholic; O fatal ten o'clock at night! The spectacle and rumour having left, sadness remains.

With these places are we in the everyday or the extra-everyday? Well, one does not prevent the other and the pseudo-festivities break out only apparently from the everyday. They prolong it by other means, with a flawless organization which brings together *everything* – advertising, culture, the arts, games, propaganda, labour rules, urban life . . . And the police keep vigil and watch.

Rhythms. Rhythms. They reveal and hide, being much more varied than in music or the so-called civil code of successions, relatively simple texts in relation to the city. Rhythms: music of the City, a picture which listens to itself, image in the present of a discontinuous sum. Rhythms perceived from the invisible window, pierced in the wall of the facade . . . but beside the other windows, it too *is* also within a rhythm which escapes it . . .

No camera, no image or sequence of images can show these rhythms. One needs equally attentive eyes and ears, a head, a memory, a heart. A memory? Yes, to grasp this present other than in the immediate, restitute it in its moments, in the movement of various rhythms. The remembrance of other moments and of all the hours is essential, not as a simple reference, but so as not to isolate this present and *live* it in its diversity made up of *subjects* and *objects*, of subjective states and objective figures. Here is found that old philosophical question (the subject and the object and their relationships) posed in non-speculative terms, close to practice. The observer at the window knows that he takes as first reference *his time*, but that the first impression displaces itself and includes the most diverse rhythms, as long as they remain *to scale*. The passage from the *subject* to the *object* requires neither a leap over an abyss, nor the crossing of the desert. Rhythms always need a reference; the first persists through other perceived facts. Philosophical tradition has raised half-real, half-fictional problems which by staying within speculative ambiguity are badly resolved. The gaze and meditation follow the main lines which come from the past, the present, the possible, and which join up within the observer, at the same time centre and periphery.

Here as elsewhere, opposites find and recognize each other, in a unity both more *real* and more ideal, more complex than its elements already accounted for. Which actualizes and clarifies the concept of *dialectical thought* that does not cease to fill these pages with so many questions and a few answers!

23

Rhythmanalysis of Mediterranean Cities

Written by Henri Lefebvre and Catherine Régulier, this text was first published in 1986 in issue 37 of Peuples Méditerranéens.

This work is a fragment of a more comprehensive study or an introduction to this study. The specific qualities of Mediterranean cities impress, astonish and surprise. Despite their differences, we shall try to identify some of their general features, through their diversity. The focus is on the larger historical cities which often have origins going back to Ancient Greece. As most historical cities in the world, they are fated to decline, indeed to explode into suburbs and peripheries. Nevertheless, in the Mediterranean historical characteristics appear to persist with extraordinary power more than elsewhere. To these persistences, to this maintenance, the rhythms, historical but also daily, 'closer to the lived', are not in our opinion strangers. At least the question deserves to be asked.

It is impossible to understand urban rhythms without referring to a general theory, which we will call 'Rhythmanalysis' realted particularly to these rhythms but not only these.[1] This analysis of rhythms, in all their magnitude 'from particles to galaxies', has a transdisciplinary character. Moreover, it gives itself as aim the least possible separation of the scientific from the poetic.

In this manner we can try to draw the portrait of an enigmatic personage wandering the streets of a large Mediterranean city, with his thoughts and emotions, his impressions and his wonder, and

---

[1] Henri Lefebvre and Catherine Régulier, 'Le projet rythmanalytique', *Communications*, 41, 1985.

whom we will call the 'rhythmanalyst'. More aware of times than of spaces, of moods than of images, of the atmosphere than of particular spectacles, he is strictly speaking neither psychologist, nor sociologist, nor anthropologist, nor economist. Yet, by turn he comes close to these disciplines and he can use all the instruments employed by the specialists. He therefore adopts in relation to these different sciences a transdisciplinary approach. He 'keeps his ear open', but he does not only hear words, speeches, noises and sounds for he is able to listen to a house, a street, a city, as one listens to a symphony or an opera. Of course, he seeks to find out how this music is composed, who plays it and for whom. He will avoid typifying a city by a simple subjective trait as a particular writer will characterize New York by the howling of police sirens or London by the murmur of voices and the cries of children in the squares. Attentive to time (or tempo) and therefore as much to repetitions as to differences in time, he separates by a mental act what gives itself as linked to a whole: namely, rhythms and their associations. He not only observes human activities, but he hears (in the double meaning of the word of noticing and understanding), the temporalities in which these activities take place. He can at times be closer to the physician (analyst) who examines functional troubles in terms of disfunctions of rhythms or arhythmia and at other times to the poet who can say:

O people that I know
All I need is to hear the sound of their footsteps
To be able to tell forever the direction they have taken.
                    (Apollinaire, 'Cortège')

Rhythms cannot be analysed when they are lived. For example, we do not grasp the relations between the rhythms whose association comprise our body: the heart, breathing, the senses, etc. We do not even grasp any of them separately except when we are suffering. To analyse a rhythm, you have to be out of it. Exteriority is necessary. And yet to grasp a rhythm you must yourself have been grabbed by it, given or abandoned yourself inwardly to the time that it rhythmed. Is it not thus in dance or music? In the same way, to understand a language and its rhythm one must acknowledge a principle which appears paradoxical. One only hears the sounds and the frequencies that one produces when speaking – and reciprocally, one can produce only those that one hears. What is called a loop . . .

If one attentively observes a crowd during peak times and especially if one listens to its rumour, one discerns flows in the apparent disorder and an order which is signalled by rhythms: chance or predetermined encounters, hurried carryings or nonchalant meanderings of people going home to withdraw from the outside, or leaving their homes to make contact with the outside, business people and vacant people – so many elements which make up a polyrhythmy. The rhythmanalyst thus knows how to listen to a place, a market, an avenue.

At the same time, in social practice, scientific knowledge and philosophical speculation, an ancient tradition separates time and space like two entities or two clearly distinct substances. This in spite of contemporary theories which show a relationship between time and space, or more precisely, express how they are relating to each other. Despite these theories, in the social sciences one continues to split time between lived time, measured time, historical time, work and leisure time, and daily time, etc., which usually are studied outside their spatial framework. Now, concrete times have rhythms, or rather, are rhythms – and every rhythm implies the relation of a time with a space, a localized time, or if one wishes, a temporalized place. Rhythm is always linked to such and such a place, to its place, whether it be the heart, the fluttering of the eyelids, the movement of a street, or the tempo of a waltz. This does not prevent it from being a time, that is an aspect of a movement and a becoming.

Let us insist on the relativity of rhythms. They cannot be measured like that of the speed of a mobile on its trajectory is measured, with a well-defined start (zero point) and a unit defined once and for all. A rhythm is fast or slow only in relation to other rhythms to which it is associated within a greater or lesser unity. An example is a living organism – our own body – or even a town (of course not reducing it to that of a biological organism). Which leads us to emphasize the plurality of rhythms as well as their associations and their interactions or reciprocal actions.

Consequently, every body more or less animated and *a fortiori*, all gatherings of bodies are polyrhythmical, that is, composed of various rhythms, each part, each organ or function having its own in a perpetual interaction which constitute an ensemble or a whole. This last word does not signify a closed totality but on the contrary, an open totality. Such ensembles are always in a 'metastable' equilibrium, that is, always compromised and more often restituted, except of course, in the case of profound trouble or catastrophe.

There is another important point: rhythms imply repetitions and can be defined as movements and differences in repetition. Yet, there are two forms of repetition: cyclical and linear. Inseparable even if the analysis must distinguish and separate them. Thus mathematicians clearly distinguish two types of movements, rotations and trajectories, and have different measures for these two types. Cyclical repetition is easily understood if one considers days and nights – hours and months, seasons and years. And tides! The cyclical is generally of cosmic origins: it is not measured in the same way as the linear. The numberings which suit it best are duodecimals, that is, based on twelve: the twelve months of the year, the twelve hours of the clock, the 360° of the circumference, the twelve signs of the zodiac and even the dozen of oysters and eggs, which means that the measure by twelve extends itself to living matter in direct provenance from nature. Cyclical rhythms, each having a determined frequency or period, are also rhythms of new beginnings: of the 'returned' who is not opposed to the 'become' to paraphrase René Crével. Dawn is always new. On the other hand, the linear is defined by the consecutiveness and the reproduction of the same phenomena, identical or almost at more or less close regular intervals. For example, a series of hammer blows, a repetitive series in which are introduced stronger and weaker blows, and even silences – but at regular intervals. The metronome is also an example of linear rhythm. This generally emanates from human and social activities and particularly from the motions of work. It is the point of departure of all that is mechanical. Attaching itself to the identity of what comes back, the linear and its rhythms have a tendency to oppose themselves to what is becoming. According to Crével, 'The returned conflicts with the become'. Following this pattern, the linear, including lines, trajectories and repetitions is measured on a decimal base (the metric system). If therefore the cyclical and the linear can be clearly distinguished, the analysis which has separated them must rejoin them, for they enter into a perpetual interaction and are even relative to each other, to the point that one becomes the measure of the other. An example: so many days of work.

These points being established, what will the rhythmanalyst say of Mediterranean cities? Again we must insist that he remains attentive to the relativity of rhythms. Any study of rhythms is necessarily comparative. Therefore we will begin by briefly indicating certain contrasts between Mediterranean and oceanic cities. The latter are governed by the cosmic rhythms of the tides – lunar rhythms! As for Mediterranean cities, they skirt a sea with almost no tide and therefore the cyclical time of the sun takes on a predominant importance. Lunar cities of the ocean? Solar cities of the Mediterranean? Why not?

But Mediterranean shores are not homogeneous. Everyone knows that they differ by their settlements, ethnicities, history, the specific features of their economies, cultures, and religions. How can the oriental Mediterranean not be distinguished from the occidental Mediterranean, the Aegean sea and the Adriatic sea, the northern Mediterranean which is part of Europe and the southern Mediterranean, part of Africa? Nevertheless, the Mediterranean itself imposes common features upon these cities, as a relatively small, closed and limited sea. All those who have been at sea more than a little know that the waves of the Mediterranean are not the same as those of the oceans; a simple but significant detail – the waves have and are rhythms. The climate also imposes a certain homogeneity: all around the Mediterranean are the olive tree and the vine, etc. As for the ports of the Mediterranean, they are characterized by their commercial relations which were the beginnings of Greek civilization. The resources which most of these cities extract from their hinterlands are limited. Industrialization has taken place unevenly and with difficulty; it does not seem to have altered in depth habits or traditions of exchange. Very early, on this basis of limited exchanges political powers and policies were constituted which attempted to dominate the city by dominating space. These powers have used and are still using space as a means of control and as a political instrument.

The shores of the Mediterranean gave rise almost 2,500 years ago to the City-State which dominated a territory usually small but none the less protected trade which extended as far away as possible. In this trade material exchange has always been mixed with an extreme sociability and also paradoxically, with piracy, plundering, rivalries and naval wars, conquests and colonizations, features which can already be found in Homer's *Odyssey*. Mediterranean cities are therefore political cities but not in the same way as the cities which border the oceans. The State which dominates a city and its territory is both weak and violent.

It always vacillates between democracy and tyranny. One could say that it tends towards arhythmy. In its interventions in the life of the city it finds itself at its heart but this heart beats in a way both violent and intermittent. In the city, public life orders itself principally around exchanges of all kinds: material and non-material, objects and words, signs and products. If, on the one hand, exchange and commerce never are reduced to a strictly economic and monetary aspect, on the other the life of the city seldom has a political objective – except in cases of revolt. In this public life, men are not linked together by the ties that made Nordic cities communities guaranteed as such by oaths, pacts, charters, so that every action was constantly civic and political. One cannot but notice these founding differences between the great independent Mediterranean cities and the free cities of Flanders, Germany, the north of France and of Europe. The great Mediterranean cities appear to have always lived and still live within a regime of compromise between political powers. Such a 'metastable' state results from the fact of the polyrhythmical. One could not over-emphasize this form of alliance, the compromise which historically differs from that of the 'Sworn Community'. This historical difference has had repercussions up to our time and in our view influences the rhythms of the city.

Without laying claim to a complete theory but as a hypothesis, we give much importance to those relations between cities and especially ports with (cosmic) space and time, with the sea and the world: to what unites these cities to the world through the mediation of the sea. If it is true that Mediterranean cities are solar cities, one can expect a more intense urban life than in lunar cities, but also one richer in contrasts inside the city itself. In Nordic and oceanic cities one can expect more regulated times, linked to contractual rather than ritual forms of association and at the same time more restrictive, more disembodied and more abstract. On the Atlantic and in the north, engaged as individuals in their relations of exchange, members of the urban community abandon to it a large part of their availability, and therefore of their time. In the Mediterranean State-political power manages space, dominates territories and as we have already said, controls external relations without being able to prevent the townsmen-citizens of disposing of their time and consequently of the activities which rhythm them. This analysis helps to understand that in the Mediterranean, birthplace of the City-State, the State, whether it be inside or outside the city, always remains brutal and powerless, violent but weak, unifying but always undermined, under threat. In the oceanic cities where the State and the political have penetrated with less difficulty and thus with less violence and drama, they are deeply involved in individual and social activities. The separation between the private and the public, and therefore between the outside and the intimate takes place wherever there is civil and political society, but it always has its own distinctive features. The idea and the reality of the private/public separation are not identical everywhere. More concretely, it is not always the same things that one hides, that one shows, that one goes to see outside.

If our hypothesis is correct, in the lived of everyday, in practice, the social relations of Nordic cities are based on a contractual and thus juridical basis, that is, on reciprocal good faith, while relations in the Mediterranean would tend to base themselves either on tacit or explicit alliances going right up to the formation of clans (clientelism, mafias, etc.), or on the contrary, the refusal of alliances leading even to open warfare (vendettas, etc.). Explanations from ancient history or from the survival of peasant customs appear to us inadequate to explain the persistence and resurgence of social relations. Codes function durably, more or less tacitly and ritually; they organize and rhythm time as well as relations. These are not strictly rational laws, acceptable to all, if not accepted, which govern relations. The word 'code' does not have here the same meaning as in the north and besides, we introduce it in order to designate an ensemble of gestures, of conventions, of ways of being. Coding completes itself with a ritual and inversely.

Relations and refusals of alliances interest the rhythmanalyst to the extent that they intervene in the production of social time. They take place and deploy themselves inside this social time which they contribute to produce (or reproduce) by imprinting on it a rhythm. Our hypothesis is therefore that every social, that is collective rhythm, is determined by the forms of alliances which human groups give to themselves. These forms of alliances are more varied and contradictory than one generally supposes, this being particularly true in the big cities where class relations, political relations, although not only these, intervene.

Does the characteristic ambiguity of Mediterranean cities in relation to the State manifest itself in the rhythms of social life? It could be that around the Mediterranean, where are maintained ancient codes and powerful rhythms, the rhythmanalyst must look from this point for the secret of rhythms. In fact, rituals have a double relationship with rhythms. Each ritualization creates its own time and its particular rhythm, that of gestures, of solemn words, of prescribed acts with a particular sequence; but also rituals and ritualizations intervene in daily time and punctuate it. That happens more often during cyclical times, at fixed hours, dates and occasions. Let us note that there are several rituals which *punctuate* daily life:

1   Religious rituals, their irruption and also their intervention in daily life; for example fasting, prayers, ablutions, the muezzin, the angelus and ringing of bells, etc.
2   Rituals in a larger sense of the word, both sacred and profane such as festivals and carnivals which inaugurate or terminate a period, rites of intimate conviviality or external sociability.
3   Finally, political rituals, that is, ceremonies, commemorations, votes, etc.

In short, we place under this label all that includes the daily to imprint on it an extra-daily rhythm without as such interrupting it. The analysis of these multiple rhythms would according to us enable to verify that the relation of the townsman to his city (and area) – notably in the Mediterranean – does not consist only of a sociological relationship of the individual with a group. It is on the one hand a relationship of the human being with his own body, with his tongue and speech, with his gestures, in a certain place and with a gestural whole, and on the other hand, a relationship with the largest public space, with the entire society and beyond it, the universe.

Here a hypothesis takes shape and becomes more precise. The analysis of speech distinguishes two kinds of expression; one formal, rhetorical and frontal, the other more immediate and spontaneous. In the same way the analysis of social time can also differentiate two kinds of rhythms. Borrowing from Robert Jaulin, we can enumerate them: rhythm of the self and rhythm of the other.[2] The rhythms of 'the other', would be the rhythms of activities turned outwards, towards the public. One can also name them 'the rhythms of representation'; more contained, more formalized, they correspond to frontal expression in speech. As for the 'rhythms of the self', these are associated to

[2]   Robert Jaulin, *Gens de soi, gens de l'autre*, UGE. 10/18, 1973.

rhythms more deeply inscribed, organizing a time turned more to-wards private life, thus opposing to representation the presence to the self and then to the forms of speech, of more silent and intimate conscious forms . . .

This polar opposition should not make one forget that between these poles there are multiple transitions and imbrications; the room, the apartment, the house, the street, the square and the area, the city – the nuclear family, the extended family, neighbouring or friendly relations – and the city itself. The Self and the Other are not cut off from each other. The study of the space of the Muslim city shows these imbrications, these complex reciprocities and transitions between the public and the private.[3] Closer to the body, the difference between these two kinds of rhythms are found in the most everyday (preparing food, sleeping) and the most extra-daily (dancing, singing, making music), in gestures, in mannerisms and habits. The extra-daily rhythms the daily and conversely. No more than the linear and the cyclical, rhythms of the 'self' and rhythms of 'the other', those of presence and those of representation, cannot be separated. Entangled, they permeate practice and are permeated by it. This seems to us true of all spaces and times, whether urban or not. What then is specific to Mediterranean cities? It seems to us that in these, urban space, that is public space, becomes the site of a vast scene-setting where are shown and deployed all those relations with their rhythms. Rituals, codes and relations become visible and are acted out. It must be recognized that a deserted street at four o'clock in the afternoon has a meaning as powerful as the swarming square during during hours of trading or encounters. In music and in poetry, silences also have their meaning.

Is it not this especially the case of Venice? Is this city not a theatrical city not to say a theatre-city – where actors and the public are the same in the multiplicity of their roles and relations? Accordingly, one can imagine the Venice of Casanova, and Visconti's *Senso*, as the Venice of today. Would it not be so because what is given free rein in this space is a privileged form of civility and freedom, founded on and in a dialectic of rhythms? This freedom does not consist in being a free citizen of the State but of being free in the city outside the State. Political power dominates or attempts to dominate space, hence the

---

[3] Paul Vieille, 'L'État périphérique et son héritage', *Peuples Méditerranéens*, 27–8, 1984.

importance of monuments and squares, but if palaces and churches have a political meaning and goal, the townsmen-citizens divert them, and appropriate this space in a non-political way. The citizen resists the State by a particular use of time. A struggle therefore unfolds for appropriation in which rhythms play a major role. Through them social, therefore, civil time, seeks and manages to shield itself from State, linear, unirhythmical measured and measuring time. Thus the public space, space of representation, 'spontaneously' becomes place of promenades, encounters, intrigues, diplomacy, trade and negotiations, theatricalizing itself. Time is hence linked to space and to the rhythms of the people who occupy this space.

The comparative analysis of urban rhythms identifies them only to bring them together. In this particular case, this analysis sometimes manages contrasts or strong oppositions, but more often nuances. The analysis of the Hispanic city obviously nuances that of the Islamic or Italian city. Yet, common aspects come to light through nuances and contrasts. An illustration of this thesis: in whatever country around the Mediterranean, many cities have been built on escarpments which dominate the sea. These cities have an upper and lower city and the connecting stairs play a very important role. In a general way there is around the Mediterranean a remarkable architecture of stairs. A link between spaces, stairs also ensures the link between times: between the time of architecture (the house and the enclosure) and urban time (the street, the open space, the square and monuments) They link private dwellings and houses with their distribution in urban space. Now, are not stairs the paramount localized time? In Venice, do not stairs rhythm the walk through the city, while at the same time serving as transition between different rhythms? Let us conjure the steps of the Gare St Charles in Marseilles. They are an obligatory, even initiational, passage for the traveller to the descent towards the city and the sea. More than that of a door or of an avenue their blatant monumentality imposes on the body and consciousness the exigency of passage from one rhythm to another rhythm, as yet unknown, to be discovered.

We have hitherto stressed the historical weaknesses of the Mediterranean City-States. They could never either join forces against common enemies, nor confront effectively the great conquerors and founders of great empires. The victory of Athens over the Persians remains an exceptional event. Thus the succession of empires which since antiquity until now have attempted to dominate or encircle all the Mediterranean. All the conquerors have conquered the cities, but all the cities have resisted. How and why? In our view, by times and rhythms. Which underscores the solid and consistent character of urban times in the Mediterranean in relation to politically dominated space.

A few words here on tourism, this modern phenomenon which has become essential and which in a curious way prolongs the historical problematic of conquests. Here again a paradox is revealed: tourism is added without making it disappear, to traditional and customary uses of space and time, of monumentality and the rhythms of 'the other'. For example, in Venice tourism does not quell the theatricality of the city, but would seem to reinforce it, even if it means that dramatic representation acquires some buffoonery. It cannot modify its depth or deny its principle. Hence this surprising fact: the most traditional of cities accept modern tourism; they adapt themselves by resisting the loss of identity which these invasions could incur. Would this not be the case not only for Venice, but also for Syracuse, Barcelona, Palermo, Naples and Marseilles? Cities given over to tourism who fiercely resist homogenization, linearity, rhythms of 'the other'? Tourism can disfigure space without however deforming lived time and making it a stranger to itself. To understand this situation, we have seen that we must call upon all of history. We must remember that the long predominance of commercial and cultural exchanges has produced a mixing of diverse populations, migrations and cohabitations. Which confirms this kind of alliance in the compromise which characterizes the history of rhythm in these cities – and moreover maintains and consolidates clans. In other words, as solid and durable relations in conflict as well as in alliances. Which places the emphasis on another paradox: how such durable historical compromises have been able to be founded upon such a powerful Manichean basis? The answer: they are founded upon the organization of time and rhythms, an organization at the same time private and public, sacred and profane, apparent and secret.

The State and the political are not the only ones refused by the intimate; repulsed, even expelled from their space by a strong rhythmicity – which does not prevent them from returning with equal force to what has refused them. Every form of hegemony and homogeneity are refused in the Mediterranean. It is not only the rhythms imposed by the State-political centrality which are perceived as rhythms of 'the other'. The very idea of centrality is refused because each group, each entity, each religion and each culture considers itself a centre. Now, what is a centre, if not a producer of rhythms in social time? The polyrhythmy of Mediterranean cities highlights their common character through their differences. Such an urban practice raises a question: how does *each* (individual, group, family, etc.) manage to insert its own rhythms among those of (different) others, including the rhythms imposed by authority? In this insertion of rhythms of 'the self' into the rhythms of the other, what is the share of radical separation and that of compromises, of tolerance and violence? It is a known and ordinary fact that in all large cities of the Mediterranean periphery everyone from childhood hears several languages. This cannot but have consequences for the spontaneous or 'native' acceptance of diverse rhythms and the perception of the diversity of the rhythms of 'the other'.

The enigma of practical and social life could thus be formulated: how are the rhythms of 'the self' and those of 'the other' determined, oriented and apportioned? The refusals and acceptances of alliances are regulated according to what (civil) principles? Polyrhythmy always results from a contradiction and also from a resistance to it – of resistance to a relation of force and eventual conflict. Such a contradictory relation can be defined as the struggle between two tendencies: the tendency to homogeneity and the one to diversity – the latter being particularly vigorous in the Mediterranean. In other words, there is a tendency towards a globalizing domination of centres (capital cities, dominant countries and cultures, empires) which attacks the multi-dimensionality of peripheries, which in turn perpetually threatens unity. We can say in terms of rhythmanalysis, that there is a struggle between a measured, imposed and exterior time, and a more endogenous time. If it is true that in the Mediterranean city diversity always takes its revenge, it is never able to conquer the inverse tendency towards political, organizational and cultural unity. Everything takes place as if the Mediterranean could not renounce the unitary principle which has founded and still founds its identity. Nevertheless ideologies of diversity confront to the point of violence identical and unitary structures. We cannot here but think of Beirut.

When relations of power take over relations of alliance, when the rhythms of 'the other' make impossible the rhythms of 'the self', then a total crisis explodes, with the deregulation of all compromises, arhythmy, implosion–explosion of the city and the country. It seems to us that this extreme case, cannot but acquire the value and meaning of a symbol. Twenty to fifteen years ago Beirut was a place of compromises and alliances which now seem miraculous; the place of a polyrhythmy realized in an (apparent) harmony.

This brutal arhythmy poses a question which concerns every Mediterranean project and every perspective of unity and globality in this part of the world. Will such a project collapse before this tragedy? It is not up to the rhythmanalyst to pass judgement: at the most can he maintain that the analysis of rhythms would bring non-negligible elements to all questioning of this nature.

Applied to the urban, the rhythmanalytical project may seem disparate, as it requires notions and aspects to be linked to it that analysis too often keeps separate: times and spaces, the public and the private, the State-political and the intimate – finding itself as having alternative points of view. It can thus also seem abstract, for it calls upon very general concepts. We could have avoided these reproaches and not leave behind such an impression, by either meticulously describing a privileged and known place, or throwing ourselves into a lyricism aroused by the splendour of the cities evoked. Now this was not our purpose. We have wanted to introduce into the debate concepts and a general conception: rhythmanalysis. This conception has very diverse origins: the theory of measure, the history of music, chronobiology and even cosmological theories. We have wanted to verify them within the realm of the possible by proposing here a few hypotheses in the hope that they will be taken up and brought forward by others. We have therefore attempted to outline a paradigm: a table of oppositions constituting an ensemble. We then have examined the specifically Mediterranean content of this construct, and the entry into practice of these oppositions. By this, virtual and actualized conflicts, relations of power, threats of explosion have been revealed. This paradigmatic chart related to practice has become dialectical. Thus, the paths taken by the concepts open onto finer analyses – to be undertaken.

Index

Made in the USA
Lexington, KY
08 October 2013